INQUIRY-DRIVEN
INNOVATION

INQUIRY-DRIVEN INNOVATION

A Practical Guide to Supporting School-Based Change

LIZ DAWES DURAISINGH AND ANDREA SACHDEVA

JB JOSSEY-BASS™
A Wiley Brand

Jossey-Bass
A Wiley Imprint
111 River St, Hoboken, NJ 07030

www.josseybass.com

Library of Congress Cataloging-in-Publication Data is Available:

ISBN 9781119675358 (paperback)
ISBN 9781119675433 (ePDF)
ISBN 9781119675471 (epub)

Cover Design: Wiley
Cover Image: Andrea Rose Sachdeva

FIRST EDITION

SKY10026930_051021

For Manoj, Joseph, and Tom - my home team
For Marc, Aarav, and Jaya - my guiding stars

CONTENTS

ACKNOWLEDGMENTS

We would like to begin by thanking our colleague, Edward P. Clapp, who co-directed the Creating Communities of Innovation project from which this book emerged. He played an integral role in developing the concept of inquiry-driven innovation, as well as many of the tools in *The Toolkit for Inquiry-Driven Innovation*. His insights, vision, and knowledge helped to shape many aspects of the work reflected in this book.

The Creating Communities of Innovation project was generously supported by GEMS Education. The content of this book was developed through a process of collaborative inquiry over several years with a devoted cohort of educators in Dubai and Abu Dhabi in the United Arab Emirates (UAE). We would like to especially thank Sunny Varkey, Founder of GEMS Education, as well as Dino Varkey and Sir Christopher Stone for backing this work. We would also like to thank Michael Gernon and the Innovation Research and Development and GEMSx teams, and Dr. Linda Rush and the TELLAL team. We are further grateful to Nicholas Bruce, Vicki Hallatt, and Helen Loxston-Baker for the leadership roles they have played on this project. Additionally, we would like to express our gratitude to Kalimullah Muhammad Siddique, Ibadet Ullah Khan, and Hunzullah Khaliqnoor for all of the camaraderie and support they offered to us during our time in the UAE. This book would not have been possible without the hard work and support of the teachers, principals, and leadership teams at all of the participating schools. We are especially grateful for the contributions of Jennifer Parker, Cathy Sciolis, Abhishek Singh, Peter Thorpe, and Principal Dr. Katherine Miner at GEMS American Academy—Abu Dhabi; Rob Darby, Zoe Downes, Ruth Farmer, Harriette Gardner, Rebecca Goodman, Neil Matthews, Nicola Matthews,

Simon Murphy, Simone Rapsey, Zoe Tostevin, and Principal Stephen Sharples at GEMS FirstPoint School—The Villa; Sudharani Attili, Suby Bimal, Lourdes Oliva Mascarenhas, Mareen Mathew, Gauri Meghani, Sharmi Rodgers, Rana Sabohi, Bhawna Sajnani, Zahra Shirazi, Sreeja Unnithan, Deepa Varghese, Latha Venkateswar, and Principal Asha Alexander at The Kindergarten Starters; Ritesh Vrajlal Dhanak, Juliana Li, Sharada Kenkare, Reshmi Suresh Menon, Malini Murali, Priyadarshini Prakash, and Principal Nargish Khambatta at GEMS Modern Academy; Venetia Jayaraj, Nahmiya Ambala Kandy, Stella Laus, Christine De Noronha, Teresa Rusten, and Principal Fatima Martin at GEMS New Millennium School—Al Khail; Nicholas Bruce, Majd Hadad, Vicki Hallatt, Andy Williams, Sarah Wright, and Principals Ruth Burke and Maryssa O'Connor at GEMS Wellington International School; and Anthony Loxston-Baker, Helen Loxston-Baker, Emma MacDonald, Tracy Moxley, Shafaque Riaz, and Principals Damian Bacchoo and Elizabeth Stanley at GEMS Wellington Academy—Silicon Oasis. We are indebted and especially grateful to Christine Nasserghodsi for all of the effort and intellectual spirit she brought to this work as our devoted project liaison on the ground in the UAE. The Creating Communities of Innovation project would truly not have been possible without her tireless efforts.

In addition to our collaborating teacher and administrator partners on the ground in Dubai and Abu Dhabi, we are also grateful for the contributions of various colleagues at the Harvard Graduate School of Education. We thank the research assistants who helped at different times with the project, including Alen Agaranov, Iman Allawzi, Katy Bullard, Cortney Evans, Adriana García Nuñez, Audrey Pindell, Aneeqa Rana, and Giiti Wassie. We are also grateful for the support of our colleagues at Project Zero, including our director Daniel Wilson, our finance director Faith Harvey, and the Project Zero core team, including Sarah Alvord, Tina Blythe, Jordy Oakland, Margaret Mullen, Leyla Omeragić-Buljina, and Matthew Riecken. We thank our colleagues Kristen Hinckley, Mara Krechevsky, and Christina Smiraglia for their feedback on the manuscript.

Finally, we wish to make a special recognition in memory of Sharmi Rodgers, who did inspiring work as part of the study group at The Kindergarten Starters.

FOREWORD

It has been a decade now since I took on the role of principal at Kindergarten Starters, a primary school in the heart of Dubai with 5,000 students between the ages of four and ten. The sheer size of the school, however, was not the only disconcerting issue I faced. Desks stood in neatly lined rows facing the teacher, who delivered a standard lecture, with all children presumably learning at the same pace as their peers. This is a common sight in Indian schools, and although everything was orderly, hierarchical, and well managed according to parental expectations, I knew the soul of the school was missing.

I was searching for ways in which I could make a disruptive shift in this educational model. As a principal with more than three decades of experience, I knew that this model did not meet the needs of the present generation, much less the demands of the next. My pursuit for a new way of introducing collaborative learning for the early years had taken me to Reggio Emilia in Italy, a trip that I had found deeply inspiring. It was at the same time that the research work detailed in the pages that follow began in our school community, in partnership with researchers from Project Zero, a center at the Harvard Graduate School of Education. This work brought refreshing new changes in its wake.

What I had witnessed in Reggio Emilia reaffirmed my belief that children and their teachers should make their thinking visible in order to allow their thoughts and thought processes to emerge and to increase awareness within the school community of how students learn. However, it was Project Zero that gave us the tools for inquiry and innovation, including *thinking routines*[1] that enabled us to effectively display student thinking. They also offered a structured process for thinking about how to incorporate these thinking routines into the everyday teaching practices at our school—something that was very new for us. This research work married the process of inquiry with innovation, as explained in this book, and so began a change in pedagogy that allowed children to collaborate to solve problems and to use creative approaches and analyses.

Not only did the classrooms at Kindergarten Starters undergo a physical transformation, but so did the thinking of our teachers about what learners could do as they started to encourage students to collaborate to come up with their own way of solving problems. This inquiry-driven approach allowed students to explore the world according to their own curiosities. They puzzled out the solutions and understood that there were multiple ways to arrive at them. Most importantly, they learned by trialing different processes as they found out what worked best for them.

Our parents and teachers harbored a belief that this kind of learning approach was possible only in schools with an abundance of financial resources. They soon began to realize that creativity, collaboration, innovation, and self-direction were the greatest resources and they were inherent in all children. These qualities just needed the right kind of provocation and opportunity to come to the fore. As students explored, they became fearless and confident in their abilities to search for solutions. They realized there was no one right answer and that by understanding others' perspectives they could become truly connected to the world in which they live. Parents were welcomed into lessons to see how these approaches worked first-hand so that they understood that there was no need to rely on rote memorization—because their children had developed critical thinking skills.

This was the school I had envisioned and the kind of learning that I had hoped for. I learned that we have to stop building structures into which our students and teachers have to fit. Instead, we must create an open, multidimensional approach to teaching and learning that will revitalize our education system by giving teachers and learners the autonomy to become creative, innovative, and critical thinkers. Only this can create a common culture that supports innovative education.

The Kindergarten Starters is continuing its journey of promoting inquiry-driven innovation as we now take on the challenge of embedding climate literacy into the curriculum—not only in schools belonging to the GEMS network, such as ours, but in every classroom all over the world. Project Zero and the Creating Communities of Innovation research project illustrated throughout this book have shown us that our vision is scalable and that by sharing best practices and our story we can imbue others with self-belief. The journey of innovation continues at our school as we embrace educational technologies to find solutions to problems both in our local communities and the wider world in order to preserve the humanistic and developmental purpose of education.

Inquiry-driven innovation is about solving problems that are commonly experienced and for which collective thinking is required—because, as individuals, we may not always have the best answers. That is why it is necessary to create communities of innovation within your schools. Working together to create your own success stories of innovation will support the creative flow that is contagious not only to your community, but also to the world at large. Dreaming to designing and then making that dream a reality is an energizing process as you will discover in *Inquiry-Driven Innovation: A Practical Guide to Supporting School-Based Change*.

Asha Alexander

Principal and Executive Leader—Climate Change

GEMS Education

Endnote

1. Thinking routines are defined in the Glossary at the end of the book, alongside other key terms.

INQUIRY-DRIVEN INNOVATION

PART I

INQUIRY-DRIVEN
INNOVATION IN SCHOOLS

CHAPTER 1

INQUIRY-DRIVEN INNOVATION:

An Introduction

The school library offered cozy spaces for students to settle down with a book or study quietly. Colorful posters adorned the walls. One particularly prominent poster used giant letters to offer this exclamation: "Take time today to LEARN something NEW!" Now, however, as early morning sunshine streamed through the windows, adults rather than children were gathered in groups among the bookcases. They were part of a two-year collaborative research project exploring inquiry and innovation in education. Study groups from seven schools serving different communities across the K–12 spectrum within the United Arab Emirates (UAE) were participating in this project, including today's host school located off Dubai's busy Sheikh Zayed Road. They were convened for one of the project's tri-annual in-person gatherings that included *exhibitions* of each school's work. A genuine buzz filled the room: participating educators expressed excitement about the opportunity to catch up with one another and to find out how their different innovation projects were progressing. There was also a palpable sense of being engaged in work that mattered—not to mention a small dose of friendly competition.

The innovation projects on display were varied: one was about promoting the use of *thinking routines*[1] across grade levels to make student thinking more visible; another involved the development of a schoolwide rubric to promote critical thinking; another was about pro-

3

moting positive dispositions with regard to online learning; yet another was about introducing student-led assessment; and a further one presented the idea of using the local
landscape to establish a "desert school" (a tortoise crawled through the space to bring life
to this proposal). Working together in small groups—called *study groups*—the participating
teachers and administrators had been engaging in the process of *inquiry-driven innovation* for
about a year. As part of that process, each study group had spent months learning to look
at its teaching and learning contexts with fresh eyes. The groups had collectively identified potential changes they would like to see in their schools, established an inquiry focus,
and then developed innovations to help make those changes happen. They had piloted
their innovations and were now iterating on their initial designs. This morning they had
brought along posters and visual displays to update the other study groups about their
work, as well as to receive and offer constructive feedback. What did they most appreciate about one another's innovation projects? What connections were they making to
their own? What puzzles or questions did they have? The educators listened attentively
to one another.

■ ■ ■

Three Key Elements: Innovation + Inquiry + Community

This book is about inquiry-driven innovation: an ongoing process that empowers individuals and communities to pursue positive school-based change that is relevant and
responsive to local contexts. Three key elements are integral to the Framework for
Inquiry-Driven Innovation: innovation, inquiry, and community. Given the demands of
our fast-changing contemporary society—and the need to prepare young people for the
complexities and challenges of the world in which they are growing up—each of these
elements has been acknowledged as vitally important in schools. Innovation, inquiry, and
community are integrated within this framework in a way that both builds on and extends
current thinking and practice, as discussed in the chapter that follows. Importantly, while
the collaborative research that led to the development of the framework was initially
focused on promoting innovation, it quickly became apparent that the professional
growth—or "lift"—that the participating teachers and administrators reported experiencing was tightly bound up in the process. This book is therefore as much about empowering
individual educators as it is about promoting innovation in schools. Powerful professional
development and positive school-based change, as others have pointed out, go hand in

hand (e.g., Schleicher, 2011) and the Framework for Inquiry-Driven Innovation offers a fresh approach to strategically combining them to the advantage of both. It is important to note that this book takes a highly expansive view of what counts as innovation, interpreting it as the act of trying out anything that is new within a given school context, even if it involves practices that are quite commonplace elsewhere. This and other key terms are defined as they are used in the book in the Glossary at the end of the book. Additionally, the term *educator* is used throughout the book to refer to both classroom teachers and administrators.

The framework consists of key concepts and principles, a suggested process or "roadmap" for enacting inquiry-driven innovation, and a range of over twenty practicable tools that were collaboratively designed and field tested with educators engaged in a design-based research project called Creating Communities of Innovation led by the Project Zero research center at Harvard Graduate School of Education in collaboration with GEMS Education.[2] The framework is intended to be used flexibly and to serve educational practitioners working at any grade level and with any content area or curriculum. A series of case studies and *innovation journeys* in Part Two shows how the framework can play out in different ways according to the local school context and the team of practitioners engaged with it. Part Two also includes an examination of the ways in which individuals experienced professional growth through this work.

This opening chapter introduces the overall concept and essential qualities of inquiry-driven innovation. It also previews the contents of the rest of the book, offering suggestions on how to read and use it. The following chapter describes how the Framework for Inquiry-Driven Innovation was developed and loosely situates the framework within the broader educational landscape.

Figure 1.1 shows how the elements of innovation, inquiry, and community are tightly connected and mutually supportive within the framework.

This book shows how:

- Innovation practices are enhanced when educators use an inquiry approach to pursue locally relevant innovations in collaboration with one another and in the service of specific communities about which they know and care.

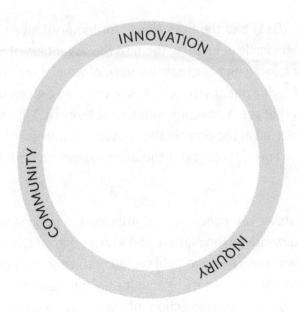

Figure 1.1 The key elements of inquiry-driven innovation.

- Inquiry practices are enhanced when they are focused on innovation projects that are meaningful to a group of participants who have the opportunity to learn both with and from one another.
- Community-building or collaboration practices are enhanced when there is a clear purpose for educators to work toward collectively and they are given relative autonomy to promote change that is meaningful to them and their communities.
- Individual teacher professional development and community building or collaboration practices are mutually supportive: while this book emphasizes the collective pursuit of inquiry-driven innovation, it also features powerful stories of individual growth.

The Five Principles of Inquiry-Driven Innovation

Now it is time to unpack the five key principles that are integral to the Framework for Inquiry-Driven Innovation. As Figure 1.2 shows, the framework promotes work that is purposeful and intentional, attentive to multiple perspectives, adapted to the context, sustained and iterative, and structured and supported. No one principle is more important than the others and all connect to form a coherent whole, encircled by the key elements of innovation, inquiry, and community.

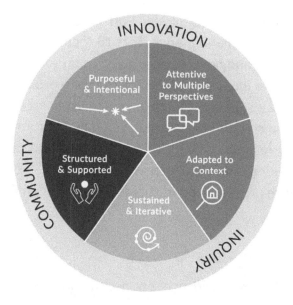

Figure 1.2 The key elements and principles of inquiry-driven innovation.

Principle #1: Inquiry-driven innovation is purposeful and intentional

It addresses a specific need or interest and involves deliberate design choices throughout the process.

The framework supports educators to work on innovation projects that address a specific need or interest—that is, to develop innovations that are purposeful and explicitly designed to promote positive change within their local contexts rather than innovating for innovation's sake. For the schools featured in this book, this kind of positive change meant different things. In one school, it meant radically overhauling kindergarten teaching practices to enable young learners to express their ideas and develop a passion for inquiry. In another, it meant promoting critical-thinking skills across the curriculum to improve students' capacity for analysis and discussion. In still another, it meant supporting students to develop positive dispositions toward online learning so that they could take greater advantage of the school's blended learning model.

Educators are also encouraged to be intentional throughout the process in terms of making choices or decisions that seek to advance the intended purpose of their innovation.

For example, some of the tools presented in Part Three, such as *Population, Innovation, Outcome* and *Theory of Action,* help educators to focus in concrete ways on who or what they want to impact and how they are going to do so. The iterative nature of the recommended process for inquiry-driven innovation also promotes intentionality. From the outset, educators are supported to observe and listen carefully to what is happening in their schools and classrooms before developing their innovation projects. Later on, they are asked to respond thoughtfully to the data and documentation they are collecting and interpreting in order to further advance their innovation projects. Reflection is key to the entire process, a point that is emphasized in Chapter 6 on individual teacher growth.

Principle #2: Inquiry-driven innovation is attentive to multiple perspectives

It engages educators who offer a variety of perspectives and considers insights from diverse literatures and stakeholders.

The Framework for Inquiry-Driven Innovation recommends that educators come together in study groups that are intentionally designed to engage a variety of perspectives. Part of the power of the framework comes from facilitating learning experiences that bring together professionals who do not habitually work together and who perhaps underestimate how much they could learn from one another's expertise and practices. Accordingly, it is generally recommended that study groups include members who differ by role and level of responsibility within the school, degree and type of professional experience, subject area, age level taught, and personal identity—for example, by gender, race/ethnicity, religion, age, sexual orientation, and/or national or regional identity. In this regard, the framework reflects research that indicates that diverse groups tend to be more effective than more homogeneous groups in terms of problem-solving and generating creative ideas—in no small part because of the different perspectives and ways of thinking that diverse group members can bring to the table (Hong & Page, 2004). Furthermore, drawing study group members from different areas of a school means that the group's innovation focus is likely to be relevant to a wide variety of stakeholders and to then take hold and be scaled throughout the institution. However, depending on the local context and impetus for engaging in inquiry-driven innovation, it might make sense for study groups to bring together educators who fulfill similar roles within a school (Weinbaum et al., 2004). In the case of the Kindergarten Starters School, for example, the two study groups were mostly comprised of teachers working at the same grade level.

The framework also fosters attentiveness to multiple perspectives in ways that go beyond the composition of study groups. The tools shown in Part Three, some of which build on decades of research, are designed to generate or bring to the surface multiple ideas and perspectives. They encourage those engaged in inquiry-driven innovation to observe and listen carefully to a variety of stakeholders, including students, teachers, parents, and other community members, as they conceive of, initiate, and develop their innovations. These tools also encourage educators to consult with and draw inspiration from a variety of sources, including ones that lie beyond the field of education. Finally, the concept of building community across as well as within schools means that study group members are introduced to a variety of practices, ideas, and learning environments beyond their immediate contexts, as indicated by the opening vignette. This kind of cross-fertilization among educators can serve to encourage or endorse the work that study groups are doing; at other times it calls into question some of their assumptions or generates new ideas.

Principle #3: Inquiry-driven innovation is adapted to context

It responds to local conditions and addresses specific needs or interests, fostering a sense of local ownership.

Innovations are far more likely to take hold if they are relevant and responsive to the local communities that they are designed to serve. The framework's recommended process begins with the development or refinement of inquiry skills that are designed to promote educators' attentiveness to their local context and the viewing of it with fresh eyes. From the start, they are encouraged to develop innovations that make sense within their local contexts and that draw from multiple perspectives. This emphasis on local adaptation helps to empower educators because it enables them to tap into their own experiences and knowledge of a particular context to generate innovations that address local needs or interests. As a result, educators are likely to experience a great deal of ownership and satisfaction. For instance, several of the study groups who helped to develop the Framework for Inquiry-Driven Innovation gave specific names to their locally adapted innovations as a means of signaling that these innovations were unique to their schools and a source of pride. For example, the study group that promoted critical thinking across the curriculum gave their rubric a whimsical name that incorporated their school's initials ("WISical Thinking," as featured in the case study in Chapter 5). Meanwhile, the school that promoted positive dispositions toward online learning gave their framework the acronym "CRUISE".

Principle #4: Inquiry-driven innovation is sustained and iterative

It involves ongoing individual and group commitment, with the process requiring revision and refinement over time.

As already noted, school-based change and individual professional growth go hand in hand. Inquiry-driven innovation stands as a counterpoint to ad hoc or scattered approaches to professional development in schools. The framework is intended to be implemented over a period of at least one to two years, with the resultant innovations and practices enduring well beyond. It promotes the concept of sustained and ongoing learning journeys—at the individual, study group, and whole community levels. As part of the framework, study groups are invited to reflect on and develop their own collective stories of developing an innovation together, including the challenges or obstacles that they have overcome (see the *Project Journey Mapping* tool in the Toolkit). A great deal of individual and group commitment is required for this kind of work. However, many educators are looking precisely for this kind of sustained professional development, which enables them to continue to evolve their practice and empowers them to make original and positive contributions within their local contexts.

The framework proposes an iterative approach to innovation in which innovations are developed by educators through a process that involves ideating, piloting, implementing, evaluating, and then eventually scaling their innovations, all the while deploying inquiry skills to help them refine and further develop their innovations and take stock of the impact they are making. The tools presented later in Part Three are designed to be revisited and reused over time; for example, the *Theory of Action* tool guides the creation of a living document that is continually being revised and updated.

Principle #5: Inquiry-driven innovation is structured and supported

It follows a coherent trajectory from conceptualizing the innovation to scaling it up, and involves using or adapting specifically designed tools, resources, and structures.

Educators need structures in place to facilitate their growth and development: most individuals working within schools are simply too busy to carve out enough time for sustained professional development or to engage in coordinated networking with other colleagues.

This framework proposes weekly study group meetings that follow an arc of activities, as well as periodic cross-study group community meetings that can happen in person or virtually.

Inquiry-driven innovation requires commitment and ideally direct involvement from administrators and leaders within a school. While study groups may need to develop creative ways to meet or coordinate with one another because of scheduling constraints, they will ideally have protected time to be able to meet with one another on a weekly basis. As already noted, any type of collaborative work in schools needs at least some level of approval and support from those with administrative authority within a school; the *Spreading, Scaling, and Sustaining* and *Spheres of Influence* tools shown in Part Three recommend involving and engaging administrators and other stakeholders to help promote and develop the innovation.

The framework crucially involves supporting educators to develop innovations that matter to them and their schools, with the energy and psychological support that they derive from working in community, making the experience more satisfying and impactful. It is not easy to take risks through innovation. By supporting one another to overcome challenges and by having a shared collective experience, educators who work together are able to achieve much more than they can working solo. Moreover, they can develop very close bonds with one another in ways that can sometimes be surprising if they are working with people with whom they would ordinarily have little contact. As the opening vignette indicates, educators can become invested in one another's work and feel a sense of collective pride in being involved in a larger network that speaks to their broader professional identities in ways that transcend local school contexts.

How to Use This Book

This book offers a practical guide to promoting school-based change through the Framework for Inquiry-Driven Innovation. This chapter has introduced the key concepts and principles of inquiry-driven innovation. To recap, the three key elements of inquiry-driven innovation are innovation, inquiry, and community, and the framework represents work that embodies five major principles: purposeful and intentional, attentive to multiple perspectives, adapted to context, sustained and iterative, and structured and supported.

The next chapter focuses on how the framework was developed and how it is situated relative to existing practice and research in education.

Part Two, "Inquiry-Driven Innovation in Practice," offers a range of innovation journey maps and case studies to show how the framework was variously implemented on the ground in schools; these stories are offered as a source of inspiration and indicate the inherent flexibility of the framework. Part Two also includes a chapter on individual professional growth, showing how the lifting of individual practice was bound up with the collective pursuit of inquiry-driven innovation—with openness, purpose, and reflection emerging as key aspects. The third and final part of the book is called "Creating *Your* Communities of Innovation." Here, readers will find guidelines and resources for establishing their own innovation communities centered around inquiry-driven innovation, including a suggested process "roadmap" and over twenty pedagogical tools to support this work. The book and framework are intended to be both flexible and dynamic: some readers may wish to use just a few ideas, while others may prefer to follow the framework and suggested process more carefully. Regardless, the intent of this book is to support educators—both individually and collectively—on their own paths toward generative school-based change, to the benefit of the students and communities whom they know and serve. In the book's conclusion, the authors share their own perspectives on what they have learned through the process of developing inquiry-driven innovation, calling on *all* schools to embed more innovation, inquiry, and community into their practice to better serve young people.

Endnotes

1. Thinking routines and other key terms are defined in the Glossary at the end of the book.
2. The primary researchers working on the project from Project Zero were Edward P. Clapp, Liz Dawes Duraisingh, and Andrea Sachdeva. The primary liaison for GEMS Education was Christine Nasserghodsi.

CHAPTER 2

THE STORY OF INQUIRY-DRIVEN INNOVATION

This chapter describes the process or methods by which the Framework for Inquiry-Driven Innovation was developed. It also situates the framework within a broader existing field of practice and research.

Where the Framework Was Developed

The framework emerged from a close collaboration between Project Zero, a research center at the Harvard Graduate School of Education, and approximately fifty educators at seven schools working within diverse contexts in the United Arab Emirates (UAE). Close to 90 percent of the UAE population is made up of non-citizen residents; given that government-provided education is reserved solely for Emirati students, an array of independent schools has sprung up in the UAE to cater to the various communities who live and work there. Among these educational providers is the GEMS network of schools, which runs over forty different schools in the UAE, as well as a number of schools in different countries.[1] The GEMS schools that helped to develop the framework followed various international curricula, served different communities within the UAE, and represented different levels of tuition, thereby differing in terms of available resources and facilities. The table in the Appendix summarizes key details about the seven participating schools, who all chose to participate in the project.

This diversity among the participating schools provided an important opportunity to develop a framework that would be relevant to a variety of school systems and contexts. It is fair to say that the UAE offered a particularly conducive setting for promoting innovation in schools given its government's emphasis on creating an innovative, future-leaning economy. However, it is important to note that the educators associated with this collaboration were subject to a strict annual government inspection regimen to determine their schools' official ratings, as well as the demands of various external examination bodies. Moreover, the schools were operating within a highly competitive school market, thereby increasing the pressure on them to produce strong inspection and educational results. In other words, the educational professionals who helped to develop the framework were not operating in a "blue skies" scenario, but rather experienced similar pressures and constraints as those faced by many educators around the world. The innovation journeys and case studies offered in Part Two of this book provide some sense of the local variation from one school to another and how they adapted the framework to deal with various constraints and challenges.

How the Framework Was Developed: Collaborative Design-Based Research

Collaborative design-based research takes into account and indeed embraces the messiness of the real world, with the overarching goal of creating usable knowledge and resources for practitioners (The Design-Based Research Collective, 2003). In that spirit, Part Two of this book is laden with specific real-world examples of what inquiry-driven innovation can look like on the ground in schools and Part Three consists of ready-to-go tools for practitioners to do this work. Furthermore, the work that led to the development of this framework involved researchers actively collaborating with their practitioner colleagues. Educators contributed to the shaping of the framework by giving feedback on its key concepts and principles, piloting and offering feedback on the suite of pedagogical tools found in Part Three, and helping to document and shape the stories that are told through the case studies and journey maps of their innovation projects in Part Two. Throughout the process a local GEMS Education liaison, Christine Nasserghodsi, played a vital role by coordinating and supporting activities and offering advice regarding next steps.

Design-based research involves initially designing something based on existing knowledge and research and then iterating on the design as it plays out in practice and more is learned about what works well and what does not. In this case, the broad design remit was to help the GEMS network to support and promote more innovative teaching and learning in its schools and, more specifically, in the seven schools that volunteered to participate in the project. The initial design drew from decades of research into effective teaching and learning, much of it from the researchers' home institution of Project Zero. The first step was to form study groups of educators in each of the participating schools, with each group or team initially made up of five to eight members. An overall strategy or arc of activities was developed for promoting innovation. This arc began by encouraging educators to look in new ways at their otherwise familiar school contexts. The arc proceeded over a two-year period to support them to ideate, prototype, implement, evaluate, and scale an innovation project that was customized to their school. Some of these innovations included ones already mentioned in Chapter 1, such as: introducing more learner-centered, Reggio Emilia–inspired practices at the kindergarten level; developing a school-wide critical thinking rubric; and developing a framework for promoting positive dispositions toward online learning. Other innovations included developing new interdisciplinary curricula for middle-school–aged students; introducing the practice of thinking routines across all grade levels and subject areas; developing an Open Doors policy to build trust with parents; and creating opportunities for student-led assessment. While the roadmap in Part Three is an "ironed-out" version of the overall process, the various school innovation journeys in Part Two show that there was considerable room for variation in terms of how schools chose to engage with the materials and strategies developed by Project Zero in conjunction with the participants.

To be clear, the research team did not set out with a preestablished framework that was then rolled out and tested with educators. The framework and indeed the very concept of inquiry-driven innovation emerged *through* the work with the educators who were participating in the research *over time*. Design-based research aspires to create solutions and/or products to address immediate needs in the moment *and* to develop knowledge that is relevant to contexts beyond the ones involved in the original design. Accordingly, this book represents a distilled version of what was learned from the project in the hopes that it will help promote similar school-based change elsewhere. At the same time, it documents what educators actually did as a means of providing both illustration and inspiration to others. Where possible and as indicated below, the approach taken by the research team members as they developed the framework parallelled the kinds of inquiry-driven processes that educators were engaged in as they developed their innovations: an attempt to "walk the talk" as it were. There was also a concerted effort to collect data in ways that served to enhance the learning experience of the educators involved—for example, by encouraging reflection on what they were doing and why, or by offering a new tool that they could use within their practice.

Specific Research Methods

Specific research methods were embedded within the overall collaborative design-based research approach previously described.

Documentation. Documentation is an important practice that builds on decades of collaborative work between Project Zero and educators in Reggio Emilia, Italy, with the goal of deepening or extending learning by "making learning visible"(Giudici et al., 2001; Krechevsky et al., 2013). It involves closely observing, recording, and reflecting on learning and gathering data in a variety of media forms such as photographs, typed or handwritten notes, audio or video recordings, examples of learner work, or other artifacts of learning. Just as the *Documentation* tools in Part Three promote this practice as part of inquiry-driven innovation, the research team also sought to document the emerging thinking and collective work of the educators throughout the study. Accordingly, when the research team traveled to the UAE for site visits, they ran whole-group and school-based workshops that featured activities designed to "make visible" participants' thinking and learning about their innovation projects—and then made sure to capture that thinking by photographing or recording the evidence and to subsequently interpret and reflect on what might be learned from it. The *Project Journey Mapping* tool, in particular, was an opportunity for study groups to reflect on the documentation of their story so far and try to make sense of it; their story maps then provided important information for the development of the case studies and innovation journeys shown later in this book (see Part Two). The community-wide exhibitions, as featured in the opening vignette of the book, served as another means to document the evolution of the various study groups' thinking. In between site visits, educators were encouraged to update one another and the research team on the progress of their innovations asynchronously via a customized online platform. Through this platform, participating educators posted updates about their innovations through videos, text, and images and also responded to each other's posts by asking questions or offering feedback. Additionally, they used the online platform to post documentation of how they used many of the tools from Part Three of this book.

Observations and school visits. Members of the research team visited the UAE three times a year for a week at a time over the two years of the Creating Communities of Innovation research project that led to the development of this framework. The first visits were focused on understanding the teaching and learning contexts of the different schools and getting to know the participating educators in person. There was also an opportunity to visit classrooms, enabling the team to witness the innovation projects in action and to offer targeted feedback. The team sought to engage in the kind of *slow looking* promoted by the framework in order to push past first impressions and to notice revealing details or underlying systems at play. It is worth noting that the research team continued to visit GEMS schools after this period in a light advisory capacity and to document how inquiry-driven innovation played out with an expanded cohort of schools, which is further detailed in the book's conclusion.

Surveys. Educators were asked to complete online surveys at four different times. The surveys allowed educators to give feedback on aspects of the process that were going well for them and aspects they would rather change. Later on, the surveys were also used as a means to solicit input on emerging concepts such as the five principles of inquiry-driven innovation featured in the previous chapter. While there was an interest at the start of the project in understanding the kinds of teacher attitudes or mindsets that might facilitate change or innovation in schools, that focus later shifted to how and why educators thought they were experiencing powerful professional growth. The surveys invited educators to describe their current thinking about various aspects of their work including school-based or classroom-based innovation, effective teaching or learning, their personal professional development or growth, and ways to collaborate with colleagues.

Interviews. Approximately half of the educators were interviewed about their survey responses, with participants chosen to include voices from each of the schools and to represent a variety of perspectives. These interviews allowed research cohort participants to explain their answers more thoroughly and to reflect on differences and similarities between earlier and later survey responses. The research team followed the techniques recommended by the framework's *Interviewing* tool. Transcripts of the interviews were then analyzed in a way that is consistent with the *Data Analysis* suite of tools, which recommend combining both a top-down (etic) and bottom-up (emic) approach to examining data. In other words, the research team was alert from the start to evidence of educators feeling more comfortable with incorporating innovation into their everyday practice or adopting more learner-centered, inquiry-driven practices. At the same time, the team wanted to remain open to the unexpected and to learn from educators by listening carefully to their perspectives. An iterative and collaborative process was followed to distill key themes from the interviews. Participating educators were then consulted to make sure that these themes and how they were presented resonated with their own experiences.

It is important to acknowledge the limitations as well as the possibilities opened up by this kind of collaborative, design-based research. This book does not statistically prove the positive impact of teachers participating in inquiry-driven innovation in their schools. Nor can it claim that this process would work in all school contexts, even though it was developed across different kinds of school settings. Furthermore, the educators who volunteered to help develop this framework were, by definition, particularly motivated practitioners— and although inquiry-driven innovation is intended to be incorporated into everyday practice rather than experienced as an additional duty, their considerable commitment may have been unusual or reflective of particularly supportive school environments. Educators also operate within larger ecosystems: it is unclear, for example, if the framework would get the same traction in an American, British, or Indian curriculum school operating outside of the UAE. Yet while each school's innovation was unique to the specific context, that is in many ways the point of this framework. It is meant to be flexible and to offer inspiration rather than to mandate a particular blueprint for effecting positive change, with the varied examples developed with the collaborating teachers and practitioners intended to help other educators find resonance with their own practice.

Situating Inquiry-Driven Innovation within Existing Practice and Research

Many of the components of the Framework for Inquiry-Driven Innovation are already recommended by educational researchers and leaders. In fact, much of the framework reflects current thinking around effective practices regarding teacher professional development and effecting positive change in schools. It is the *way* in which innovation, inquiry, and community are strategically combined that makes this framework original, as well as the collaborative development of the concepts and principles, process, and set of tools with educators and administrators working in different kinds of schools serving a variety of communities. What follows is an explanation of how the elements of innovation, inquiry, and community, as they feature in the framework, relate to existing practice and research.

Innovation

When people speak of innovation in education they may mean integrating new technologies into classrooms or building makerspaces in schools. In other cases, they may mean adopting the practices of project-based learning, flipped classrooms, blended learning, or using design thinking protocols. And in yet other cases, innovation may simply mean adopting an "imagine if . . ." mindset and experimenting with new approaches to practice or doing things differently than they have been done before. As already noted, this book embraces an extremely broad definition of *innovation* so that it includes trying out anything that is novel for a particular school or classroom, even if it is well established in other settings. This innovation may be incremental rather than dramatic and many of the innovations described in Part Two are what could be termed "everyday innovations." This book also emphasizes that there is not one but rather many paths for pursuing school-based innovation, and that context matters a great deal.

Inquiry-driven innovation is primarily about practitioners working collaboratively to initiate, pilot, implement, evaluate, and then scale school-specific innovations—broadly defined—in order to promote positive change in schools. Education systems are notoriously impervious to change, with many of today's schools still resembling systems that were built to fulfill the needs of industrial economies rather than today's innovation or creative economies (Sawyer, 2006). Even schools that are concerned with following generally agreed-upon best practices within the field often lack a nimbleness in terms of meeting students' needs. A teacher who participated in the research project behind this book made the following comment about her prior experiences of trying to initiate change within her school:

> I felt like every idea I threw out there was, like, "Well, no, because what research do you have to back that up? What's been tried and true that shows that's going to really work?" And I was like, "That's great. But some of those practices that were really well-researched were done in the '90s. Does that mean that we still have to be doing it today? Is there not something new we could be trying?"

This book by no means suggests that existing research or practices be disregarded. In fact, the Framework for Inquiry-Driven Innovation actively encourages practitioners to seek out and build on existing practices and research to address local needs. However, educators also need to develop practices that are responsive to the continually evolving larger realities of the complex world in which we live *and* the needs of the specific students and local communities whom they serve (Hargreaves & Fullan, 2012).

Relatedly, much has been written in recent years about the need to nurture young people who are, among other things, capable of innovating and thinking innovatively (P21, 2019; Sawyer, 2006; Wagner & Dintersmith, 2015), with Wagner (2012) even describing innovation as "the most essential real-world skill." A growing literature offers suggestions on how to promote innovation among students. Couros (2015), for example, provides an extensive range of tools for promoting an "innovator's mindset," while Juliani (2018) emphasizes the need to foster "intentional innovation" within schools by explicitly promoting innovation and risk-taking in terms of what is praised, prioritized, permitted, and assessed. Literatures on design thinking and maker-centered learning similarly emphasize the need to nurture students who are inclined and able to create new things, ideas, and systems, or to be proactive in changing elements of their environment that could be improved (Clapp, Ross, Ryan, & Tishman, 2016).

The Framework for Inquiry-Driven Innovation echoes or complements existing practices and thinking about innovation in education in several ways. First, the framework offers a set of principles, a process, and a series of tools for promoting innovations that are designed for local contexts. It helps teachers, administrators, and other educational leaders to rethink existing educational practices so that they can better meet the needs of young people today, including helping prepare them for a world that will require them to be innovative, creative, and adaptive. Second, while this book is not explicitly about how to nurture young innovators, the expectation is that students will be the main beneficiaries—not just because of specific innovations enacted within their classrooms and schools, but also because their educators will model, value, and promote innovation. Educators cannot be expected to facilitate types of learning experiences they have not experienced themselves: the active learning promoted by this framework is intended to empower educators to adopt a more innovative stance toward their practice. Finally, individual components of the framework can be implemented in various ways to help promote specific skills or strategies related to innovation. In particular, aspects of the tools in Part Three were adapted by participating educators for use in their classrooms and schools so that they could share specific learning strategies that they themselves had found to be powerful. For example, teachers tried out strategies from the *Slow Looking* tool, various thinking routines such as the one embedded in *Documentation Part II*, and the dialogue toolkit recommended in *Exhibiting Your Work* (all in the Toolkit in Part Three).

Inquiry

This book also reflects a broad movement to make teaching a more "research-informed and research-engaged profession" (Darling-Hammond, 2017). Increasingly, part of this engagement with research involves educators conducting action research with colleagues to meet specific challenges within their schools (Deluca et al., 2014). Inquiry-driven innovation resonates with established practices associated with action research, and has a similar remit to improve schools while empowering educators to become researcher-practitioners capable of enacting locally meaningful change (Mertler, 2017). Furthermore, some of the tools in Part Three, as well as the overall flow of the recommended inquiry-driven innovation process, are similar to ones that can be found in action research guides (e.g., Baumfield et al., 2013; Stringer, 2013).

However, inquiry-driven innovation differs from action research because it places greater emphasis on the process of initiating, piloting, implementing, evaluating, and scaling *innovations* to address specific challenges or gaps in practice, and on doing this work in community. Indeed, several teachers who participated in the study leading to this book contrasted inquiry-driven innovation with their previous experiences of engaging in solo action research projects. It is also worth noting that the innovations featured in this book are about generally improving learning for all students rather than explicitly promoting social justice or more equitable educational outcomes—a key impetus behind an important strand of the action research movement, particularly in the United States (Mills, 2017), but one that did not particularly resonate with our UAE-based educators at the time of our collaboration. Nevertheless, inquiry-driven innovation holds great promise for inspiring innovations that are concerned with addressing historic and structural injustices within schooling systems, and as is pointed out in the book's conclusion, *all* students and teachers should have access to the kinds of opportunities and learning cultures facilitated by inquiry-driven innovation.

Meanwhile, *collaborative inquiry* has been steadily gaining traction in schools in recent years as approaches to teacher professional development shift away from one-time workshops to structures that promote sustained collaboration and reflection, which are more embedded in practice and provide opportunities for meaningful intellectual growth and development (Nelson et al., 2008; Weinbaum et al., 2004). While approaches to collaborative inquiry—or promoting *inquiry as stance* (Cochran-Smith & Lytle, 1999, 2009)—are varied, they are generally viewed as cyclical processes that are grounded in socio-constructivist approaches to teacher learning. That is, teachers are assumed to learn best and more deeply when they are actively learning and co-constructing their under-standings with one another in localized contexts rather than merely receiving knowledge from outside experts. The Framework for Inquiry-Driven Innovation's sustained and iter-ative process and its emphasis on active inquiry make similar assumptions about what effective pedagogy looks like, as well as the need to blur traditional boundaries between research and practice. Furthermore, the study groups and associated practices that lie at the heart of the framework accord with those proposed by collaborative inquiry and other inquiry-driven professional development approaches.

Inquiry-driven innovation also generally promotes inquiry-driven principles of teaching and learning within schools—that is, principles that encourage learners to actively and critically inquire about the world. Most of the innovations described in this book involve practitioners trying to shift teaching and learning practices at their schools to ones that more closely align with what is known about how the human mind works and what makes for powerful individual and collective learning. It has already been noted that teachers cannot be expected to facilitate powerful learning experiences for their students if they have not had such experiences themselves. This framework enables educators to engage in meaningful inquiry, thereby, in turn, informing and energizing their work with students. Indeed, as previously mentioned, some of the tools and strategies included within the framework can be applied directly to classroom teaching.

Community

Although an inherently social activity, teaching can be a lonely and stressful profes-sion (Johnson, 2019). Since the 1990s, there has been an increase in the formation of professional learning communities (PLCs) to address this challenge, with the collaborative inquiry approach referred to above one relatively recent variation on this theme. Such groups offer professional development that is ongoing and embedded in daily practice, which, as noted, is generally viewed as more effective than one-off workshops. However, professional collaboration often goes awry if it is framed as a way to implement policy, which can feel contrived or imposed to those experiencing it (Datnow & Park, 2018).

Meanwhile, numerous studies have shown that collaboration among teachers is associated with improvements in student achievement (Hargreaves, 2019). However, teachers merely talking to one another does not necessarily amount to collaboration and the most powerful collaborations involve teachers working purposefully and interdependently (Little, 1982). A primary aspect of this framework is that educators within a school—many of whom might not ordinarily work together—come together to co-create and implement an innovation that feels relevant and responsive to their local school community. Ideally, they also connect in authentic ways to a broader network of inquiry-driven innovators located in different school contexts. Of course, attention has to be paid to *how* exactly practitioners work together: the *Toolkit for Inquiry-Driven Innovation* and *Roadmap for Inquiry-Driven Innovation* in Part Three are intended to provide scaffolding in this regard. While there is some evidence that innovation as a focus for collaboration can be particularly powerful (Meirink et al., 2010), it is worth noting that other kinds of school-level supports have also been found to be important for effective collaboration, such as an open and collaborative culture, supportive leadership, and sufficient time and resources (Admiraal et al., 2016). The detailed case studies in Part Two indicate that important supports were indeed in place in those schools, suggesting that study groups pursuing inquiry-driven innovation need at least somewhat conducive conditions to succeed.

Nevertheless, implementing inquiry-driven innovation was by no means without its challenges for the study groups involved. Some study groups struggled to find the time to meet. Others found it difficult to identify a coherent innovation or one that felt "right" for their group and school. Some faced setbacks in the process of trying to implement their innovation. But they came out on the other side feeling proud of what they had accomplished and having implemented positive change in their schools in different ways and to different degrees. Building community was key, as were the elements of inquiry and innovation.

Endnote

1. More about the history of GEMS Education, as told by the company, can be found at: www.gemseducation.com/why-a-gems-education/our-heritage/. It was founded as Global Education Management Systems.

PART II

INQUIRY-DRIVEN INNOVATION IN PRACTICE:

School-Level Change and Individual Professional Development

CHAPTER 3

FROM THEORY
TO PRACTICE

Part One introduced the underlying concepts of the Framework for Inquiry-Driven Innovation. Part Two explores what inquiry-driven innovation looks like in practice, offering varied examples of real-world application from schools in the participant cohort of the Creating Communities of Innovation research initiative. These examples go beyond the school-based innovations themselves—the new equipment, spaces, curricula, programs, or resources that educators created to effect change—to also shine a spotlight on the *process* of innovating, and the individual and collective changes that took place as educators went through this process.

As previously indicated, the process started with study groups forming at each school: five to eight individuals from different parts of the school who met weekly over the course of two years to engage in inquiry-driven innovation. The research team recommended study groups of this size: the goal was to form groups small enough for close collaborative work but large enough to represent a range of perspectives and also allow for any attrition. These groups began by looking and listening around them to see their own teaching and learning contexts in new ways, using tools provided by the research team to do so (see Chapter 8). The inspiration they gathered through these explorations led each group to identify a unique *inquiry focus*—a question of practice that motivated and focused the group's work. Refined versions of these initial inquiry foci inspired the development and implementation of defined *innovation projects* through which each study group introduced practices, resources, or approaches that were new to its particular school context. While in many groups all group members worked collaboratively on one or more innovation project(s), some groups divided up for parts of their work so that individuals or small subgroups could explore separate projects related to the group's overall inquiry focus. Study groups pilot-tested, refined, and eventually scaled and shared these innovations across their schools. Study groups in different schools also met periodically to share their work with one another and eventually with broader audiences. These key milestones in the inquiry-driven innovation process appear in the stories of change that make up the rest of Part Two.

The first chapter in this section distills the innovation journeys of four of the original research cohort schools, including the pedagogical tools that were particularly important to their processes. These innovation journey maps indicate the diversity of paths that schools can take in innovating through the approach presented in this book—though there are certainly many more possible paths than those shown. Next, three in-depth case studies explore in more detail how three additional schools innovated within their unique teaching and learning contexts. In addition to providing rich examples of the innovations themselves, the cases draw out broadly applicable themes and learnings that should be useful to others interested in implementing the Framework for Inquiry-Driven Innovation. The final chapter in this part focuses on the professional lift that took place among participating educators—with the elements of openness, purpose, and reflection emerging as particularly salient for elevating individual practice. This chapter shows the impact that engaging in inquiry-driven innovation can have on individuals, and speaks to the tight connection between professional development and the promotion of positive change in schools.

CHAPTER 4

SCHOOL CHANGE STORIES:

A Bird's-Eye View of

Four Innovation Journeys

The following innovation journeys describe an arc of experience for four study groups: GEMS American Academy—Abu Dhabi, GEMS FirstPoint School—The Villa, GEMS New Millennium School—Al Khail, and GEMS Wellington Academy—Silicon Oasis (Figures 4.1 through 4.4). The research team provided an overall structure for the work of these schools that loosely aligns with the *Roadmap for Inquiry-Driven Innovation* in Chapter 7. The journeys show how each group chose to travel through this general process, and which pedagogical tools felt especially important to each study group, with all tools included in Part Three of this book.

These innovation journeys were developed and written in close collaboration with each of the four study groups represented. The research team supported the study groups in looking at the documentation they had collected while implementing their innovations and reflecting on their experiences. In particular, they prompted the study groups to develop timelines of their innovations by identifying and then connecting pivotal moments in their work. In some instances, these pivotal moments included new insights or "aha" moments for the participating educators, who were at times supported by specific pedagogical tools from Part Three. But in other instances, they included failed attempts, wrong turns, or unexpected surprises that changed the course of their work. The research team then used

(text continues on page 38)

GEMS WELLINGTON ACADEMY - Silicon Oasis | Innovation Journey
STUDY GROUP MEMBERS: Anthony Loxston-Baker, Helen Loxston-Baker, Emma MacDonald, Tracy Moxley, Shafaque Riaz

CREATING THE STUDY GROUP

GEMS Wellington Academy – Silicon Oasis (WSO) has a school-wide focus on innovation and helping young people develop as creative individuals. The WSO teachers that formed the school study group had a particular interest in innovative uses of technology, and settled on an exploration of blended learning practices as their group's inquiry focus. Early on in their work, they considered the parts, people, and systems related to blended learning in their school.

BUILDING INQUIRY SKILLS

Study group members began to visit each other's classes to conduct informal observations about teaching and learning and explore how teachers were using blended learning in classrooms. They also interviewed teachers about their approaches to blended learning and flipped classrooms.

Related Tools:
- Slow Looking
- Interviewing

DEVELOPING AN INQUIRY FOCUS

The group's first ideas on an inquiry focus were related to exploring the impact that technology could have in classrooms. They began a debate on the desired outcomes of using digital technologies in classrooms, considering long-term developmental or skill development outcomes for learners.

From these experiences, study group members started to read literature on digital learning approaches.

Related Tools:
- Wishes, Challenges, and Opportunities

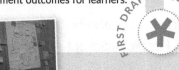

FIRST DRAFT INQUIRY FOCUS

GATHERING INSPIRATION

REFINED INQUIRY FOCUS

Study group members refined their inquiry focus and decided to explore the dispositions and learning needs of students in blended learning environments, including how feedback might best support learning.

Related Tools:
- Population, Innovation, Outcome

Over the summer school break, study group members continued to read background literature to explore concepts that might relate to their work, including the idea of "digital natives" and "digital immigrants."

Upon returning to school, study group members shifted their focus from ideas to action, envisioning four school Innovation Projects in a Theory of Action diagram:

Related Tools:
- Theory of Action suite of tools

MAKING A PLAN

Project 1: Creating online courses that help learners to self-pace and take responsibility over their learning

FIRST DRAFT INNOVATION PROJECT

Project 2: Helping teachers understand their role in a blended learning environment

FIRST DRAFT INNOVATION PROJECT

Project 3: Trying out alternative forms of feedback for students

FIRST DRAFT INNOVATION PROJECT

Project 4: Exploring how students experience flipped learning contexts

FIRST DRAFT INNOVATION PROJECT

Figure 4.1 GEMS Wellington Academy—Silicon Oasis | Innovation Journey.

PILOT-TESTING

To test out some of their ideas about blended learning models for students, some study group members created an online course through a virtual learning environment already in use at the school.

Another member of the study group started to try out alternative methods for giving feedback to students, including giving audio feedback.

From this piloting, the group realized that although their learners were digital natives, they didn't necessarily have strong skills in digital literacy.

At this point, the study group members' work across four innovation projects began to come together. They developed an overall philosophy around what it takes for learners to engage in high-quality, technology-rich learning environments

Building on the overall philosophy and group discussions, group members began to prototype a toolkit to foster positive dispositions for digital learning.

The group piloted the toolkit, gathered feedback about it from students, and started to code and analyze students' comments on online forums.

 Related Tools:
- Prototyping a Tool or Resource
- Data Analysis suite of tools

REFLECTING AND SHARING

The study group shared its work with other schools in an exhibition format, received feedback, and engaged in discussions with those schools that wanted to try out some elements of their digital dispositions work. One of these schools struck up a discussion about how difficult it can be to get students to participate in online forums, and the study group began to think about a toolkit to support learners in this kind of work.

 Related Tools:
- Exhibiting Your Work
- Theory of Action Tuning Protocol

PILOT-TESTING

WORKING WITH DATA

 ADVANCED INNOVATION PROJECT

MOVING FORWARD

SCALING UP & REACHING OUT

The study group continued to develop online courses and developed the "Let's Cruise" toolkit to support dispositions for digital learning and incorporate what the group had learned about giving feedback to students.

Toward the end of their first two years of work, study group members reflected together and considered how to scale their new toolkit to additional classrooms.

Related Tools:
- Looking Ahead
- Spreading, Scaling, and Sustaining

At the start of the next school year, group members also scaled up the study group model to engage over 100 teachers at their school in their own innovation projects.

GEMS NEW MILLENNIUM SCHOOL - Al Khail | Innovation Journey
STUDY GROUP MEMBERS: Venetia Jayaraj, Nahmiya Ambala Kandy, Stella Laus, Christine De Noronha, Teresa Rusten

CREATING THE STUDY GROUP

GEMS New Millennium School – Al Khail (NMS) is an Indian curriculum school serving students from pre-kindergarten through grade 11. Its diverse student body includes learners from 40 different nationalities.

DEVELOPING AN INQUIRY FOCUS

Stemming from overall priority areas at NMS that built on school inspection results, a study group was created that began its school year by looking at assessment of learning as its inquiry focus.

GATHERING INSPIRATION

Reflecting on what they saw and heard, study group members recognized the challenges their learners were facing in terms of language skills and ability to express themselves. Students entered the school throughout the academic year and with widely varying skills in the language of instruction. Study group members referred to this idea of a shifting student population as "student mobility."

The study group began its exploration of assessment by looking at how feedback was given to and received by students at the school. They practiced observing students at work and listening to how they expressed themselves. *Related Tool:*
🔧 • Slow Looking

FIRST DRAFT INQUIRY 3

REFINED INQUIRY FOCUS

BUILDING INQUIRY SKILLS

GATHERING INSPIRATION

Study group members realized that promoting learning and development of student expression was more relevant to the school than the issue of assessment. The study group decided to shift its inquiry focus to an exploration of how to help learners develop into expressive, high-achieving, and flexible global citizens.

The study group gained exposure to Project Zero *thinking routines* through presentations from research cohort Liaison Christine Nasserghodsi and GEMS Modern Academy, another research cohort school. They thought these thinking routines might support NMS learners in the area of self expression.

FIRST DRAFT INNOVATION

PILOT-TESTING

They began by using the See—Think—Wonder thinking routine in English, Math, and Science lessons. They started to hear learners express themselves in ways they had not before—asking questions, making connections, and gaining confidence in sharing their own ideas. Study group members felt that the thinking routine helped learners to go beyond initial impressions and a search for the "correct answer."

Figure 4.2 GEMS New Millennium School—Al Khail | Innovation Journey.

BUILDING INQUIRY SKILLS

The study group also interviewed teachers involved in pilot-testing the use of thinking routines in order to gain feedback that helped them refine their approach to implementation. They collected documentation of student work as they used the thinking routines.

During this initial piloting, students told their teachers that they liked the thinking routines and wanted to use them regularly as part of their lessons. Teachers encouraged students to begin finding additional thinking routines online.

Related Tools:

- Interviewing
- Documentation suite of tools

The study group expanded to include more teachers, and began to support the use of thinking routines across the school. To learn more about how these thinking routines were being used, study group members observed lessons. Building on a question brought up by another research cohort school, they started to wonder how expressiveness might be measured and created an Expressiveness Rubric to use during class observations.

BUILDING INQUIRY SKILLS

They found that even teachers who had been apprehensive about trying out new practices were excited to integrate the thinking routines into their lessons. Students also took a leadership role and created a Student Thinking Routine Squad to train additional teachers at the school to use thinking routines in classes.

Study group members began to share their work with other research cohort schools through cross-school exhibitions. They also recorded videos on their use of thinking routines with teachers at other GEMS schools. Members of the Student Thinking Routine Squad were involved in many of these efforts to share the study group's work with other schools, and began to develop their own thinking routines.

 Related Tools:

- Exhibiting Your Work

REFLECTING AND SHARING

WORKING WITH DATA

Members of the study group began to assess the impact of their work by looking at documentation and data collected over months of teachers' use of thinking routines in the classroom. They noticed increases in learners' critical thinking, expressiveness skills, and self-empowerment. They continued to think of new ways to scale the use of thinking routines at NMS, and to share their work with others.

 Related Tools:

- Data Analysis suite of tools

GEMS FIRSTPOINT SCHOOL - The Villa | Innovation Journey

STUDY GROUP MEMBERS: Rob Darby, Zoe Downes, Ruth Farmer, Harriette Gardner, Rebecca Goodman, Neil Matthews, Nicola Matthews, Simon Murphy, Simone Rapsey, Zoe Tostevin

CREATING THE STUDY GROUP

GEMS First Point School – The Villa (FPS) is a British curriculum school that enrolls learners ages 3 to 18. Members of both teaching staff and high-level school administration came together to form the FPS study group. As a new school at the start of its involvement in the research cohort, the study group's work in creating new initiatives was integrally tied to thinking about the overall approach to innovation at FPS.

Early in their work, two members of the study group were inspired by a conference talk on interdisciplinary learning. They shared their enthusiasm with other study group colleagues, and together began to think about what an interdisciplinary curriculum might look like for FPS learners. They also began to explore how an interdisciplinary curriculum might foster creativity and innovation, and how looking at student attainment and progress could measure the impact of such a curriculum.

GATHERING INSPIRATION

BUILDING INQUIRY SKILLS

Group members began to explore the current context at their school through lesson observations and "slow looking" at the school environment.

Related Tools:
- Slow Looking

These areas of interest came together as the study group created a first draft inquiry focus, asking the question: *How does student-led learning promote creativity, innovation, and improved attainment and progress?*

FIRST DRAFT INQUIRY FOCUS

DEVELOPING AN INQUIRY FOCUS

During a visit by the research team, study group members were asked to critically evaluate their draft inquiry focus and articulate what they meant by keywords including "innovation" and "creativity."

Related Tools:
- Population, Innovation, Outcome

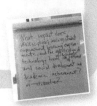

The study group also chose a target population of year 5 – 8 students. They framed their new focus as: *What impact does interdisciplinary learning, student empowerment, learning environment, and the application of technology have on year 5 – 8 students' personal and social development and academic achievement?*

REFINED INQUIRY FOCUS

Figure 4.3 GEMS FirstPoint School—The Villa | Innovation Journey.

MAKING A PLAN

New members joined the study group, and the group's first innovation project began to take shape.

A new interdisciplinary learning curriculum was envisioned for the school that spanned across grades 5 – 8. As study group members considered how this new curriculum would take shape, ideas for additional innovation projects emerged and were taken on by pairs of study group members.

Related Tools:

- Theory of Action suite of tools

Project 3: New learning environments were envisioned for FPS, including Corridor Classrooms that helped make use of hallway spaces for student learning, as well as an outdoor Desert School to promote experiential education opportunities.

Project 2: A "Bring Your Own Device" (BYOD) initiative helped the study group try out a new way of incorporating technology at the school.

Project 1: A PASS (Pupil Attitudes toward Self and School) survey was disseminated throughout the school and the resultant data analyzed in order to better understand FPS learners and eventually be able to better support student empowerment.

Corridor and classroom displays to reflect the rainforest features.

As the school year progressed, study group members reflected on their first run of the innovation projects and created a series of resources that would help others at the school to implement them. Study group members began creating new methods of staff support for those implementing the interdisciplinary curriculum at the school, and piloted models of the BYOD policy, an outdoor Desert School classroom, and several Corridor Classrooms. Their interest in student empowerment led them to create resources that would help FPS teachers to better understand student learning through the use of established assessment models.

MOVING FORWARD

By the end of the school year, teachers felt more empowered to implement new teaching and learning strategies including self-directed interdisciplinary projects. They were able to see impacts on students such as increased student engagement. The interdisciplinary learning curriculum rolled out to all teachers in grades 5 – 8, and additional teachers began creating their own Corridor Classrooms. The outdoor Desert School classroom began to accommodate more students, and the school's use of technology expanded from the BYOD policy to additional technologies including educational robotics kits.

A new study group formed and began to identify additional opportunities for innovation within the school.

GEMS AMERICAN ACADEMY - Abu Dhabi | Innovation Journey
STUDY GROUP MEMBERS: Jennifer Parker, Cathy Sciolis, Abhishek Singh, Peter Thorpe

CREATING THE STUDY GROUP

GEMS American Academy (GAA) is an American curriculum school located in the Emirate of Abu Dhabi. The school operates on a holistic education model guided by the International Baccalaureate Scope and Sequence and Project AERO (American Education Reaches Out/Common Core) curriculum standards, among other models. It has a school-wide focus on developing global citizenship and a nationally and ethnically diverse student body.

The GAA study group included one classroom teacher, two members who shared teaching and administrative roles, and the school's Vice Principal. Early interests of the group included developing a set of common teaching practices across the school, using technology in new ways, and assessing student learning outcomes.

Members of the study group wondered if there might be a connection between student motivation and assessment at GAA. Group member Jen questioned: "If the way you're being assessed is boring then how are you going to be excited about the learning that leads to it?"

GATHERING INSPIRATION

In an effort to better understand some of the challenges and opportunities for innovation at GAA, the study group engaged colleagues in a conversation about students' current strengths, and the strengths that GAA staff wanted to see them further develop. This conversation revealed a gap between aspirations for students and current student development.

BUILDING INQUIRY SKILLS

To learn more, study group members and their colleagues interviewed GAA students to solicit their thoughts. They also observed students in learning environments. Student engagement and the subject of assessment both came up frequently.

 Related Tools:
- Slow Looking
- Interviewing

DEVELOPING AN INQUIRY FOCUS

Study group members felt that student-driven assessments could be a way to increase engagement, and developed an initial inquiry focus: *How do we use assessments as tools to get students more excited about their learning?*

The study group began to refine its focus by considering a specific target population and desired outcome for its work. Group members also started to gravitate toward the idea of student-designed assessments. Their inquiry focus evolved into the question: *What is the impact of student-designed assessment on grade 9 & 10 students' engagement in learning in core academic subjects?*

 Related Tools:
- Population, Innovation, Outcome

Figure 4.4 GEMS American Academy—Abu Dhabi | Innovation Journey.

BUILDING INQUIRY SKILLS

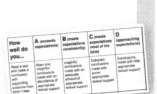

The study group consulted with colleagues as they considered different options for piloting student-designed assessment.

Study group members again looked to students for more information, distributing a survey to 9th and 10th grade students to better understand learner engagement in school.

The vision for the group's innovation project came together and they developed an approach where students were asked to propose their own ways of demonstrating what they had learned in class, including creative projects such as games or artistic representations. These were paired with a teacher-designed rubric for translating students' submissions into academic grades. Study group member Cathy began to pilot-test this approach in her classroom.

FIRST DRAFT INNOVATION PROJECT

PILOT-TESTING

The study group iterated on their initial design, adjusting the language and framing of the student-designed assessment approach in ways that they thought would ease student anxiety and lead to better results. They began to think about how to measure impact, and the school's Learning Support Staff team was recruited to help scaffold the approach for students.

As Cathy and other teachers pilot-tested the new approach to assessment, they learned that many students were uncomfortable with having so much freedom in self-defining how to demonstrate their learning, and in being asked to demonstrate learning through creative projects.

 Related Tools:
- Data Analysis suite of tools

ADVANCED INNOVATION PROJECT

SCALING UP & REACHING OUT

REFLECTING AND SHARING

Seeing exciting student projects and promising learning outcomes, study group members collaborated with colleagues at the school to pilot the new assessment approach in additional school subjects. They also presented their work to other members of the school that were interested in trying out inquiry-based projects of their own.

the study group–created timelines, as well as other documentation and data collected by the study groups over the course of implementing their innovation projects, to develop drafts of the innovation journeys that appear on the following pages. Journey maps were then revised and refined by each study group. This general process is detailed in the *Project Journey Mapping* tool in Chapter 8, which can be used by educators to create their own timelines and journey maps.

While the schools generally went through the same sequence of activities, the innovation journeys illustrate how each study group's experience was somewhat different. Collectively, these journeys help to illustrate the diversity inherent in the ways that different educators will approach inquiry-driven innovation based on their unique contexts and the highly personal goals and purposes that drive their desire to innovate. For example, in addition to seeing variety in each study group's innovation project(s), readers of these innovation journeys will also notice some differences across study groups in terms of their exact innovation processes and the setbacks and successes they experienced along the way. These innovation journeys also help to show the ways in which some study groups worked as a full team on one or more projects for the duration of their work, while other groups split up to work as individuals or subgroups at certain times.

Just as these journey maps show diversity across study groups, they also highlight similarities among the schools' innovation journeys. This is particularly noticeable in the pedagogical tools from Part Three that were noted by the study groups to be especially important for their overall journeys; tools such as *Slow Looking*; *Population, Innovation, Outcome*; *Theory of Action*; and the *Data Analysis* suite of tools were recognized as important to multiple study groups.

Overall, these innovation journeys can help readers to envision how the Framework for Inquiry-Driven Innovation detailed in Part One plays out in real-world settings in a quick and accessible way. They also provide support for the idea that engaging in inquiry-driven innovation is a winding path that can take very different forms and yield different kinds of positive school-based change.

CHAPTER 5

SCHOOL CHANGE STORIES:

Three In-Depth Case Studies

The following case studies show inquiry-driven innovation in action at three of the original research cohort schools: The Kindergarten Starters, GEMS Wellington International School, and GEMS Modern Academy (see the Appendix for further details about the schools). The case studies were developed collaboratively, with the research team first creating draft timelines of the case schools' innovations by pulling out key moments in the work, including setbacks as well as positive developments. Each school study group then revised those timelines and participated in group interviews with the research team to discuss what was included in the final timelines, and why. The research team incorporated these timelines with other data collected through school visits, interviews, focus group conversations with study group members and other associated stakeholders at each school, and documentation from workshops and study group meetings. Together, these data helped the research team to craft a selective retelling of each group's innovation story, with key learnings then distilled about what it can mean to engage in inquiry-driven innovation within diverse contexts. The cases were then written up by the research team and approved by study group participants.

While these case studies delve into unique stories of inquiry-driven innovation, they are meant to offer food for thought to other educators, who are likely to find resonance with some or perhaps many aspects of the specific contexts and scenarios.

Case Study 1: The Kindergarten Starters (KGS)

Re-Envisioning Roles and Expanding Conversations

Innovation in educational contexts often places a focus on the tangible products or "stuff" of innovation such as expensive curricula, cutting-edge technology, or shiny new maker-spaces. But how does innovation happen in a school that is not bursting at the seams with financial resources? The Kindergarten Starters (KGS) school did invest in some new "stuff" as part of an ambitious school change initiative to shift from traditional and teacher-led classrooms to more student-centered educational approaches. KGS is a school with limited financial means, and what is arguably more compelling about KGS's change story is how it invested not in tangible stuff, but in people. By giving time and attention to the personal and professional development of teachers, and by inviting more stakeholders into conversations about teaching and learning, the school succeeded in transforming the experiences of KGS students, teachers, and families.

This case study begins with a brief and selective history of KGS, including the story of its two study groups and the innovations they initiated as part of a broader school transformation. Next, the case study explores the ways in which KGS changed its approach by re-envisioning the role of the teacher, and opening up conversations about teaching and learning at the school. It then shares implications for practice and outstanding puzzles and insights.

Finding the "Soul" of Teaching and Learning: The Story of Inquiry-Driven Innovation at The Kindergarten Starters

Founded in 1990, KGS (see Figure 5.1) has a co-ed population of more than 5,300 students. Of this total population, 2,300 students are in kindergarten classrooms and the remaining 3,000 are in grades one to five. School fees at KGS are more than 80 percent lower than the Dubai average. The school's overall educational approach was founded on the Central Board of Secondary Education (CBSE) model, the current iteration of the Boards system established in India beginning in the 1920s. Today, the CBSE approach provides guidelines on a variety of aspects of schooling, including among others the learning environment, curricular approach, assessment, teacher development, and teacher quality measures. Like many other Indian schools in Dubai, the majority of

Figure 5.1 The Kindergarten Starters School, Dubai.

teachers, students, and parents at KGS are of Indian origin and teachers grew up in many different parts of the Indian subcontinent.

Building on What Came Before: Previous Practices at The Kindergarten Starters

The school's approach in its initial decades stood in contrast to the hands-on and interactive approaches found in many other early childhood education settings. Even the youngest learners were expected to sit in rows of desks and listen attentively to their teachers. While this approach is not mandated by the CBSE, many members of the school community, including both parents and teachers, grew up in teacher-directed classrooms similar to those at KGS. As teachers described their own schooling in India, they noted a lack of opportunities to ask questions or stray from the planned curriculum. Sreeja,[1] a participating teacher, said, "I had questions, but no opportunity to ask them," and her colleague Mareen explained, "We didn't miss out on any learning, but there was no opportunity to nurture inquisitiveness." This teacher-directed paradigm naturally informed how the school was run in its first years.

As the school approached a leadership change in 2011, it was assigned an Acceptable rating from Dubai's Knowledge and Human Development Authority (KHDA)—which is designated the minimum level of acceptability required for Dubai schools. The 2011–2012 KHDA report noted positive aspects of the school, including student attitudes, older students' understanding of economic and environmental issues, and parent partnerships. The same report recognized the school's institution of new initiatives in teacher planning, sharing best practices, and recognizing students' varying abilities. But along with these achievements, the report commented that "many of these initiatives had not been fully implemented and were not, as yet, showing enough impact on students' learning" (Knowledge and Human Development Authority, 2012, pp. 3–4). Shortly after this report was released, new principal Asha Alexander began her tenure at KGS.

Seeing with Fresh Eyes: A Change in School Leadership

As indicated in her foreword to this book, Asha had her own observations about KGS's key strengths and challenges as she assumed leadership in 2011. Visiting classrooms in her new school, she observed that kindergarteners were not able to clearly express their thoughts or share their ideas. Asha said she felt there was "no soul" in the kindergarten classrooms at KGS, and questioned: "Were they learning language; were they learning to speak? We didn't know because they weren't allowed to speak." She felt an imperative to find a different model for teaching young children at KGS.

But in order to change course, she needed the teachers at her school to be on board. She wanted to help them find the passion and excitement that she felt was missing in the classroom. Inspired both by her own observations and by KHDA recommendations, Asha worked with her vice principal[2] and others at the school to begin an ambitious school change process that replaced the desks in rows with carpet squares in circles and chalkboards at the front of the classroom with wall space to hang student work and classroom documentation. She started using e-learning resources instead of textbooks, and encouraged group- and play-based learning.

But these changes did not always come easily. Asha recalled making rounds of the school after removing chalkboards and seeing that teachers had hung chart paper in their place to continue teacher-led instruction. She also noticed that some teachers had arranged the carpet squares in rows to recreate the structure of desks. Teachers were not the only ones with concerns about changes at the school. KGS parents did not understand why their children came home at night with empty notebooks—a result of the school's recent switch from traditional textbooks to e-learning resources. And when parents saw their kindergarten children sitting on carpets on the classroom floor, they asked Asha, "Has the school become so poor that we don't have desks for our children?"

Change Starts to Take Off

Alongside those still getting used to the changes, others at KGS were excited by the transformation underway. As teachers noticed positive impacts on student learning, they began to get on board with Asha's overall change mission. At this point, Asha and her teaching and leadership staff continued to broaden their approach to address changes to the school curriculum. From 2013 to 2015, the school began to implement new student-driven pedagogies with its older students (grades 4–5) and invested in a school-wide focus on service and giving back. Staff was trained in the delivery of a digital curriculum using the school's new e-learning platforms, and it started to look more critically at its work and its impacts through individual action research projects. New STEM programs in robotics, engineering, and design were developed, and the school's musical theater program was enhanced.

As part of the school's curricular and pedagogical overhaul, Asha continually searched for existing educational models that might be relevant for KGS. In this process, she visited early childhood centers in Reggio Emilia, Italy, to gain a first-hand view of a powerful early childhood education model. In particular, she gravitated toward practices from Reggio Emilia, including group learning, exhibiting student work, documenting the ideas of young children, and supporting student-led projects both within and outside school walls. Asha shared some of these ideas with staff through professional development sessions. With the implementation of a wide variety of new initiatives, the school's CBSE curriculum was becoming enriched with strands from international curricula—creating an academic approach that was unique to KGS.

Taking on the Charge of Inquiry-Driven Innovation

Within this overall change process, the school began to participate in the research project described throughout this book. Adopting an inquiry stance, teachers and school leaders started to pay close attention to their surrounding school and classroom contexts, looking anew at the educational approaches that some of them had been practicing at the school for years. From a group of volunteer participants that included teachers, school administrators, and school principal Asha, two study groups emerged. One group focused on kindergarten learners (aged 4–5) and the other looked at grade 4 learners (aged 9). In this setting, the responsibility to see with fresh eyes was not only placed on Asha, but was also extended across members of the study groups. Using some of the tools shared in Part Three of this book, they began with a broad inquiry focus that they described as "play, learning and the Indian context." Over time, study group members started to take ownership of new initiatives at the school, whether developed at KGS or brought in from existing models in the field of education.

One of the study groups focused on kindergarten-aged learners, building on ideas shared from Asha's visit to Reggio Emilia and from Project Zero about making student thinking and learning visible (Project Zero, n.d.; Project Zero & Reggio Children, 2001). They began to think about how to capture and collaboratively interpret student voices and classroom activities. They explored the practice of classroom documentation as used by educators in Reggio Emilia and researchers at Project Zero, in which learning artifacts are carefully collected, interpreted, and shared in order to enhance the learning of both learners and educators (Krechevsky et al., 2013). They used Project Zero *thinking routines*—simple structures or protocols that extend and deepen student thinking, and become integrated into the daily workings of a classroom (Project Zero, n.d.)—to guide learning and gain a better understanding of students' thoughts and ideas. They also documented and displayed learners' ideas and work through hallway bulletin boards and displays (see Figure 5.2). Inspired by an existing educational approach called Emergent Curriculum (Jones & Nimmo, 1994), kindergarten teachers began to experiment with curricula in which children were able to engage in material exploration and thematic projects that provided opportunities for teachers to build and adapt curriculum in response to how learners approached various provocations and open-ended tasks.

The other study group, focused on fourth-grade learners, began to experiment with interdisciplinary project-based approaches that challenged learners to design solutions to real-world opportunities and problems. These approaches loosely fell under the STREAM

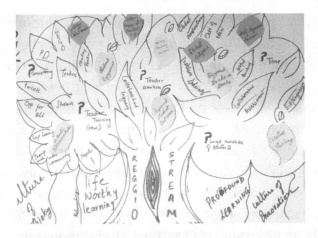

Figure 5.2 The study groups at KGS articulate their Inquiry Focus at the start of the inquiry-driven innovation process.

(Science, Technology, Research, Engineering, Arts, and Math) disciplines. They encompassed programs that helped learners build engineering and design skills, create multimedia stories, and envision and enact projects to address global issues like natural disasters, poverty, and human rights. For KGS, the STREAM approach meant finding interdisciplinary ways to approach any topic through mapping curricular themes that cut across classrooms and academic subjects. Across the school, students in multiple grades learned about the country of Malawi and raised funds to build a school there for other children. In another school-wide project, students learned about endangered species and wildlife protection, and visited conservation centers in Oman and Abu Dhabi. Eventually, they adopted and followed the progress of a sea turtle named Cookie and held a "turtle parade" around the school to raise awareness about the conservation of endangered species.

Through their work on these innovation projects, teachers engaged in an overall process of looking and listening to their surrounding context with an inquiry stance in order to see what new insights, learnings, and surprises might emerge. In weekly study group meetings, they increasingly listened to one another and this commitment to listening started to spill over into the classrooms as teachers began to listen to their students more and in different ways. Zahra explained the change she saw through her work in the kindergarten-focused study group:

> In the culture of the school [before our inquiry-driven innovation work], I felt the teachers were not ready to listen to one another. Even me. . . . I maybe wasn't ready to listen. There was a very rigorous reflection required on our part. . . . So it took us a long time and there were roadblocks where the teachers felt, "No, this is crazy. What rubbish." When they actually started [trying out thinking routines] they started believing in this because they could see it in fact in the children; they were learning even better. . . . [The teachers are] surprised now the way the children are talking. . . . [Teachers collect documentation and] they get back to it, they reflect, they read it again, they analyze: so it's becoming more authentic. [Before starting this work] we were documenting, no doubt about that, but we were missing all the important aspects, missing all the important things, missing all the important links to what's the progress. So all of this has changed. The entire culture I feel is changing.

Having embraced inquiry-driven innovation, including its incorporation of local ownership of innovations and attentive listening to multiple and diverse voices, teachers and school leadership saw that they were still leaving an important stakeholder out of the classroom: parents. Instead of being deeply embedded partners in the school's change process, many parents instead learned from their children about changes after they had been put into effect. To help bring parents into the change process, the school began to institute an Open Doors initiative that continually invited parents into KGS classrooms to help them get a better sense of the teaching and learning practices at the school. After class visits, parents were asked to share reflections and feedback with school supervisors, who then shared this feedback with individual teachers. Dialogues began between parents and school staff about how the school was using parent feedback to make changes at KGS. By the end of the study group's initial two years of work, nearly 5,000 parents had visited KGS classrooms as part of Open Doors.

Moving Forward, Together

In a short period of time, this work extended beyond the efforts of the study groups, and teachers across the school began using similar pedagogical approaches and increasingly listening to colleagues, students, and parents. KGS began to explore spreading Open Doors to other schools. The practice of documentation and the use of thinking routines and cross-disciplinary projects continued to grow and become embedded in their day-to-day approach to teaching and learning. Over time, the new practices at KGS started attracting positive attention from other schools and even the local press, as well as the Dubai School Inspection Bureau that assigns school ratings. By 2016, KGS had moved from a rating of Acceptable to Good on this all-important rating scale. School achievement measures in Science and Math also rose significantly on the Trends in International Mathematics and Science Study (TIMSS).

Over the course of several years, members of the school community—teachers, parents, and learners—were asked to embrace the visible and tangible changes at the school, such as getting rid of desks and printed textbooks. But more importantly, the school community was asked to rethink some of the intangible aspects of school: beliefs about how learning happens and who is involved. This required letting go of how the adults in the KGS community had grown up learning, incorporating more stakeholders into the dialogue about teaching and learning, and creating spaces for listening, collaboration, and trust. Much of this challenging work happened through a process of personal and professional growth for teachers that led to a re-envisioning of the role of teachers and an expansion of conversations about teaching and learning.

Re-Envisioning Roles and Expanding Conversations

This case study now shifts to look at the personal, professional, and dialogic changes that were intertwined with the school's transformation, distilling themes that could prove useful to educators and educational leaders working in contexts strikingly different from KGS. As the Framework for Inquiry-Driven Innovation sits at the nexus of innovation and professional development, many of the school's changes were caused by—and led to—changes in teachers' professional and personal development. The framework also promotes innovation that is responsive and relevant to its surrounding educational context, inviting educators to think about and listen more broadly to diverse peers and stakeholders. Thus, the analysis of how innovation happened at KGS is deeply enmeshed in a story of how the educators and their conversations about teaching and learning changed during the overall process of reshaping the school.

Re-Envisioning the Role of the Teacher

As mentioned earlier, KGS educators' own learning experiences as children were significantly different from the types of learning experiences they were tasked with implementing following the school's pedagogical overhaul. Previous research has shown that embracing this kind of shift can be a formidable task. While teachers' own schooling experiences can occur decades before they enter the classroom as educators, these childhood experiences—or what Lortie (1975) calls "apprenticeship[s] of observation"—can have profound and long-lasting impacts. Making an intentional and conscious separation from one's previous classroom experience often involves not only learning new practices, but also *un*learning preconceived notions and deeply held beliefs—a process that can have a strong affective component and be deeply entwined with explorations of one's own identity (Dede, 2020).

Given the importance and the challenges involved in teachers separating themselves from their own previous experiences, it is all the more striking to consider the changes that took place at KGS. In contrast to teachers' own learning experiences in which they felt they were not allowed to ask questions and were expected to follow the teacher's lead, KGS teachers were now offering students a more inquiry-based approach to learning. Learners were allowed to find multiple pathways toward a final answer, encouraged to debate with each other and admit when they did not know how to answer a question, and were not penalized for making mistakes. This shift involved changing the teacher's role at KGS. When Asha began her principalship, teachers at KGS were seen as the experts in the classroom. They were in charge of managing the curriculum and ensuring that students mastered certain vocabulary words or learned preestablished content, and making targeted decisions about what information to cover on a day-to-day basis in the classroom. During the school's overall transformation, these roles of the teacher as expert and curriculum manager had to be questioned and reconsidered in order to create the space for more learner-centered pedagogies to develop and thrive.

From Teachers as Experts to Teachers as Learners

Asking teachers to learn new classroom practices was an inherent part of Asha's approach to implementing school-based change. Through their involvement in the research leading to this book, KGS study group members were further asked to become learners by taking on an inquiry-based and reflective approach toward their classrooms, including engaging in *slow looking*. KGS teachers were asked to let go of their role as experts and become learners themselves. This shift helped teachers better understand the student experience, try out approaches that were markedly different from their own school experiences, and gain confidence in implementing new practices.

For the *Slow Looking* tool used by this study group, see Part Three.

Some of this work happened experientially in continuing professional development (CPD) sessions at the school. Educators described these sessions as important spaces for colleagues who did not normally have shared planning or meeting time to come together, collaborate, and exchange ideas. In CPD sessions—which were required for all teachers, including those participating in the research—KGS teachers debriefed from the week's classes, collaborated on curriculum plans, and analyzed classroom data and documentation. Asha also began to use these sessions as safe spaces where teachers could role-play new practices. With some teachers trying out new practices and others acting as students, teachers grappled with what it might feel like to be students engaging in types of learning that were different from previous practices at KGS.

See the *Prototyping an Experience* tool used by this group in Part Three.

For example, in beginning to explore the idea of *provocations*—questions and materials within the Emergent Curriculum approach that were used to generate student interest and inquiry—Asha asked teachers to play at a classroom water table, exploring the qualities of water and the questions they raised without specific directions for what to do next. This modeling in a safe space provided an opportunity for teachers to understand the student experience before trying out the Emergent Curriculum approach in class. Teachers also role-played the use of Project Zero thinking routines and received feedback from colleagues who had acted as students in the role-play scenario.

As they built confidence through trying out new approaches to practice, teachers began to worry less about the specific scripts or steps of the thinking routines and more about how to iterate on these routines in ways that were best suited to their school, their classrooms, and their students. Teachers also cascaded their learning as those who had tried out new pedagogies or approaches to practice shared their experiences with other teachers. At times, they shared this learning with educators outside of KGS by presenting their work at convenings organized by Dubai's KHDA to facilitate exchange of best practices in schools.

This openness to being learners and supporting each other's learning was embraced in a holistic way by teachers as they recommitted to ongoing learning and professional growth. Sreeja described feeling a "collective responsibility" toward good teaching at the school, saying that she felt free to support other teachers by telling them what worked well in her classroom—as well as what *did not* work. Teachers described having to be more "on their toes" in order to keep up with what was happening in their classrooms. As class lessons were increasingly guided by student questions and interests, teachers were compelled to do more research so that they could support learners to delve into unanticipated questions. Veteran teachers began to reinvest in ongoing learning in order to be more up to date on what they were teaching. Sreeja said: "[I've become] more responsible for my own learning. I have been teaching for years before KGS, then comes the last two years. In these two years, [I have begun to] understand I need to be more updated to allow my children to think—when they think, I also need to be thinking."

Author Erica McWilliam (2008) describes this role as different from both the *Sage on the Stage* and *Guide on the Side* paradigms in teaching; she refers to the *Meddler in the Middle* for the teacher who is able to experiment, fail, take risks, and design along with students. Embracing experimentation and risk-taking at KGS played out not only in how teachers transitioned from being positioned as experts to being positioned as learners, but also in how they shifted from curriculum managers to owners of and innovators in their classroom practice.

From Teachers as Curriculum Managers to Teachers as Owners and Innovators

Prior to changes at the school, teachers—under the guidance of the principal and the guidelines of the CBSE—were the main managers and decision-makers in classroom curriculum development and delivery. Some teachers continued this role after the changes initiated by Asha by using models and curricula brought into the school from elsewhere. But for others, these externally developed models were only a starting place.

These teachers began to take on ownership of models developed outside of KGS, in part, by taking control of the language of teaching and learning at the school. In framing its initial inquiry focus at the start of its engagement with inquiry-driven innovation, one of the study groups described its focus as looking at how "Reggio practices" could impact student outcomes. The other study group wanted to look at how STREAM approaches affect student learning. Encouraged by the research team and project liaison Christine Nasserghodsi to clarify what concepts like STREAM and Reggio approaches meant at KGS, teachers began to refine their understanding of these concepts, identifying the core elements that seemed most important for KGS learners. The group that aligned itself with practices from Reggio Emilia distilled its interest to four core Reggio-inspired ideas: documentation of learning, child-constructed learning, respect for children, and observation. The STREAM study group honed in on how interdisciplinary learning approaches might help teachers support students to problem-solve for real-world challenges—a strategy that was key to many of the school's community service projects and design-based thinking programs.

Teachers also developed the confidence to iterate on the educational models that inspired their changes in pedagogy. Teachers in the kindergarten-focused study group recounted that in the early days of the school's changes, they constantly looked back to the way things were done in Reggio Emilia centers to ask: "How do they do what they do?" But little by little, they became more confident in adapting ideas in ways that would work best in their own school. Zahra explained:

> On our journey from Reggio to Emergent Curriculum, where we started was superficial, it was just an idea about exploring materials, but now we've moved on. . . . [We're

thinking about] how to make better use of materials, and how to inquire about it, how to get students to think about it.

Describing this shift toward greater improvisation, Olivia said: "We used to be Reggio-inspired; now we're KGS-inspired." And Radha reflected:

> *Now teachers have the liberty to take learning in the way they want it to be, the way they want to do it. . . . Before, they were told how to go about things. Now you can tweak the lessons as per your understanding, you know what will work and what won't.*

Teachers said that their confidence in trying out new approaches continually increased as they saw the positive impacts of the approaches on student learning. And as adapting current practices became the norm at KGS, school leaders increasingly took changes to practice in their stride. Gauri, the school's Head of Curriculum, said she began to feel that members of the KGS community had become ready to innovate on anything, anywhere, at any time.

While principal Asha—as previously mentioned—was key to bringing new practices and approaches to KGS, the ownership of this process was not exclusive to this one pivotal person. As teachers reflected on their work about a year into their involvement with the research project, they said that the ideas had started with Asha, but had then filtered down to the study group members who were asked to take on the mantle of innovation and eventually pass it on to the rest of the teachers at the school. Rana said that innovating through the study groups differed markedly from previous attempts to innovate at the school because it involved sharing innovation work with others. She felt that this sharing, in turn, helped teachers to gain confidence and reflect on the changes they were effecting in the school as they shifted their role from curriculum managers to owners and innovators of new practices.

While the shifting role of the teacher was critical to the innovation process at KGS, another key and related change lay in expanding conversations on teaching and learning to include those whose voices hadn't been heard as loudly before: students and their parents.

Making Room in the Conversation: Expanding Conceptions of Who Gets a Say in Teaching and Learning

As part of its sweeping changes, KGS's school community had to think more expansively about who would be invited into conversations about teaching and learning. When asked by the research team to be attentive to multiple perspectives within the school community—one of the five principles of the Framework for Inquiry-Driven Innovation discussed in Part One—study group members were challenged to create the time and space to seek out and consider new voices by carefully listening to and observing various stakeholders. Through these activities, the voices of students and parents were brought into the school conversation on teaching and learning in ways they had not been before.

Student Voice in Teaching and Learning

The general shift at KGS to allow greater student voice within the classroom was, of course, not a new idea: early in the twentieth century, John Dewey wrote about the importance of promoting active engagement and democratic ideals in classroom experiences, and of striving to make education meaningful and relevant to learners (1916, 1963). More recently, ideas such as student-centered learning, student agency, and self-directed learning have gained wide adoption in the field of education. But in spite of their long history in the field, these ideas remain easier said than done and teacher-driven patterns of interaction tend to be the norm around the world (Watkins, 2017).

Gauri, the Head of Curriculum, said that teaching changed "drastically" at KGS to let students assume ownership, set the course for learning, and voice their interests and opinions. Teachers described this change not only as a process of students stepping *up*, but also of teachers stepping *back* and allowing their learners to take the reins. Rana, a kindergarten teacher, described this idea of stepping back:

> It was difficult because [for me] . . . as a student I'd always seen my teacher coming in with a book in her hand; she kept [talking] and we kept looking at her and nodding our heads; she kept dictating and we kept writing our notes; she kept writing on the board and we kept copying. . . . Even after I've seen my teachers like that, I wasn't like that [as a teacher] . . . . But still it was difficult for me to step back and wait and see students perform. . . . Every time I thought they would need my help [I'd say], "I'm here to help you," but they didn't [need it]. . . . [Asha said to me:] "You don't have to say anything. You just have to give [them a task] and see and they'll surprise you . . . just leave it to them and they'll do it."

Mareen said she began to think of effective teaching as "[giving] students the freedom to choose the method of learning." And Bhawna said that her involvement in the project helped her to "remove the boundaries [for students] and . . . give them the opportunities and platform where they can think out of the box. They should not be limited by my activity as a teacher [saying]: 'Okay, this is the start to the activity, this is the methodology, this is [what] I wanted to teach them today.'" In this new paradigm, learners gained a voice in conversations about teaching and learning at the school. And nowhere was this more apparent than in the school's Emergent Curriculum and STREAM learning approaches.

In the Emergent Curriculum, kindergarten teachers started a curricular unit with a loose overarching plan of what they might explore around a given topic. They introduced *provocations* (Wien, 2008): objects, materials, events, and ideas intended to inspire student curiosity and motivate them to learn more. They then used mind maps to document student questions and ideas brought about by the provocations. In one early pilot of the Emergent Curriculum, kindergarten teachers chose animals as a curricular theme. Rather than crafting lesson plans around biodiversity or animal species, teachers instead created a pretend zoo in each classroom and invited children to explore it. Instead of asking predefined questions, teachers observed their learners and documented the questions they came up with on their own. While teachers made decisions about which student-generated questions made the most sense to carry further in class, student brainstorming sessions and mind maps (see Figure 5.3) were the starting point for proposing where the curriculum would go next.

Figure 5.3 Documentation of student ideas raised during brainstorming sessions in the Emergent Curriculum approach.

Similarly, with the school's interdisciplinary STREAM initiatives that asked students to design solutions for real-world challenges, teachers used global issues and design challenges as the catalysts for fourth-grade student projects. School programs that focused on engineering and design challenges, multimedia storytelling, and raising funds to support less financially resourced school populations in other countries, all intentionally began by soliciting student ideas and interests. Through this work, teacher Suby said she had learned "to make a student-centered classroom environment where [students] are given the responsibility to choose, observe, think, and reflect independently and by making connections [from] what they have learnt to how they apply their learning in real-life situations." These curricular approaches meant that teachers had to transition from a lesson-planning model—led by what teachers thought students should learn—to a collaborative approach to curriculum planning that stemmed from questions brought up by students themselves.

Another key change that cleared the path for students to have a voice lay in removing the stigma from making mistakes in class or not immediately arriving at what the teacher deemed to be the correct answer. Olivia explained:

> *Initially teachers felt that the students should give perfect, complete work with the proper format, otherwise it's not correct. Now teachers [think], even if the format isn't good but the child can explain [her work], it's still right. Teachers do that because they're listening to the child's explanation. . . . That's the difference—the teachers had the mindset of needing [something] perfect and that is what is right. They would be giving feedback on an outcome they have seen, not on the process of the outcome.*

By creating the space for mistakes and acceptance of alternative answers, teachers let go of having pre-set correct answers be the sole guides in the classroom and began to hear their learners' misconceptions and ideas that were still in development. KGS teachers used the word "fearless" to describe how their students approached learning following changes at the school. Sreeja described this change from her perspective as a parent of a KGS fourth-grader, saying that she saw her daughter begin to feel empowered to bring questions to her teacher even if that meant not being able to finish her assigned homework due the following day. Teachers talked at length about seeing their students gain confidence through this process, expressing their thoughts more frequently and losing their fear of speaking. Mareen described how she saw her learners become more empowered to disagree with their peers and have debates in class. Overall, teachers were impressed by the quality of learners' ideas and realized that greater teacher attention to student voice would encourage learners to speak up even more in class and help them understand that their ideas were valued. Reflecting on her work as a study group member, Sharmi commented: "Students have the opportunity to express their thoughts and sometimes take us aback with their answers or queries."

Seeing the powerful results achieved by giving greater attention to student voice, KGS teachers and school leaders began to consider other missed opportunities for hearing new voices that could impact learning. In particular, they began to think about learners' parents. While school inspection reports cited the relationship between parents and the school as a point of strength for KGS both before and after the school's sweeping pedagogical changes, school leadership and teachers recognized the unfulfilled potential for parents to be true partners in supporting student learning and high-quality teaching. This potential went beyond parent–teacher conferences that foregrounded teachers' perceptions of what was happening in class, to inviting parents to visit KGS classrooms and form opinions and impressions of their own.

Parent Voice at KGS

In remembering what the school–parent relationship was like prior to the pedagogical changes at the school, longtime teachers from KGS reported that parents did not know what was happening in their children's classrooms. Twelve-year veteran teacher Olivia reflected that parents were happy with the type of homework their children received prior to changes at the school—written assignments in workbooks—because that was the type of homework that parents themselves had received when they were school-aged learners. In spite of the generally positive school–parent relationship at KGS, parent surveys around the start of major changes at the school showed that only half of responding parents felt the school was listening to them. This scenario is not uncommon around the world: comparative studies have shown that the degree to which parents have a voice in their children's schooling or are treated as partners to the school varies widely, particularly on matters that go beyond the practical or logistical (OECD, 2006). KGS had the ability to recognize that, despite its history of strong relationships with parents, it had further room to grow in this area.

As KGS began to make significant changes, school leadership had to figure out ways to bring parents into the change process. Asha explained:

> While we had the changes in pedagogy very clear in our head that definitely we [needed to] deviate from our textbook-oriented rote learning and regurgitation of knowledge; we definitely wanted parents to understand that learning has evolved, it has changed since they went to school. . . I knew we would be less successful if we denied them that transparency. . . We could see while teachers were moving towards their new way of thinking and new approaches [and] children were excited in the classroom, we were leaving a huge section of the stakeholders who are crucial to the success of these ventures out there with little or no understanding about the changes that we were effecting.

The school's study groups took on this charge, creating the Open Doors innovation project that invited parents into KGS classrooms (see Figure 5.4). They created a *Theory of Action* for parent involvement, outlining how participation in the classroom would deepen parents' understanding of how students learn and eventually lead to stronger parent–teacher bonds, improved quality of instruction, and better learning outcomes for students. By making opportunities for parents to visit classrooms and see the changes at the school for themselves, Open Doors explained new teaching and learning approaches to parents in a way that a presentation or a letter sent home could never fully convey. Different from school models in which a small group or council of parents is tasked with speaking on behalf of the entire parent community, the aim at KGS was to have *every*

Figure 5.4 Parents sit in on classes and participate in their children's learning as part of the school's Open Doors initiative.

parent involved—and not just in periodic or strategic meetings, but in the day-to-day life of teaching and learning at the school. When some parents did not respond to the initial invitations to visit classrooms (for a variety of reasons), Asha challenged her staff to continue getting in touch with parents who had not yet visited a classroom, seeking to encourage full participation across the parent body.

> See Part Three of this book for the *Theory of Action* and *Theory of Action Tuning Protocol* tools used by this group.

Teachers said that prior to Open Doors, when they asked parents for help or support in implementing school strategies at home, the parents did not understand how these requests fit into their children's learning. Gauri, the Head of Curriculum, said she felt a "resistance to change" among parents in the first two years of significant transformation at the school. But as parents started visiting classrooms, teachers saw them realize almost immediately that their children were learning in a fundamentally different way than they themselves had learned in school. Parents noticed their children working with different materials, and saw that they were being given opportunities to explore and express their feelings in class. These visits had a noticeable impact. In reflecting on the changes that Open Doors effected at the school, Zahra said: "Parents are *with* us now, they know that this kind of approach is helping to build up the skills in the children. So they are more focused, they know why we are doing what we are doing." Study group members felt that this experience enabled parents to better support their children's learning at home. Parent complaints about changes at the school also lessened.

But Open Doors was not only useful for parents. Teachers and school leaders also benefited from having someone with another point of view give feedback on what they saw in classrooms. Asha saw how parents noticed things that school supervisors might not: the temperature in the classroom, the dimness of the lights, and other factors that could disrupt learning but were not necessarily front of mind for those focused on pedagogy and managing a school. In inviting parents into the school on a daily basis, teachers also became more open to having visitors in the classroom. Radha commented that teachers made an effort to be better prepared with their lessons and classroom resources when they knew that another adult would be paying close attention to what happened in class.

Asha also noted the motivational and emotional value of having parents provide praise to teachers through their feedback on class visits. In many cases, parents gave positive feedback and support for what teachers were doing and created some external validation for the school's new approaches. Asha said this endorsement made its way into learners' homes as well, as students began to hear their parents' transition from making complaints about the school to talking positively about what they had seen in classrooms. She asked for daily reports from her staff to ensure that all parents were consistently being invited into classrooms. She committed the school to engage not only with parents who were already highly involved, but also with parents with lower levels of involvement at KGS or those whose children were struggling in school. In each case, parents were contacted by school supervisors following their visits in order to solicit their feedback. Supervisors also followed up with parents to tell them how their feedback was being incorporated into ongoing changes at the school.

With a regular presence in the classroom and a voice in how learning and teaching happened at KGS, parents began to transition from being school outsiders to classroom insiders, involved and vocal in their children's learning. In turn, teachers—after some initial hesitation—came to view parent visits as an integral part of building trust and support among families for student learning and as a source of valuable feedback. Beyond these impacts, a wealth of research indicates that strong parent–school relationships accrue benefits for learners themselves, ranging from increased educational attainment to more positive behaviors and enhanced motivation for learning (Henderson & Mapp, 2002; Gonazlez-DeHass et al., 2005). Far from simply shifting the conversation on teaching and learning, literature indicates that KGS's work to include the voices of learners and their parents in the everyday life of the school set children up for powerful long-term benefits.

Takeaways

KGS's overall transformation was personal and unique to the context and the individuals involved. However, many of the challenges and opportunities that were part of this transformation are not unique to this one context and this specific group of people. The following section of the case introduces some takeaways that emerged from the KGS story, but will be applicable to many other teaching and learning contexts.

Consider the *Who*, the *How*, and the *Why*

Oftentimes, the conversation around innovating in education starts with questions of *What*: What new curricula, supplies, equipment, or technology will drive learning in our context? What "stuff" do we need to purchase in order to innovate? The Framework for Inquiry-Driven Innovation challenges innovators to consider not only the material needs that are part of an innovation initiative, but also the purposes, stakeholders, and unique contexts that are involved. As can be seen in the case of KGS, questions of *Who*, *How*, and *Why* in educational innovation were at least as important as questions of *What* in the changes that took place at the school. Transformational innovation that has deep and long-lasting impacts requires engaging new stakeholders and expanding conversations with those who are already part of the school community. It demands taking another look at how teaching, learning, and leadership happen in a given context. And it must be founded on a critical examination of the purposes that guide the way a school does its work.

Start by Exploring Assets

Relatedly, the question of the assets required for innovating in education frequently begins with financial assets—how much money a school has to spend on innovation initiatives and what facilities and equipment it has available for new programs. This creates an "innovation is expensive" narrative that can deal a blow to the morale of schools without large budgets to spend on innovation initiatives, but with a wealth of other assets on which to draw. While there are undoubtedly schools with far fewer financial resources than KGS, within the context of Dubai, this school is certainly at the more modest end of the scale in terms of financial assets. Recognizing the nonfinancial assets and strengths of a school and its surrounding community is critical no matter what the school budget. The Framework for Inquiry-Driven Innovation explicitly asks educators to consider and draw on these assets by engaging diverse stakeholders and creating innovations that are responsive to and draw on their surrounding school contexts. At KGS, this meant building on the strengths and passion of the people in the school community, reframing who could help bring new ideas to the school, and adapting approaches from elsewhere to make them bespoke to the KGS context.

Gain by Letting Go

Educational innovation, in many cases, involves bringing novel ideas and practices to an existing context. But alongside bringing in the new, there is often a need to let go of what already exists—even aspects of the context with long and deeply embedded histories. At KGS, various members of the school community let go of beliefs about teaching and learning and their understandings about the expected roles of the teacher and other school stakeholders. The process of letting go required uncovering, reexamining, and dismantling long-held beliefs—both conscious and unconscious. But the possibilities that opened up by going through this examination made the process worthwhile. The powerful transformation at KGS shows how school stakeholders—including members of the teaching staff and parent community—changed from skeptics of the school's changes to some of its greatest advocates and champions. Rather than losing something by letting go of past practices at the school, stakeholders across the school community gained a great deal by being willing to pick up and integrate practices that for them were new.

You Do Not Have to Re-Invent the Wheel

In this story of school-based innovation, much of the change involved emulating or using practices that were already developed and established within the field of education. But KGS's "new to you" innovations amounted to radical and inspiring change within their local context; furthermore, the way in which they combined new ideas and made them their own over time reflected the kind of intentional innovation that Juliani (2018) advocates fostering within schools. In other words, the Framework for Inquiry-Driven Innovation by no means stipulates that educators need to be creating new practices or tools from scratch for what they are doing to be considered innovative. This case also suggests it may be helpful to consider the significance of school-based innovation at both the micro and macro level: while KGS's work may be viewed as an incremental innovation for the field of education as a whole, within the local context it was experienced as radical change.

Outstanding Puzzles

While this case study may offer inspiration to other schools, a number of puzzles remain. The next section draws attention to potential aspects of the KGS story that might be hard to replicate in other settings and/or might inadvertently bring up new challenges.

What Is the Role of a Leader in Innovation?

Asha used the metaphor of jumping into a swimming pool to describe how her school's teachers negotiated change, with the swimming pool representing new and unfamiliar pedagogical approaches. Asha said she would not "drag" teachers into the pool, but that she knew many were "sitting at the side of the pool" and would gain the confidence to jump in on their own. Here, a question exists about what would happen if they never plucked up the courage to jump. What should the specific role of a principal or school leader be in the process of innovation? Is a visionary leader required to make the kinds of transformational change proposed by the Framework for Inquiry-Driven Innovation, or can groups of teachers instigate change in the absence of a school principal or leader as proactive and sure about leading and implementing change as Asha? And, is there a point at which a leader could push too much or too hard toward innovation? Questions about the best way to lead toward innovation, and how to support educators themselves to lead innovation, are raised by the KGS case.

Where Is the Point of Innovation Saturation?

The use of Reggio-inspired approaches, thinking routines, and interdisciplinary curricular themes at KGS are just three of a wide range of initiatives that were part of the school's overall change process. The large number and diversity of approaches at the school that were introduced concurrently surfaces a question of whether or not there is a tipping point where too much change might be happening all at once in a given educational innovation context. David Perkins and Jim Reese have noted the difficulties that can arise when trying to implement many different initiatives at a school, each with their own timelines and frameworks. Perkins and Reese (2014) write:

> In such a situation, there's no common language for sharing practice and building collegiality, and therefore no real community of innovation. Teachers frequently respond with initiative fatigue: Next year will bring another new thing. . .let's not try too hard. (p. 44)

Nearly a decade into Asha's tenure as principal at KGS, new initiatives continue to be introduced with regularity. The question of whether or not the school will ever reach a point of saturation with new programs and approaches remains to be seen as its long-term trajectory continues to unfold.

Whose Values Are in Focus?

While the positive impacts of changes at KGS seem to demonstrate the value of a move away from educational approaches including rote learning and teacher-driven instruction, this move carries an inherent value judgment. KGS's teachers and principal embraced and championed a departure from the way that they—and many students' parents—had learned when they were growing up. Perhaps all change initiatives have at their core a value judgment about what has happened before, and the aspirations for what may happen in the future. But how might creating a deficit framing of one's personal experiences, or of certain models of education, be avoided? The road toward change may straddle a fine line between hopefully looking forward and disparaging what came before. Asha seems to have negotiated the journey along this road, as she received much support for the school changes from both within and outside of KGS. In any school change initiative, a constant examination of personal assumptions, value judgments, and asset versus deficit framing seems to be vital to the work.

Final Thoughts

As part of an ambitious and overarching change initiative, KGS transitioned from rote learning and teacher-driven classrooms to an educational approach centered on student interests and inquiry-based practices. Feelings of ownership and excitement for the school's changes spread across the school community and eventually led to learners and parents being invited to have an important and respected voice in conversations about teaching and learning. Principal Asha was widely recognized as the catalyst for this work from the beginning of her tenure at KGS in 2011. However, participants, including Asha, credit their engagement with inquiry-driven innovation with helping the school to slow down, reflect, share, and gain confidence through the process of introducing new initiatives at the school. Collectively, the school's commitment to trying new practices and its move toward inquiry-driven innovation led to changes that not only impacted how students learned, but also how teachers and school administrators thought about professional development, ongoing learning with peers, and the roles that teachers play at the school. While some aspects of the KGS case are obviously unique, as is the particular context of Dubai, implications can be drawn for school change and educational innovation in other settings.

Overall, the story of change at KGS shows that innovation does not have to be expensive, and that a school with a modest budget but a sincere and ambitious desire to change can build on a wealth of non-monetary assets within its context and community. This work may require seeing with fresh eyes, being humble, and reexamining or unlearning perceived best practices and deeply held beliefs and assumptions. The story of innovation at

KGS is inextricably linked to a story of personal and professional development within the school community. And it may encourage readers to consider where there is room in their own contexts for a more inclusive approach when considering questions about innovating in teaching and learning—one that includes more ideas, more voices, and more stakeholders. While school change is often evaluated in terms of changes in test scores, there is also great value in the changes that take place in the people involved: their roles, their confidence, their identities, and their place in collective conversations about teaching and learning.

Case Study 2: GEMS Wellington International School

Forging Cohesion through Innovation

Innovation is often thought of as shaking things up—quickly unsettling the norm and going into the sometimes uncomfortable space of new ideas or changes in practice. This case, focused on GEMS Wellington International School (WIS), does focus on one such school-based change: a new way of thinking about teaching and learning through the development of a school-wide, cross-disciplinary rubric for promoting critical thinking— playfully called *WISical Thinking*. However, rather than breaking up ossified or stagnant ways of doing things at the school, this case shows how both the process and resultant product of inquiry-driven innovation at WIS had the effect not of unsettling and creating discomfort, but of forging greater cohesion within a busy, initiative-rich school.

The case begins by providing background context for the school and five of its educators who formed a study group as part of their involvement in the research project detailed throughout this book. It then offers a selective timeline that outlines the group's development of the idea of WISical Thinking from its initial inception to a whole-school scaling effort. The case zooms out to consider how cohesion was promoted in different ways through this journey, including the coalescing of individual educators into a purpose-driven and action-oriented study group team; the development of a cross-curricular product that was distinctively homegrown and bespoke to WIS; and the whole-school implementation of the WISical Thinking rubric after close consultation with colleagues and students. The ways in which diversity, purpose, and ownership played a role in developing and spreading innovation at the school are also discussed. The case closes by exploring some broader implications of the school's innovation story and poses outstanding questions and puzzles.

Coalescing around a Shared Focus: The Story of Inquiry-Driven Innovation at GEMS Wellington International School

Set alongside one of the busiest throughways in the UAE, a brightly colored sculpture of a camel greets visitors to WIS. Once inside—and out of the heat—one will find the pace of this British curriculum school to be no slower than the traffic zipping by its front doors. But this fast pace does not imply a lack of welcome or friendliness: students, faculty, and staff pause to greet guests and are eager to share their pride in this impressive school. WIS was established in 2005 and is located in Al Sufouh in Dubai (see Figure 5.5). It hosts approximately 2,700 co-ed students from Foundation Stages (ages 3–5) to Year 13 (ages 17–18). The student and faculty population at WIS is largely British, although many other nationalities are represented throughout the school. WIS follows the National Curriculum for England (NCfE) from Foundation Stages up to year 11 (age 16). The International Baccalaureate (IB) Diploma Programme is available for students in Years 12 and 13 (ages 16–18).

Like all other independent schools in Dubai, WIS is overseen and supported by the government's KHDA. For eight years as of the writing of this case, WIS was continuously categorized by the KHDA as an "Outstanding" school—the highest attainable standard on the KHDA rating system. In 2018, WIS was profiled by the UAE-based website Schools Compared where it was awarded the grade of A+. Although excelling in almost every content area, in recent reports around the start of its involvement in the research project, KHDA noted that the Arabic and Islamic studies programs at WIS could be improved. While WIS was proud of its KHDA status and other accolades, as the school began engaging with inquiry-driven innovation, the leadership at WIS had felt challenged by the badge

Figure 5.5 GEMS Wellington International Schools, Dubai.

of "Outstanding"—especially in regard to internal and external murmurings that suggested that WIS had been "coasting" on its "Outstanding" status. The school wanted to prove that it could carry the badge of "Outstanding," "move beyond coasting," and continue to excel.

In addition to being a KHDA-certified "Outstanding" school, it should also be noted that WIS is considered a "Premium" school within GEMS Education, the school network of which WIS is a part. The designation of "Premium" signifies that the tuition and fees associated with attending WIS are at the highest end of the GEMS spectrum. In fact, at the time that the study group began its innovation work, WIS was the seventh-most expensive school in Dubai. As a result, the school is well-resourced, boasting a rede-signed library and cafeteria space and even one of the few astronomy observatories in the UAE. Nonetheless, students attending the school come from a variety of socioeco-nomic backgrounds. The "Outstanding" and "Premium" status of the school, coupled with the student, faculty, and staff's desire to excel, contributed to WIS's reputation as being a fast-paced teaching and learning environment. This aspect of the school resulted in increased workloads—and stress—for the school's faculty, staff, and students.

Formation of the Study Group

Once WIS signed on to participate in the research cohort of educators implementing in-quiry-driven innovation, then-principal Ruth tasked Andy, the Deputy Head of Teaching and Learning and a member of the Senior Leadership Team, with forming a study group (see Figure 5.6). Andy alerted the staff of the opportunity via email, and the study group was formed through a self-nomination process. However, in addition to the participants' own interest, Senior Leadership also played an important role in forming the study group by nudging some individuals to participate.

Figure 5.6 Members of the WIS study group:
(from left) Majd, Vicki, Nick, and Sarah.

Majd, an Arabic teacher, had expressed interest in participating in the study group because she saw it as an opportunity to improve student engagement in Arabic as a second language—what is called "Arabic B" within the Dubai education system. At WIS, as with other schools in the UAE, the approach to teaching Arabic is based mostly on a curriculum established by the UAE Ministry of Education. Improving the approach to Arabic language teaching is recognized as a continual focus across GEMS Education schools in the UAE, and both schools and teachers are on a perennial quest to ensure that the Arabic curriculum is interactive and engaging for students. As Majd noted, "We have a challenge to make this class or this subject interesting for students." She was interested in joining the study group as an opportunity to think differently about the school's application of the Arabic curriculum.

Meanwhile, Vicki, a history teacher and the school's IB coordinator, joined the WIS study group partly as a way to revisit her interest in inquiry-based learning—but this time in a group setting. Initially nudged by the Head of the Secondary School to participate in the study group, Vicki had recently completed a graduate degree in history education and through her degree had conducted action research into how writing can help improve class discussions. Vicki soon learned that the structure of inquiry-driven innovation offered a different approach to inquiry and research. Whereas her previous action research work had been a solitary experience focused on her own classroom, being part of a study group was a welcome change for Vicki. "It's different this time," she said, "because it's as part of a group, whereas before it was just my own thing and I had to go and sit at home every weekend and just do something entirely by myself."

Along with Majd and Vicki, two English teachers, Sarah and Nick, volunteered to join the study group. In addition to their teaching positions, Sarah served as the English department chair and Nick was the English department's intervention manager. Nick joined because he was interested in engaging in action research "and creating something new and innovative for the school." Sarah, on the other hand, cited her attraction to the project's focus on teaching and learning, as well as the opportunity to work with teachers from other schools through the broader research cohort.

Interestingly, the professional roles of each of the members of the study group changed over the course of their involvement in this work, with many members receiving promotions. Together, the five study group members represented staff from a variety of different departments and levels of leadership. Had it not been for the opportunity to engage in this research, this set of players would likely not have had the chance to work together closely.

Tackling the Badge of "Outstanding" and Coasting

As the study group was forming, group members began to consider what to pursue as their inquiry focus—that is, a question of practice that could motivate and focus their innovation work. Concurrently, the school as a whole was at an important moment. For one, the KHDA was conducting its yearly inspection at WIS—a process that brought with it significant pressure, preparation requirements, and demands on the time of WIS teachers and administrators. WIS had been performing as an "Outstanding" school for eight years, but as noted, there was an impression that WIS was riding on the "Outstanding" ratings of prior years—and the senior leadership at WIS was concerned that not enough effort was being applied to sustaining that rating.

Aside from this pressure, the school had a history of taking a demanding approach to innovation and instituting new practices. At WIS, many new initiatives and projects had been conceived, drafted, and implemented at a very rapid pace. It was the norm that projects would be announced one week and implemented the following week. This was one of the aspects of the school culture that contributed to its fast pace. "Our work is so fast," Vicki noted, "the [WIS administration] come up with a new idea and it has to be actioned immediately." The speed of change was also something that affected the school's students, and, as a result, it became an early area of interest for the study group. "This working environment is very fast-paced," Nick mentioned. "It takes an outside influence to suggest slowing down." Engaging in the process of inquiry-driven innovation presented itself as an opportunity to investigate the pace of the school—and to potentially develop a way to slow things down.

As it happened, while the study group was getting started, school-wide initiatives were being launched to address "pace and time management." The study group felt that their innovation needed to be related to some of these schoolwide concerns about coasting and the pace of the environment. "When we came to the very first meeting," recalled Vicki, "we thought, because of the aims of the school, that we would have to do a project relating to pace and challenge." As a preliminary idea, they decided to focus on the role of time in teaching and learning.

Coming Out of Inspection: Establishing a Study Group Dynamic

After the important school inspection, which went well, the study group had signifi-cantly more time to dig into its inquiry focus—and to bond as a team. Even though study group meetings follow a nonhierarchical format, in effect the team was led by Andy who, as previously noted, was the Deputy Head of Teaching and Learning, and thus, part of the school's Senior Leadership Team (SLT). Traditionally, one of the main responsibilities of a person working in this position is to review and improve the performance of head teachers and staff. Andy, however, was known for breaking boundaries. In this spirit, he committed to becoming an active team member rather than simply reviewing and assess-ing the group's progress. Reflecting on Andy's participation in the project, Vicki noted, "Andy was part of the team, he was leading it, but he came to all the sessions and was in it as much as the rest of us." Not only was Andy an active participant in the study group, he was also critical in setting up a team culture that was positive and empowering for all members of the group.

Narrowing the Focus

With time and innovation as its inquiry focus, the study group used the *Slow Looking* tool to observe how school staff spent its time. While study group members did indeed find that a scarcity of time was an issue for many of their colleagues, they also noticed something else.

For the *Slow Looking* tool used by this study group, see Part Three.

Coupling what they observed in classes with their prior experiences at the school, study group members began to feel that WIS students, in their words, "struggled with 'thinking' as a concept." As an IB Diploma Programme school, WIS educators worked across grade levels to prepare students for the IB Learner Profile that students would be expected to meet in the school's highest grades (Years 12 and 13, or 16–18 years old). Among other skills and competencies, this Learner Profile included students' ability to take risks and "[apply] thinking skills critically and creatively" to the work they were doing both within and outside of class.[3] In order to begin reinforcing these aptitudes early in the student trajectory, study group members felt it would be important to begin to introduce key thinking skills in Key Stages 3 and 4 (11–16 years old), with the idea that by introducing thinking skills earlier, they would become instinctual and built into students' ways of approaching concepts and problems by the time they reached the higher grades. They decided to start with the students on the younger end of this age spectrum, who they noticed sometimes found it challenging to articulate their thinking and to apply critical thinking skills. Study group members summarized: "We want our students in Year 7 to be able to articulate how they think and how they are able to sort pieces of information. We want our students to apply these skills to solve real-world problems. This will ultimately help them to achieve in exams at school and set them up for real life so they can apply the skills to anything."

As the study group turned its attention toward the issue of critical thinking among students, the members were still uncertain about how to move this interest forward in a way that was tailored specifically to their school and to WIS learners. Interestingly, waiting outside together during a fire drill at the school one day, members of the team came up with a term that—although still undefined—captured what they were interested in exploring: *WISical Thinking*. By establishing the name WISical Thinking, the study group set an intention to develop an approach to critical thinking that was bespoke to its unique teaching and learning environment, and designed specifically for WIS students across all subject areas.

Refining and Piloting the WISical Thinking Rubric

Now with an idea in mind, the WIS study group team began to pursue an innovation that would establish the components of WISical Thinking. To this end, group members delved into readings on critical thinking while reflecting on the realities of their student population. One reading, a piece on critical thinking within the nursing field, catalyzed the team's search for the components of WISical Thinking; the group was inspired by the way in which it provided concrete statements of what critically thinking nurses should be able to do. Working together, the study group developed six components of critical thinking that were specific to its school and began to establish a rubric: analysis, applying standards, categorizing, focused information seeking, reasoning routines, and predicting and transforming. The initial sketch for their rubric is shown in Figure 5.7. The purpose of the rubric was not to assess critical thinking, but rather to support the development of critical thinking within the student population. By developing this rubric, the WIS study group hoped to establish a set of skills that WIS students would aspire to achieve, and to enable students to reflect on where they were in the spectrum of skill development.

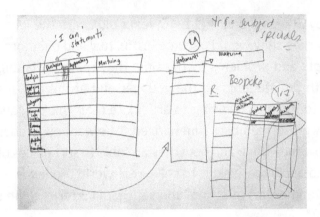

Figure 5.7 An early sketch of the study group's
WISical Thinking rubric.

These skills were wide-ranging. For example, they included highlighting the key points in a text, persevering when faced with a challenge, categorizing information, identifying a problem that needs to be solved, and predicting an alternative outcome. While this work was energizing and exciting for the group, it did not strike group members as especially fast-paced. They reflected: "It has surprised us how difficult it has been to move forward once we had the idea [for WISical Thinking]. The process is quite slow in order to think carefully and we are not used to working slowly."

Almost a year into their work as a study group, Andy left his position at WIS to assume a role at another school. His role as study group convener at WIS was quickly assumed by Vicki. By the time Andy left, the team had already become cohesive and the study group was able to continue with its shared vision for WISical Thinking. Around this same time, Vicki received a promotion to Deputy Head. Following this shift in roles, the study group decided to try out the WISical Thinking rubric during a Global Innovation Week event that was being held at the school. At this event, students created and presented technological solutions to global and corporate challenges. The study group tried to apply the rubric to student entries to get an idea of the degree to which they incorporated some of its components such as analysis and reasoning. This pilot-testing yielded valuable feedback from colleagues and the realization that as a study group the members needed to incorporate more instructions into the rubric. Initially, they had envisioned that the rubric would be used mostly by students with guidance from their teachers to help them reflect on and develop the abilities shown in the rubric categories. However, they realized that

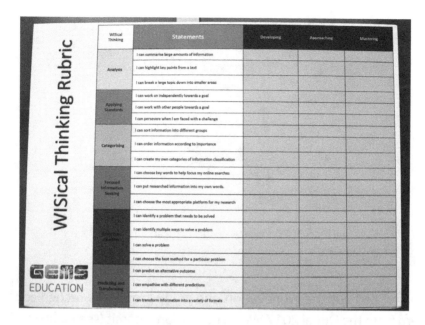

Figure 5.8 A refined version of the WISical Thinking rubric.

the rubric might be better used as a pedagogical tool to help teachers work with students to develop their critical thinking skills, and educators therefore became their target user population. The study group refined the rubric and trialed it once more in a Year 9 English class. After receiving more feedback, the team further tinkered with its innovation before arriving at the final product shown in Figure 5.8.

Gaining Traction and Exposure

After several trials of the WISical Thinking rubric in a variety of settings, the study group began to roll it out strategically to additional colleagues. The group members did this work slowly over time, and in fact at the beginning of introducing it to colleagues, they did not reveal the name WISical Thinking because they thought it would seem as if they were presenting a finalized product. But, over time, many colleagues at the school engaged not only in pilot testing the rubric in their classrooms, but also in giving feedback and making tweaks to the rubric based on what would work best in their own settings. By the end of the study group's two years of participation in the research cohort, the WISical Thinking rubric had a presence in nearly every classroom throughout the school. A corps of WISical Thinking Ambassadors was also created to engage colleagues from outside the study group in spreading the work to additional departments and classrooms. And not long

Figure 5.9 The study group proudly displays its
award from the World Education Summit.

after they had rolled out their innovation, the study group was recognized for its work
with an award from the Dubai 2017 World Education Summit (see Figure 5.9).

Forging Cohesion through the Study Group, the Product, and the Process of Scaling

This case now zooms out from the details of WIS's innovation work to consider what can
be learned from how that work unfolded—a discussion that brings to the fore the overarching theme of forging cohesion through innovation. The section begins by considering how a diverse group of individuals who had not previously worked closely with one
another emerged as a tight-knit group and why their sense of unity was important for their
innovation's ultimate success. Next, it discusses the WISical Thinking rubric itself and how
this innovation, with its catchy name, promoted a sense of collective ownership and pride
within the study group. The discussion then turns to the study group's inclusive approach
to rolling out the WISical Thinking rubric across the school and how that approach involved
sharing ownership of the product more widely. By pursuing cohesion in these various ways,
WIS educators were able to purposefully and strategically harness the innovation process
to improve teaching and learning within a fast-paced, initiative-heavy school environment.
Various ideas are introduced and considered through this exploration that may be useful to
educators working in a wide variety of teaching and learning contexts.

Establishing Group Cohesion

The story of inquiry-driven innovation at WIS involved individuals from different parts of
the school voluntarily coming together in the study group, and then bonding over time

to become a united force working together to innovate and spread innovation across the school. Their story, as previously recounted, shows how they coalesced from a group of individuals with diverse backgrounds into a cohesive and action-oriented team united by a common purpose. Three factors seemed to drive group cohesion: excitement about working as a diverse group, a collective purpose and sense of ownership over the work they were doing together, and a strong team identity.

Excitement about Working across Usual School Divisions

One of the most salient findings from WIS's story is the power of bringing together teams of practitioners whose membership is diverse and whose work is informed by multiple perspectives. As with many schools around the world, teachers at WIS were not only very busy, but also isolated from one another based on curricular content areas. As a result, WIS educators rarely had the opportunity to speak with one another, much less to actively collaborate with one another across departments. Furthermore, different professional roles were very well defined at WIS, as they are in many schools, and there were seldom opportunities for people from different roles or tiers of leadership to engage in projects together. The WIS study group broke from the norm on both of these counts, joining together educators from across content areas and levels of leadership.

Interestingly, the study group was not engineered to be diverse in the ways that it was: although Vicki was encouraged to participate, the group otherwise emerged organically according to people's interest in the project. The uniqueness of this opportunity to work across the usual silos was not lost on group members. Vicki, for example, noted that it was especially unusual for the Arabic department to be integrated into an initiative such as this:

> Often what happens in schools is, the Arabic department tends to get left out of things that are going on. . . . Personally, I've never worked with the Arabic team here at all, so to have Majd on board has been fantastic because she has some really, really good ideas, and she thinks about things in a different way and she's coming from a different perspective to the rest of us. And even Sarah and Nick, I know them from in school, but I've never sort of sat down in a meeting [with them].

For her part, Majd commented on the reciprocal benefits that emerged from her involvement in the study group, also noting that it was not just a case of her representing a different subject area, but that she also came from a different cultural background and had received different pedagogical training from her study group counterparts:

> In our team we [came from] different backgrounds. Four of them . . . they were from England but also they had different experiences and definitely I learned a lot sharing their . . . experience in teaching. . . . I didn't have that much chance to sit with them that much of the time before. . . . But with [the study group] I had more time to deal with them and know more things they are doing in their departments and as well they knew what we are doing in Arabic B more than before.

As an example, Majd learned from Nick and Sarah how reading and analyzing novels was approached in the English department, and shared that approach with the Arabic department to spur some new ideas about how to make short story reading in Arabic more interesting and engaging for learners.

As already noted, the group was also diverse in that it included both classroom teachers and school leaders—with some group members holding both types of roles simultaneously. In terms of role hierarchies from the broader school community, Andy was the highest-ranking member as Deputy Head of Teaching and Learning. Due to his role at WIS, he was familiar with the entire faculty body and helped the group to gain buy-in and collaborators for their work. Andy's role, coupled with the fact that he had initially invited others at the school to apply for involvement in exploring inquiry-driven innovation, made Andy the de facto leader of the group. Andy was humble in his approach. He took on his role in the study group as an equal group member rather than as a supervisor, thereby helping to establish a positive and empowering culture for all group members. Sarah also described different roles that emerged as part of the study group's work together. In addition to the leadership roles that Andy and then Vicki took on, Nick and Sarah often made the first attempt at designing resources and Majd thought deeply about applications of the WISical Thinking work to the Arabic department and helped the group to stay organized.

Group members noted that this diversity deeply affected how the study group was able to understand student needs across the school, allowing group members to make observations and form opinions that cut across departmental areas and professional roles. While the group in its later stages used formal data collection tools, including surveys to gain this understanding, its initial framing of student areas of strength and weakness was more anecdotal and came from each group member's personal experiences with students—a perspective that incorporated each member's work in different roles and content areas, and across learner age groups.

The diversity of the group also affected how the idea of WISical Thinking was applied across the school. The study group's focus on critical thinking initially seemed more readily applicable to the humanities than to other subjects, but some of its earliest trials also took place in Arabic classrooms due to Majd's involvement in the group. Majd recalled, "It was a bit challenging for the Arabic department to think about how to apply [the WISical thinking work] in the Arabic curriculum. We started to simplify the steps and do it step by step and share it with the team." The diversity of the group may have also helped in eventually gaining buy-in about the scaling of WISical Thinking across the school, as the study group was able to present it as a resource developed across departments rather than something developed by one department or a discrete group of teachers with their own interests in mind.

The idea that there is a benefit to assembling diverse teams with multiple perspectives (in contrast to homogeneous teams) is not new (Rock & Grant, 2016). This idea also relates to the concept of *functional diversity*. While there are various ways of describing this concept (Bunderson & Sutcliffe, 2002), here it can be used to describe the degree to which team members differ in their backgrounds and experiences. Interestingly, associations between the functional diversity in a group and a group's innovation capacity are mixed or inconclusive (Cheung et al., 2016). However, some studies indicate that various mediating factors such as trust among team members, working toward a shared vision, interacting frequently, and reflecting as a team—all of which are embedded within the process of inquiry-driven innovation—tend to increase the relationship between a team's functional diversity and its propensity to innovate (Ibid.; Hofhuis et al., 2018). The study group members appreciated the fact that they combined to form a diverse yet cohesive group, citing the collaborative aspects of the work as a highlight of the overall inquiry-driven innovation experience.

Shared Purpose and Ownership

The process of inquiry-driven innovation also helped to unite study group members through a sense of collective purpose and group-level ownership—a dynamic that developed over the course of time. Group members had started out assuming that they would focus their innovation work on coasting and/or time management because those were stated school-wide priorities. However, when they engaged in inquiry-based practices such as observation, interviewing, and documentation of teaching and learning, they found a more compelling focus: as they surfaced the need to strengthen students' critical thinking abilities, they found a purpose for innovating at WIS that was truly their own. As Majd pointed out, they did, in fact, find a way to address their initial concern about the perception of coasting—but they did so in a way that was compelling for their study group: "It wasn't on purpose that we moved from coasting to critical thinking. When we started on critical thinking, it wasn't like 'we need to do this because of our coasting perception.' But [the WISical Thinking rubric] will have an impact on the coasting [perception]." Moreover, this revised inquiry focus was explicitly connected to students' well-being and to the overall betterment of the school, two driving forces mentioned by study group members as personal motivators in their professional lives. Nick reflected: "We are here to produce something which is going to benefit our students and the school. And that, fundamentally, is why we work well together, because we're not doing it to kind of bolster reputation, it's something we want to do for the good of our students and the school."

This focus on long-term improvement was a core aspect of what drove the study group in its work. Sarah pointed to the group's focus on action as a key differentiator between this group and other groups of which she was a part at the school. As a point of contrast, she described her regular meetings with other department heads or with members of the English team. These meetings tended to be more functional and focused on immediate tasks rather than any longer-term vision. She reflected:

> A lot of the conversations that happen with the heads of department are all like, "What have you done about this? Have you done this?"—kind of like a tick list for the week. . . . "What are the results looking like here?" . . . In terms of WISical Thinking, we're trying to apply it to the school, so we're trying to create something new. Whereas, within the [heads of] department meetings . . . it's more a case of discussing what we're doing.

While Sarah still had numerous demands on her time and work pressures to deal with when she entered her study group meetings each week—meetings that came with their own to-do's and task lists—she felt that the space of the study group afforded her a time to be creative and think toward purpose-driven actions that went beyond just getting things done or checking off to-do lists. She described these study group meeting times as "invigorating."

Team Identity

A third driver behind the group cohesion that arose was the social and community-focused pull to be part of a team. Study group members mentioned the importance of bonding as a team on the bus rides to and from research cohort meetings or exhibitions with study groups from other schools. During those bus rides, they formed a stronger sense as a team as a result of being able to spend time together in an informal space beyond school walls. These informal conversations helped the team to form social bonds and gain excitement about its work together. By the time of Andy's departure from the school, a positive group culture was already in place, and Vicki was able to step into an informal leadership role and help the group continue its momentum. Thereafter, the composition of the study group remained the same. This consistency of membership benefited the group because members were able to establish trust and build on ideas without stopping and starting to catch new people up to speed.

Vicki noted that while each member came into the study group committed to promoting good teaching and learning at the school, "It becomes more than that when you are working with the same people all the time." The team-based element of the work was also significant:

> You've got that common thread each time you meet. . . . It's still good for the school, and of course we will begin to teach this to the kids and we of course want to increase their critical thinking, but when you're working with a group of individuals and you feel part of a team, it helps you to go on for the rest of your day.

These feelings may have been particularly salient for Vicki because she knew from the solo action research work that she completed as part of her master's studies how it can feel to plan, roll out, and reflect on a change in practice in isolation.

Research on teamwork beyond the field of education suggests that a strong team identity can aid innovation, as long as the team is encouraged to be reflexive and group members can, for example, participate in decision-making, as was the case here (Litchfield et al., 2018).

Whether or not Vicki, for example, was able to be more innovative or creative because she was working within a group rather than by herself is unclear. However, the group's overall dynamic and the ways in which as individuals they interacted with one another undoubtedly shaped the innovation they developed (Adarves-Yorno et al., 2007).

Promoting Cohesion through the Development of a Product

Unlike some of the other study groups in the research cohort, the WIS study group developed a readily identifiable product—the WISical Thinking rubric—around which the group's work centered. This rubric generated considerable pride and helped promote cohesion because of the joint sense of ownership it engendered both within the study group and across the school. Furthermore, the very premise of a rubric relevant across subject matters encouraged educators across WIS to consider the school curriculum as a coherent whole. The importance of feelings of ownership in the process of innovation has been cited by many, including in the business realm. A sense of ownership, which is often, but not necessarily, tied to a sense of agency, can encourage teachers to invest the necessary time and effort required to change practice (Ketelaar et al., 2012). More generally, developing a sense of collective ownership within an organization or professional setting typically enhances group effectiveness, in no small part because of the psychological safety it promotes (Pierce et al., 2001).

Owning the Innovation Product

Almost six months into the study group's work, and after completing several readings on critical thinking and studying its student population of interest, the study group met to boil down the core elements of WISical Thinking. With these core elements outlined, the study group was then able to implement and spread the rubric throughout the school. Participants felt that their sense of unity helped to facilitate this significant moment, which Nick reflected on several months later:

> We had collective understanding that we wanted to create something tangible. We had ideas, we wanted to create something you can see. . . . I remember the session clearly, we had readings and shared ideas. Then we all effectively came up with our rubric. We were all on the same page. It was a collective effort to create something.

In addition to cohering around the WISical Thinking rubric itself, the group came to own the concept of critical thinking as it applied to WIS's student population. When the study group first came up with the idea of focusing on critical thinking, Andy cautioned that while the concept of critical thinking is often talked about in education, many educators find it difficult to articulate what it actually means. On a site visit to the school, members of the research team encouraged the study group to consider the population, innovations or interventions, and long-term outcomes that felt most important to their work: Figure 5.10 shows how they used what became the *Population, Innovation, Outcome* tool, which can be found in Chapter 8. Researchers further pushed the group to define what it meant by "critical thinking" by asking group members to move beyond buzzwords to state in concrete terms what they were hoping to do in their work, and why.

The group thought of WISical Thinking as "adding their own spin" to critical thinking. Their approach combined existing ideas from readings with customized components developed by the study group when thinking about their own students. And putting a title on their product made a difference to group members. It gave life to the group's long-term

Figure 5.10 Ideas generated by the WIS study group using the *Population, Innovation, Outcome* tool.

work of thinking about needs at the school and potential interventions to address those needs. Nick described the naming process as giving the work "a face." Initially, group members thought that it was very important to have the name and branding of "WIS" as part of what they were doing—to the extent that they first attempted to define elements of critical thinking by creating an acrostic of their created word *WISical*. But they quickly abandoned that idea, realizing that the power of their work lay in developing a shared language about what they were working toward. While the school name still remained part of the WISical Thinking title, the group held onto that title, not because it was catchy, but because it was motivational to have the school at the heart of their work to define critical thinking.

A Product to Promote Cohesion

By its very nature, WISical Thinking sought to make connections across different subject areas rather than to emphasize difference. As already noted, the diverse nature of the study group allowed for different perspectives to be accounted for in the design of the product. Furthermore, the idea of designing the rubric so that it was relevant across all subject areas meant that it could be incorporated across the school—a great source of satisfaction for the study group, especially as it was focused on doing something concrete to help students. Nick, for example, talked about how he felt when he saw the rubric being used in other initiatives and programs across the school:

> You know, we've created resources, we've created our rubric which is still a work in progress, but it's something that did not exist and now exists. We have communicated to the whole staff about this. We've done assemblies where we've actually communicated WISical Thinking to the whole school. . . . So there's a sense of pride there. But it's the reaction from students as well . . . seeing how students are taking to it or not taking to it has been very interesting . . . already I can see ways in which I can tweak it and change it and make it better.

In this last point Nick is indicating his ongoing level of investment in the rubric and his desire to iterate on the design. The research team did not interview nonstudy group members to ascertain their level of enthusiasm for the WISical Thinking rubric. However, the rubric was displayed very visibly in the school foyer and in classrooms across the school, an example of which is shown in Figure 5.11. It was something that students would see multiple times in a given day, presumably offering some degree of continuity and connectedness as they moved from one subject area to another.

Figure 5.11 The WISical Thinking rubric on display in a WIS classroom.

While the rubric itself promoted cohesion within the study group, the way in which it was spread and scaled across the school provided another opportunity to bring people together around a shared goal.

Promoting Cohesion through the Process of Scaling

This case has so far highlighted how WIS study group members cohered around and felt ownership over the purpose and product of their work. This section considers the ways in which they extended ownership of WISical Thinking to other colleagues as they sought to scale up their innovation across the school.

Creating "Something for Us"

Creating something that could be owned by the whole school started from the very beginning of the study group's inquiry-driven innovation process: group members made efforts to tailor their work to the teaching and learning contexts they saw around them by closely observing WIS students, including their strengths and challenges. The act of including the school name acronym in the title of the WISical Thinking rubric also helped to signal that it was created specifically for WIS. In a school context that study group members had described as fast-paced and one in which new initiatives were regularly introduced and expected to be rolled out quickly, this homegrown approach was different. Sarah said that it felt important to create "something for us" (meaning the school) as the group envisioned the WISical Thinking project. She reflected that had the group branded its work as being about critical thinking, it would have seemed like an approach that was rehashing an idea that had been brought up many times before. But she felt that "WISical Thinking captures specifics of our school, and there's a lot of pride within that."

Study group members felt strongly that helping the rest of the school to feel ownership over WISical Thinking wasn't as much about putting the school name into the title of the rubric as it was about developing a resource that was inclusive and attentive to the perspectives of stakeholders within the school. Group members reflected on the question of how important the name was. Nick said that while the name was effective, without it "there would still be staff buy-in, still be that support. Because we've worked very hard to include students in the process, it's not something we created without students. And also bringing it to other members of staff was really important." In other words, WISical Thinking was not perceived to be a mere pet project of a few individuals. Vicki added that it was important that the group took their time to introduce the concept to their colleagues: "I think because it has been quite a long process, people didn't just hear about it overnight. . . . Other people did hear a lot about our process along the way as well." The "long process" that Vicki mentions unfolded over an extended period of time—more than two years—and importantly began in study group members' own classrooms within the Arabic and English departments. This approach helped to ensure that the first pilot-testers—the study group members themselves—already felt buy-in and motivation for the WISical Thinking work because they had been leaders in its development. It also allowed adjustments to happen quickly as study group members saw how the rubric worked in their own classrooms and were able to observe and reflect on it in real-time (see Figure 5.12).

Figure 5.12 Study group member Majd stands alongside a display about WISical Thinking in her Arabic language classroom.

Offering Ownership to Others–Slowly

As the group members' work progressed, they began to share ownership of their work by engaging colleagues outside the study group in pilot-testing and by seeking feedback from WIS colleagues and students. Colleagues who pilot tested the rubric were invited to hack or tweak it. Here, the thinking was that the study group could not just give final products to its colleagues to use; the group's colleagues also had to go through the *process* of using those products to see their benefits and utility. Two of the first such implementations outside of the English and Arabic departments happened in the school's Global Innovation Week and in the school's Maths department. In both cases, leaders of those initiatives and departments were invited to review and modify the rubric to suit their own purposes, tailoring it for their specific subject areas, student populations, and contexts. Presenting the rubric as a work in progress that could be hacked and tweaked— rather than as a static final product—was a strategic decision made by the study group.

Study group members also used these moments of partnership as opportunities to solicit feedback about how the rubric was developing from colleagues teaching students in the 11–16 age category. The turnaround time and process for soliciting this feedback was different from when they had tried it out informally in their own classrooms. When asking others to pilot test the rubric, they used a more formal process for evaluating its strengths and weaknesses, including asking students to fill out evaluation cards about their perspectives. In handing over some of their control, study group members shared the creative process—and ultimately the sense of ownership—with other members of the school community. In some ways, asking colleagues to engage in hacking and tweaking the WISical Thinking rubric mirrored the process the study group went through to create it. Their thinking was that people have to engage in the process in order to feel invested in the products that result from it. Majd said she felt that colleagues at the school "should own the idea and be partners in scaling it up."

Over the course of these pilots within and beyond the study group, members of the school community heard about the idea of WISical Thinking through presentations, meetings, newsletters, and conversations. This helped the school community to get used to it over time—as opposed to the "introduce it one week, implement it the next" pattern that had happened with other new initiatives at the school. WIS study group members described their approach to dissemination as being a "slow-drip" or "drip feed" approach. In this way, they slowly introduced aspects of the WISical Thinking rubric to their colleagues without giving it a name. Instead, they kept the branding of their work to themselves until they felt their colleagues had accrued enough practice with the rubric to fully understand it as a structure. Later, when the study group was ready to introduce the WISical Thinking rubric by name, it intended to make the case to its colleagues that WISical Thinking was something they were already familiar with and something they may have applied themselves in previous months. The group also created a WISical Thinking Ambassadors initiative that engaged colleagues from outside the study group in trying to get other departments as passionate about the rubric as the study group members were. Those ambassadors would also be tasked with leading the rollout of WISical Thinking within their own departments.

The experience of developing WISical Thinking stood in contrast, then, to the typically splintered and rapid implementation of new initiatives and ideas at this fast-paced school. Time and care were taken to bring people together and attend to different perspectives not just within the study group, but also in the very concept and development of the product and in the manner in which it was implemented across the school.

Takeaways

The following section of the case now turns to some takeaways from the story of the WIS study group that will be applicable to others interested in school-based innovation.

Cross Boundaries

This case is a reminder of the known benefits of working in diverse teams. Here, diversity involved the representation of different school departments—including the Arabic department which was not always at the heart of new initiatives within the school— and the involvement of people playing different roles within the school, including both teachers and school leaders. This diversity was an important motivator for the group members, who were excited to work with people outside of their immediate departments or offices; the tight bonds they created were due, in part, to the fact that they were able to create a space that took them away from the daily routines or established norms of the groups in which they usually worked. It also meant that a range of perspectives were brought to the table and informed the development of the critical thinking rubric. And later on, it meant that there was a greater chance of the rubric being adopted more widely across the school because it was not associated with a single department and the innovation design had actively taken different subject areas into account.

Be Humble

When the study group was formed, Andy took on an informal leadership role because he had convened the group and was the most senior member of the team. But he very much made himself one of the team and worked closely alongside his colleagues, helping to create the positive group dynamics that were quickly established. Vicki stepped into his shoes when he left the school, but similarly worked alongside her study group members as an equal. The group members were also humble in the way in which they developed, shared, and then sought to implement their innovation work across the school. They listened closely to colleagues' feedback. They invited people to tweak the rubric to suit their own needs and subject areas, presenting the rubric as a work in progress rather than something ready to be imposed on others. While they did, in fact, receive accolades for their work, they were generous in sharing ownership of the rubric: WISical Thinking was very much presented as something that belonged to the entire school community and something of which all school members could be proud.

Make Innovations Your Own

Relatedly, in this case it seemed important that there was a distinct naming or branding of the innovation: "WISical Thinking." As noted earlier, the broader school community did not adopt the rubric *because* of the name; as Nick pointed out, the time the study group took to listen carefully to people and to incorporate different perspectives played a much more important role in that regard. But the name did signal that this was a homegrown innovation, specifically designed for the needs of the WIS community and particularly its students. Indeed, while the study group was inspired by existing literature on critical thinking, it created an innovation that made sense for their community and which incorporated findings from their careful classroom observations and the teacher and student feedback they solicited. The WISical Thinking rubric was also a concrete manifestation of the work they had achieved together, as represented by the posters displaying the rubric that were highly visible across the school.

Allow the Necessary Time

At the beginning of the research project, the WIS study group thought it would focus on issues of time management and/or of the perception of "coasting" at its school—issues that had been identified as worrisome by leaders within the school. Although group members shifted their attention to critical thinking, somewhat paradoxically they ended up addressing issues related to time and coasting. Time, for instance, ended up playing a very significant role in what the study group learned. It discovered that it was worth investing the time to do something "properly" as Vicki put it. Group members needed time to bond with one another and to develop a sense of cohesion as a group—including time spent outside of the regular school routine such as during a fire drill or on bus rides to the research project's exhibitions. They needed time to look closely at classrooms and student work in order to develop a meaningful inquiry focus. They needed time to pilot and iterate on their rubric design. They needed time to roll out the rubric and meaningfully include other colleagues in the process. Carving out this time for a more sustained project in the end paid dividends: by finding the time to engage in inquiry and to learn from one another's perspectives, they developed an award-winning innovation that was adopted across the school and widely viewed as successful.

As individuals, the study group members came to feel that they were doing work that was important and enjoyed experiencing a sense of collective purpose that transcended the busyness of their everyday lives at school. Furthermore, by taking the necessary time, they arguably found a way to address the perceived issue of coasting by challenging students across all subject areas to engage in more rigorous critical thinking—using the rubric as a visible aspiration for the kinds of thinking they wanted to see valued and promoted within their school. Their advancement in this regard was specifically noted in their next annual inspection report, which commended the WISical Thinking rubric; indeed, Vicki credited it with helping secure a continued rating of "Outstanding" for the school.

Outstanding Puzzles

While many educators may find resonance with aspects of this case study, several puzzles remain. The following section lays out some caveats regarding the potential applicability of this case to other contexts and groups of people.

Was This Level of Cohesion Exceptional?

While Majd, Nick, Sarah, and Vicki credited inquiry-driven innovation with providing them with the tools, process, and space to create WISical Thinking, it is fair to ask if a different group of educators would have enjoyed the same level of cohesion as a group or would have achieved such success with its innovation. Were these particularly talented and motivated individuals or was there something special about the combination of personalities and expertise within the group? One strength of the WIS study group was its consistent membership and the regularity with which it was able to meet: while other schools in the research cohort overcame scheduling obstacles, such as the study group at GEMS Modern Academy featured next, is it realistic to expect study groups to be able to find sufficient space and time to develop the degree of closeness that was apparent with the study group at WIS? And what happens if someone leaves or new people want to join the study group? While the WIS study group was sensitive to the need to share ownership of the rubric innovation with its colleagues and give them the space to make it their own, the group could perhaps have become a closed-off clique—even while the diversity of its team mixed up the usual groupings of staff within the school.

Does Attention to Context Limit the Potential of an Innovation?

Another puzzle is the degree to which the WISical Thinking rubric was so specific to the WIS context that it would be difficult to spread to other schools: Would another school readily adopt a framework specifically tailored to the needs of students at a different school and also bearing that school's name? While creating an innovation that was truly "homegrown" was at the heart of the purposes, the work, and even the piloting and scaling-up processes for WISical Thinking, one has to wonder whether this way of developing the innovation necessitated any trade-offs in terms of its potential reach and applicability, and whether or not this could be problematic.

What Is the Impact of the Process of Innovation?

Relatedly, while other schools in the research cohort were interested in WISical Thinking, they were particularly focused on *how* the WIS study group developed and implemented their innovation. It is worth asking in this and other cases if the process of creating an innovation is more than or as important as the actual innovation or product itself. If so, how can the impact of a process be discerned? For example, as Chapter 6 explores more fully, the individual growth of educators was intimately tied up with the process of effecting positive change in schools, thereby creating a further legacy of the inquiry-driven innovation process. Given that members of this study group were promoted to positions of greater responsibility either during or immediately after their engagement in the project, the skills they developed during this experience may have had a ripple effect on their colleagues—but such effects are difficult to specify.

What Was the Role of the Research Project?

It is also important to acknowledge the role of the overall research project in which the study group took part in structuring and supporting the inquiry-driven innovation process for this and other study groups. For instance, while the study group members were entirely responsible for choosing which pieces of literature to explore, they may not have discovered the nursing article that kick-started their thinking about the elements of WISical Thinking without access to some of the research repositories provided by the research team. And while a major takeaway from this case is the importance of taking the time to do this kind of work in a sustained manner rather than trying to quickly launch one initiative after another, it can be difficult to carve out the time and space for this approach without having the sense of obligation that can come with being part of a larger research project—even if the very point of this book is to provide the tools and insights to enable educators outside of a formal project to embark on their own journeys of inquiry-driven innovation.

Final Thoughts

As noted at the outset of this case, innovation can be viewed as shaking up how things are typically done. But when the WIS study group encountered inquiry-driven innovation, they were operating in an environment where the pace already felt busy and multiple initiatives were continuously underway. The WIS case shows how in this kind of context the process of inquiry-driven innovation can be a powerful means to forge a greater sense of cohesion or togetherness that might otherwise be lacking in the rapid unfolding of day-to-day activities in a school. The diversity of the study group members was an important asset for promoting cohesion, both within the team itself and in terms of the innovative school-wide critical thinking rubric they developed and then succeeded in rolling out across the school. Throughout this inquiry-driven innovation process, fostering a sense of ownership was also important—from owning the process of inquiry-driven innovation and the purposes to which it was applied, to owning the innovation product, to eventually sharing the ownership with colleagues across the school.

While puzzles remain, the work of this group hopefully offers insights and inspiration to other educators. Inquiry-driven innovation can be a vehicle for bringing people together to do productive work that cuts across the usual subject area silos found in schools. The case shows how the development and implementation of WISical Thinking benefited from the diverse perspectives that informed its design. The process of creating this product, as well as the product itself, encouraged a more cohesive approach in a school where new ideas and initiatives were a hallmark and efforts to improve teaching and learning could feel fragmented and short-lived. It also points to the benefits of finding the time for this kind of work; while it can seem a luxury to do anything that is not immediately essential in a busy school, carving out time to focus on longer-term projects and to more generally strive toward improving teaching and learning within a school was, in the case of WIS at least, time extremely well spent.

Case Study 3: GEMS Modern Academy

Innovation as Construction Project

The word *innovation* is often used to describe something brand-new, a practice or idea that explores uncharted territory or distinctly sets itself apart from what came before. But not every innovation starts from scratch or fundamentally disrupts the way that a field or even a single institution does its work. The frequently-cited 70–20–10 rule of innovation—a maxim that has been widely applied to innovation approaches in a variety of fields—proposes that 70 percent of an institution's efforts to innovate should be focused on innovating its core activities, products, or services, preserving only 20 percent of such efforts for innovating on areas adjacent to what a company is already doing, and 10 percent to paradigm-changing or "transformational" innovations (Nagji & Tuff, 2012). While opinion is divided on the relative value of different kinds of innovations, particularly in the business world where the well-being of children is not generally at stake, *incremental innovations* that serve to strengthen and sustain what an organization is already doing can lead to significant positive change. Meanwhile, Robertson (2017) cautions against a binary between incremental or radical innovation, arguing instead for a focus on "little ideas" that enhance an organization's core enterprise. Many of the innovation activities of the schools described in this book could be described as little ideas or incremental innovations.

Indeed, rather than focusing on the degree of novelty of an innovation, the Framework for Inquiry-Driven Innovation promotes approaches that value and foreground the needs and interests of local contexts. While an inquiry-driven approach to innovation can encourage trying something brand-new, it also compels educational innovators to examine the structures, practices, and perspectives that already surround them. This approach to innovating is often less like a garden where innovations grow from the ground up, each starting from a separate seed, and more like a construction project in which new builds co-mingle with existing structures and employ materials already in use. This metaphor of *innovation as an ongoing construction project* can be seen in practice at GEMS Modern Academy, an Indian/International Baccalaureate (IB) curriculum school in Dubai that innovated by *building on* and *building around* existing elements of its teaching and learning context. These approaches to building, and the elements of the school context that supported ongoing construction, are illustrated in this case.

Innovating on Excellence: The Story of Inquiry-Driven Innovation at GEMS Modern Academy

GEMS Modern Academy (called "Modern") is a 30-year-old, co-ed school located in Nad Al Sheba, an eastern Dubai locality (see Figure 5.13). Over 3,700 students from pre-kindergarten to grade twelve (4–18 years old) enroll at Modern each year after applying through an entry-level assessment and interview process. Parents are highly engaged in the daily life of the school, and students are given opportunities to take on leadership roles and participate in a wide variety of extracurricular activities. As with other schools in Dubai, Modern's tuition fees increase with age and grade level. Modern's average tuition is a little over one-and-a-half times the average across all Dubai schools.

Figure 5.13 GEMS Modern Academy, Dubai.

Modern's principal, Nargish Khambatta, began her tenure in 2014. Her work is supported by a teaching faculty of nearly 230 educators, as well as a Senior Leadership Team of around 30 individuals and middle-level leaders, many of whom have teaching responsibilities at the school in addition to their leadership work. Members of these leadership teams help coordinate a "teacher quality cycle" at the school that uses a wealth of data on classroom results and teacher performance to inform coaching sessions, peer observation, and professional development.

Modern aspires to develop student skills and dispositions, including curiosity, ambition, technological competence, open-mindedness, and care for others. The school prides itself on a holistic educational model that includes a range of academic opportunities and extracurricular activities. Alongside plentiful trophies and award plaques, the school's entryway showcases posters from its Broadway-style musical theater productions, a photograph of a student research expedition to Antarctica, and stunning visual art works created by students. The school also has its own innovation agenda that includes—among other initiatives—a focus on design thinking (IDEO, n.d.) and interdisciplinary learning, both of which have become increasingly integrated into the school's activities over the past several years. Modern's approach to design thinking as a problem-solving methodology incorporates ideas from Stanford University's d.school, IDEO design firm, Google, and Design for Change. This emphasis creates opportunities for students to engage in focused, large-scale design challenges at local and global levels to support the overall approach. Modern also works to achieve cross-disciplinary learning through Science, Technology, Engineering, Arts, and Math (STEAM) programming.

Modern follows the curriculum of the Council for the Indian School Certificate Examinations (CISCE), one of several widespread approaches to education designed for Indian school children as well as the International Baccalaureate's Diploma Program for select students in grades eleven and twelve. As a school in the United Arab Emirates (UAE), Modern balances the aims of the CISCE approach with more local agendas, such as ensuring that all learners know the history and culture of the UAE and have skills in Arabic as an additional language.

Starting from a Place of Excellence

Modern has a reputation for excellence. Among many honors, it has the distinction of receiving the highest educational accolade in the Gulf region: the Sheikh Hamdan bin Rashid al Maktoum Award for Distinguished Academic and Administrative Performance.

It was also the first educational institute to receive the Dubai Quality Award. In the time period described in this case, Modern was one of only two Indian curriculum schools to earn an "Outstanding" rating (the highest on Dubai's school rating scale)—an accomplishment that it had achieved for the past eight consecutive years. As with schools across the UAE, Modern is also held to various achievement targets on both national educational goals and international assessments—and these targets are ever-present in the minds of teachers, students, and school leadership.

These various components—an engaged student and parent body, established pedagogy and staffing structures, benchmarking expectations from local and international entities, and a history of outstanding work—are part of a complex and constantly evolving teaching and learning environment at Modern.

Taking Stock: Inquiry-Driven Innovation Begins

Modern became involved in the research leading to this book at a key moment of reflection. Principal Nargish Khambatta recalled that the school's ongoing work to maintain its culture of excellence was "starting to have limitations because we felt that we were doing things in the same old, staid way." In working with her Senior Leadership Team to think about how the school might capitalize on its engagement in inquiry-driven innovation, she realized:

> It's not about doing things differently, but differently for a purpose. . . . There's so much jargon around innovation. . . . And so, as a Senior Leadership Team, we took a step back and said: "What are we encouraging?". . . We said, it's important for a school to pause frequently, to have the permission to pause, to find out what needs to be tweaked or fixed to make it better.

It was at this point that Modern's study group began its work (see Figure 5.14). Through an application and interview process, the group was carefully curated at the school leadership level to ensure diversity and combine different strengths. It included Educational Supervisor and Physics teacher Reshmi Suresh Menon, House Master and Geography teacher Juliana Li, Assistant Dean of Studies and Computer Science teacher Malini Murali, Chief Innovation and Digital Officer and teacher of the IB Information Technology in a Global Society course Ritesh Vrajlal Dhanak, Curriculum Development Officer and Assistant Dean of Studies Sharada Kenkare, and Educational Supervisor Priyadarshini Prakash. All group members[4] served on the school's Senior Leadership Team and had been

Figure 5.14 Members of Modern's study group: (from left) Juliana, Reshmi, Ritesh, Malini, and Sharada.

at the school for at least 12 years, with the exception of Sharada, who was in her sixth year. As with all staff that lead new initiatives at the school, study group members were in close communication with the principal throughout their involvement in the research.

Developing a Focus

Study group members began to think about an inquiry focus that would guide their innovation projects. Sharada recalled some of the conversations the study group was having at that time, in which the group thought: "We've reached a stage where we have everything outstanding, but is it deep enough? Is everybody benefiting out of it? What is their take on it? What is their feedback?" In considering some of these questions, the group began to wonder about redefining teacher development to reflect students' changing needs. This focus area was in line with the school's ongoing push to strengthen teaching practice through its robust quality assurance cycle, depicted in Figure 5.15. The group settled on a broad inquiry focus for its work, framed as redefining teacher development for those working with iGen students (sometimes called post-Millennial learners, grades 1–6) through use of the school's existing data and performance management systems.

In spite of having articulated this topic, study group member Reshmi recalled, "When we went around thinking over what is it that we want to focus our research on, . . . [it] was all very fuzzy, we were not clear exactly what is it that we want to do." The group's work seemed slow and somewhat unclear at this time as they met weekly to engage with activities and readings provided by the research team. One of the ideas

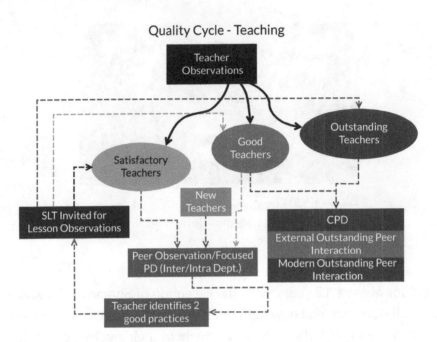

Figure 5.15 A diagram of Modern's Teaching Quality Cycle.

they gravitated toward in these meetings was the concept of *making learning visible*, as initially explored through a collaborative research project between Project Zero and educators in Reggio Emilia, Italy, beginning in the late 1990s. This work focused on group learning and ways to share thinking, making learning "visible" to others rather than keeping it inside the learner's own head, and using practices such as observation and interpretation of classroom documentation to gain deeper understandings of how and what students are learning (Project Zero and Reggio Children, 2001). The study group gravitated toward five core "Principles of Learning" at play in classrooms that make learning and learners visible, as framed in a publication from Project Zero researchers called *Visible Learners* (Krechevsky et al., 2013). The principles suggest that learning in these classrooms is purposeful, social, emotional, empowering, and representational. With this list as a starting point, study group members made their own interpretation of the principles and created what they called an "audit checklist" of indicators for each one. They observed classrooms on learning walks (Allen & Topolka-Jorissen, 2014) and used the checklist both to look for the indicators in action and to gain more inspiration for what a compelling research focus might be—something that went beyond the "fuzzy" focus area of working on teacher development for iGen students. The checklist they developed is shown in Figure 5.16.

PRINCIPLES OF LEARNING - AUDIT CHECKLIST	
Learning is Representational	**Learning is Empowering**
☐ Learners interact with appropriate representation/s,	☐ Student Voice matters
☐ Learners present information in multiple forms (Use of multi-media to display pictures/diagrams, text, animations, sound, video, equations, tables, graphs and dynamic simulations and narration)	☐ Promoting student choice/Students' choice in curriculum area/learning/ways in which they present learning
	☐ Encourage BYOD and meaningful Ed tech
☐ Informal and ungraded assessments	☐ Teacher leads by example (in activities)
	☐ Self / Peer assessment
☐ Pre-assessment/baseline assessment	☐ Refection and self-evaluation
☐ Lesson progression adjustments as per emerging needs of learners	☐ Students as teachers/Reciprocal teaching
Learning is Social	**Learning is Emotional**
☐ Coach positive social behavior (helping, sharing, waiting)	
☐ Promote respect for cultural differences in my classroom	☐ Time for reflection (reveal and reflect on feelings of wonder, surprise, pleasure and motivation)
☐ Validation of positive behavior	
☐ Use Time Out (Time Away to calm down)	☐ Avenue for feedback
☐ Use anger management strategy	☐ Diagnostic type of feedback
☐ Effective strategies to ensure discipline in class	☐ Personalization by teacher (connecting with their own experience)
☐ Use problem-solving strategy (e.g., define problem, brainstorm solutions)	
☐ Peer questioning	

Figure 5.16 The study group's "Principles of Learning" checklist.

At this point, study group members began to gather additional information to compare with the data they collected on their learning walks. A survey distributed to teachers sought to find out the degree to which they were already incorporating the principles into their daily practice. In comparing data from the learning walks and the teacher survey, a gap became apparent between what teachers planned to do in class and what actually resulted in practice. Teachers reported in the surveys that they were using problem-solving approaches in their teaching, one of the indicators identified by the study group. But during the learning walks, study group members noticed that students could not come up with solutions to new challenges and problems presented by their teachers. This finding resonated with a recent advisement from a governmental school inspection board recommending that the school increase its focus on problem-solving skills. In describing the experience of the learning walks, study group members reflected:

> Malini: *Learning was not so visible; it wasn't coming out strongly in the classroom—though teachers perceived that it's happening.*
>
> Reshmi: *Our [students] go to various competitions and . . . in those competitive pockets they do well but we wanted that same kind of culture happening in the classroom . . .*

where [all students] respond with the same kind of passion and are able to think at that level. . . . In doing the learning walks, we knew that problem-solving is that area that we actually want to focus on.

These realizations around visible learning and problem-solving skills galvanized the group and helped them to crystallize a revised inquiry focus. The study group shifted its focus from looking at classrooms in order to evaluate teacher performance to also looking for visible signs of student learning and thinking. They also determined that a sign of success would be to see more problem-solving skills at work in students' learning. Using tools from the Toolkit in Chapter 8, the study group reframed and refined its research question in order to identify the parts of the question that could be strengthened and to further zero in on the populations and outcomes that would be core to the innovation projects they would develop. They also mapped out their group's long-term plan by creating a Theory of Action diagram, shown in Figure 5.17.

> For more about the resources that this study group used to revise and refine its inquiry focus, see the *Population, Innovation, Outcome* tool and the *Theory of Action* suite of tools.

The group reframed the desired long-term impact of its inquiry-driven innovation work: while teacher preparedness continued to be a focus of the study group's work, the centrality of problem-solving skills and the role of learners in impacting their own learning and development now shared the stage.

Momentum picked up for the group. Group members zeroed in on an opportunity to innovate within their school by creating a long-term student trajectory that would routinize making learning visible and cultivate a disposition toward problem-solving from an early age. In order to do this, they needed to support teachers in adopting pedagogical models that elicited visible signs of learning and empowered learners with new thinking skills. The study group devised two innovation projects to address these opportunities.

Research Question /Inquiry Focus:

How will educators impact learning for primary students to enhance their ability to analyze problems, make decisions and design + enact solutions?

Where We Are Now: *Framing of the problem, challenge, or opportunity at your school that made you want to pursue your inquiry focus.*

- Development of problem solving skills not visible in student learning.
- Teachers would like to incorporate more problem solving activities into their classrooms, but lack the strategic approach /modification in curricular context and pedagogical models to help them facilitate their lessons.
- We can take opportunity of the gain in momentum in Innovation culture change across school.

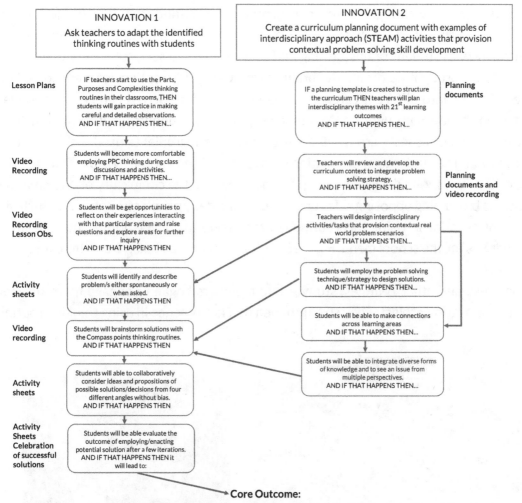

Figure 5.17 The study group's draft Theory of Action diagram.

Innovation #1: Thinking Routines to Promote Visible Learning

The first innovation aimed to use Project Zero *thinking routines* to make learning more visible in second-grade classrooms (age 7–8 years). As previously noted, thinking routines are short, simple structures and protocols that invite learners to practice and routinize ways of thinking that go beyond a surface level to engage them in deeper inquiry (Project Zero, n.d.). These routines are designed to develop not only thinking skills, but also the ability to understand when and how to apply ways of thinking across diverse contexts and academic subjects. One of the first applications of thinking routines took place in a class focused on healthy eating. The teacher introduced a routine from the Visible Thinking research project called *Generate–Sort–Connect–Elaborate*: a concept mapping protocol that starts with student brainstorming and asks learners to sort, connect, and elaborate on the ideas brought up during the brainstorm.[5] Using this routine, learners sorted pictures of foods into different categories, made connections across categories, and elaborated on the ideas brought up. As a follow-up activity, students went to the lunch hall to explore what dishes were available for lunch, the ingredients used, and nutritional information. The class was then split into groups that used another Visible Thinking routine called *Tug of War*, designed to help learners explore the complexity of dilemmas and decisions by framing opposing sides of an issue, considering their strengths, and surfacing resultant questions.[6] Using this routine led the group to conversations about healthier alternatives for the school menu. Figure 5.18 features photos taken from this class.

Using these and other routines, study group members began to engage more teachers in their innovation project. They strengthened teacher practice in using thinking routines

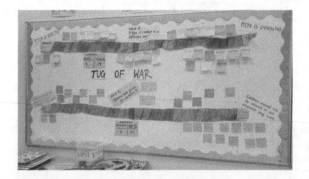

Figure 5.18 Documentation of using the thinking routines in classrooms.

through coaching and professional development, and began to see positive results. Sharada recalled:

> The impact is that teachers are able to frame good inquiry questions. And the responses that they get from students are more diverse now. And students are then able to question each other as well—otherwise, sometimes in some classes that I have been in, teachers have put forth the question in class [and] one student answers it, but it does not take the discussion forward. Here, some other students could question that student further.

The encouraging outcomes observed by study group members were echoed in student survey responses gathered by the study group, with learners reporting increases in opportunities to ask questions and challenge what they saw and heard as a result of using thinking routines in class. After some of this initial pilot-testing work with thinking routines, study group members solicited feedback and continued to refine how they supported teachers in using the routines in classrooms. Teachers became proactive in seeking out additional thinking routines to try out in class, and teachers from across academic subjects and grade levels began to use the routines. They started to pair thinking routines with other strategies to make learning visible, including peer questioning, student self-evaluation, and reflection exercises. With this initial success in place, the study group felt empowered to integrate thinking routines into its second innovation: the Futurus curriculum approach.

Innovation #2: The Futurus Curriculum Approach

The Futurus curriculum approach was designed to help Modern teachers integrate STEAM (Science, Technology, Engineering, Arts, and Math) learning, design thinking, large-scale design challenges, and thinking routines. Guided by steps of the design thinking process used by Modern that incorporated frameworks from various leaders in the field, learners engaged in problem-solving for real-world challenges. Students began by learning about potential end users and the context in which their work could have an impact, then developed ideas and solutions, and further worked to prototype, test, and refine those ideas. Along the way, teachers introduced thinking routines specifically chosen to support the work of each step and collaborated across classrooms to achieve the school's goals around interdisciplinary and STEAM learning. They piloted this approach with science and social studies classes in grade five (age 10–11 years old).

One of the first implementations of a Futurus project invited learners to envision adaptations that would better enable plants to thrive in the desert—a design challenge that students could easily imagine by looking at the sandy landscapes they passed on their journeys to school each morning. Students brainstormed solutions, in some cases envisioning new plant species and in others designing devices that would help plants thrive in harsh conditions. They then created drawings and "blueprints" of their ideas as shown in Figure 5.19, and eventually translated these into prototypes and 3D models. Along the way, teachers used thinking routines to help students approach challenges and reflect on what they were learning. In science class, students explored and evaluated structural features and adaptations that help living things to survive in their home environments. In social studies, they learned to examine how climate, habitats, and geographic location are interrelated. And in language classes, learners communicated and interpreted their plant adaptation ideas in English, Arabic, Hindi, and French. Teachers were impressed with the initial results of the Futurus curriculum approach. Study group member Priyadarshini, a grade-five supervisor and science teacher who took a lead role in piloting the Futurus approach, reflected: "The deeper understanding that the children had, the analysis and the synthesis components that we saw—we were amazed with the kind of creative ideas that the students came up with."

Figure 5.19 Student work from the plant adaptations project.

The group's hypothesis was that as both innovations were assimilated into the school's curricular approach, young learners would become comfortable with thinking routines and the kinds of thinking dispositions associated with them, drawing on them again as they entered grade five and employing thinking routines as part of an approach to real-world problem-solving through Futurus projects. With successful pilot testing of both innovations, the study group now shifted its efforts toward scaling the use of thinking routines and the Futurus approach to more teachers and classrooms.

Scaling Up and Moving Ahead

Working with the system of professional development and coaching already in place, study group members and their colleagues began to spread thinking routines and the Futurus approach across the school. Two years into their inquiry-driven innovation work, teachers of kindergarten to fourth grade had begun to regularly integrate thinking routines into their lessons. They worked together to articulate what mastery versus novice levels of teaching using thinking routines might look like, and created a video bank to showcase best practices in using the routines. Modern teachers began to present their work at local conferences, and led professional development sessions and online trainings on the use of thinking routines for other schools. They also continued to use the Futurus interdisciplinary curriculum approach in select grades within the school and planned for expansion into further grades. Finally, they used what they had learned about problem-solving skills to develop a new afterschool program.

Construction Underway: Building and Framing New Approaches to Practice in Schools

In its continuous quest to provide "Outstanding" levels of education for more than 3,000 young people, GEMS Modern Academy is always under construction. It does its work in a perennial state of building, dismantling, and improving new approaches to teaching and learning. Project Liaison Christine Nasserghodsi noted that in Modern's relentless pursuit of excellence, there can at times be "a little bit of initiative overload" as school staff try to capitalize on the large variety of new initiatives, programs, and ideas that carry potential benefit for students. Principal Nargish Khambatta described a "sense of breathlessness" that sometimes results from trying to keep up. These observations can be linked to *curriculum overcrowding* or *curriculum overloading*, phenomena that are not uncommon in schools.

Such overcrowding can lead to *initiative fatigue*—staff and faculty burnout that can result from increasing expectations and responsibilities without additional resources—an outcome that can have negative impacts on both the effectiveness of organizational change initiatives and the personal well-being of those involved (Spann, 2018). These potential risks and pitfalls point to what is at stake in introducing new practices and ideas in schools, and to the care that needs to be applied in carrying out the metaphorical "construction project."

With so much to manage, building new ideas from the ground up each time a change is warranted—creating the timetables, curricular approaches, staffing structures, and so on—can be inefficient and untenable. While some innovations at Modern do develop from scratch and independently of existing school practices, others come about in ways that are linked to what is already happening at the school. Some of these additions at the school *build on* approaches already in place and others *build around* existing constraints and structures. Both of these ways of building are seen in the story of the study group's innovations. Inner structures of the school community support and strengthen these new additions and take on many different forms. These ways of building and some underlying supporting structures are explored below.

Building On: Amplifying and Adding to What Works

Members of Modern's school community *built on* existing practices that were found to work well in the school by adding to or integrating new practices with what was already in place—an approach to innovation in which new practices amplified or augmented what had been working well at the school already. Reshmi spoke about this process as it related to the study group's innovations:

> Whatever new practices we have started have all come in from existing ones. We've looked at ways of improving the existing practices and then as an offshoot of them, something new comes up. So we're not entirely going a new way . . . I feel it helps innovation in the school, so that it's not always a hindrance to sustain it, it's a way to look at it from a different point of view and take it forward.

Enhancing Teaching and Learning with Thinking Routines

Study group members used Project Zero thinking routines to enhance teaching and learning at Modern. They reflected that teachers at the school had historically asked many of the questions that were part of specific thinking routines, but the routines themselves helped to give more cognitive structure to teachers and students. As both a study group member and a teacher trying out thinking routines in her Computer Science classroom, Malini recalled:

> Even earlier before we started our [innovation] projects, it's not that this type of thinking wasn't there. It was just that now we're adding and making it more visible— giving it a structure. Without [the teachers] knowing the thinking routine called See— Think—Wonder, they are doing activities which are tying in very well to that. But now they know, this is a scientific way, this is a structured way to go about that.

Malini also described how classroom debates changed when she began to introduce thinking routines. One routine she used from the Visible Thinking project is called Compass Points.[7] Through a series of four prompts, it asks learners to examine propositions by sharing: (1) what excites them about the proposition, (2) what they find worrisome, (3) what else they might need to know in order to evaluate the proposition, and (4) a stance or suggestion for moving forward. Malini found that this routine gave her more structure than she had had previously as she guided learners' debates in the classroom, and that this structure scaffolded class content and helped to "validate" the moves she made as a teacher. Rather than free-form debates, Malini was able to check for a more well-rounded set of student contributions to debates by making sure that her learners explored all four prompts from the routine. In introducing thinking routines, Malini built on existing classroom activities in ways that enhanced learning outcomes.

Adding to Existing Initiatives through the Futurus Curriculum Approach

The Futurus curriculum approach at Modern also began by *building on* existing practices at the school. Futurus started with design thinking and STEAM learning: two approaches with a history of successful implementation at Modern. Study group members added onto these approaches with two new sets of tools: Project Zero thinking routines and design challenges from another new program at the school that asked learners to tackle problems at the local and global levels. The design challenges helped learners to begin the design thinking process from a powerful place that encouraged deep and long-term exploration. As they engaged in this process, learners worked across different subjects in their school day in order to integrate the disciplines together through their STEAM approach. As they progressed through the different stages of the design thinking process, teachers integrated thinking routines that they felt would specifically support each stage or the transitions between stages.

Building on existing programs and approaches at the school through the Futurus curriculum not only enabled school stakeholders to add to knowledge and learnings from previous implementation of those programs. It also helped members of the study group to have a more far-reaching impact than with their previous, non-integrated approach. Ritesh reflected: "We did do design thinking before but it was done in pockets . . . [it] was not done in a structured manner. It was not done in a way that would impact the entire grade, or entire series of students." Supporting the stepwise process of design thinking and the overall approach of cross-disciplinary learning with thinking routines and design challenges helped existing school initiatives to merge and be even more successful. This new approach to problem-solving was eventually implemented across the school.

While *building on* can be a powerful way of reusing and upcycling existing assets and resources, innovation is not always a process of working with and adding onto what's already at hand. At times, it requires building new pathways around existing constraints.

Building Around: Innovating Around Unchangeable Elements of the School Context

Some elements of teaching and learning at Modern, such as the programs and class activities discussed above, are developed at the school level and are unique to Modern. Their implementation and longevity at the school are the purview of Modern's principal and staff, affording them the ability to pivot based on changing needs and learnings about what is working (or not) at the school. But other elements of the school context are fundamentally different: some aspects are developed and revised far outside school walls, and others take the form of universal and persistent challenges on the minds of educators throughout the world. These contextual elements are in place for the long haul, and innovating at Modern means learning how to *build around* existing constraints and requirements. While researchers and authors note that *too many* or *certain types* of constraints can stifle creativity and innovation, they also recognize that constraints and unchangeable factors can unlock creative potential and help innovation to flourish (Mayer, 2006; Acar et al., 2019). Many others have pointed to the power of reframing challenges as opportunities for innovation. Some of these unchangeable elements of the school context that the study group built around are discussed below.

"Curriculum Is Not a Barrier to Innovation"

The school's overall approach to teaching and learning is one such unchangeable element of Modern's teaching and learning context. As an affiliate of the Council for the Indian School Certificate Examinations (CISCE), which is regulated from afar in New Delhi, India, Modern must adhere to particular affiliation criteria, including curriculum, teacher qualifications, and even the regulation of homework. In addition to providing a curricular progression from preschool to the upper primary grades, the CISCE curriculum sets curricular themes, learning outcomes, approaches to assessment of learning, and suggested class activities—among many other guidelines. Study group member Juliana reflected: "There are a lot of restrictions imposed in terms of the kind of syllabus. And I know you can turn around your pedagogical skills to kind of make things more interesting and everything like that. But there [are] a lot of restrictions [that] kept [us] from that."

While study group member Sharada serves as a Curriculum Development Officer and Assistant Dean of Studies at Modern, she did not initially think of the school's curriculum as an area ripe for innovation. Sharada credits Modern's engagement in inquiry-driven innovation with helping the school to think about the potential to innovate with the curriculum. She recalled that before the school's involvement in this work:

> To a large extent we were restricting [ourselves] ... [in looking] at how can we innovate or do things differently. But ... the school revolves around the curriculum—whether it's the "what" of the curriculum or "how" of the curriculum. .... So that's where the focus changed. So once you are able to innovate that, I think the domino effect will be that you will be able to innovate in other areas of the school.

As already discussed, the study group at Modern started to consider how the CISCE curriculum could be interpreted more flexibly through their involvement in the research project leading to this book. As Reshmi noted, it "brought about a change in approach, a change in mindset. As educators, we really realized that curriculum is not a barrier for innovation." Malini described this approach as: "Don't change the topic, don't change the outcomes, but look at how the [curriculum] transaction can be done differently and still have the impact that you want to have." Both of the study group's innovations focused on adapting the teachers' pedagogical toolkit to help them achieve curricular content standards, rather than asking them to completely migrate away from those standards altogether.

Navigating the Pressures of Time

Much has been written about the role of time particularly in school change, and time pressures proved to be one of the unchangeable constraints at Modern. Of course, this constraint is not unique to this one school—and indeed featured strongly in the preceding case. Teachers around the world, whatever their context, echo the refrain: "I don't have enough time." Collinson and Cook (2001) note that time is consistently recognized as a formidable constraint in school change, and that the challenge of finding more time is complex and may mean different things to different individuals within a given school context. The constraint of having limited time to fulfill many priorities played out in the study group's innovations at Modern. Ritesh recounted: "We have so much activity that we are just going from one activity to another, to another, to another, and that leaves us with little time to research on a daily basis."

Initially, the idea of slowing down to reflect on opportunities for innovation was a hard sell at Modern—a place with many pressures and fast-moving parts and pieces. Members of the study group commented regularly during interviews about the struggle of finding the time to meet and work together. They frequently ended up working on their innovations at home or communicating through WhatsApp messages when they couldn't find the time to meet in person. They also used an online platform created by the research team to view and comment on the work that other schools in the cohort were doing, and recorded interviews and class observations so that different members of the study group could view and analyze them on different schedules.

But finding avenues for asynchronous work was just one part of the story. Juliana recalled another instance when the constraint of time came to the forefront as teachers at Modern were pilot-testing the use of thinking routines in second-grade classrooms:

> I remember very strongly about some teachers telling us about time. . . . While some of us in the [study] group said that, "Yes, time is always a constraint," there were other perspectives as to whether we could take . . . this time constraint to a next level and think of it very differently . . . in the sense of: "Can we make that into an opportunity? . . . Can we utilize another method, another way, by which we can counteract this problem?" . . . One person [from the group] was just looking at it as a dead end, but some of us thought of it as an opportunity to kind of, you know, further enhance the system, so to speak.

Even before the creation of the group's innovation projects, committing time to think about innovation at the school began as a leadership decision. Project Liaison Christine Nasserghodsi noted the significance of giving work time to the school's study group, which was made up of members of the school's Senior Leadership Team. She reflected:

> The commitment of that many members of the Senior Leadership Team over an extended period of time is a huge move for the school . . . . [Principal] Nargish has traditionally been willing to let the teachers make changes if they have a pretty good case for why it should happen. But giving time for the [study group] team to actually train up the teachers who are being involved was critical, too, so not just creating time for the [study group] team, but also the time for the team to engage with others.

In the end, Nargish felt that this investment had paid off. One of the principles of inquiry-driven innovation is that it be "sustained and iterative," and the recommended process that is part of the Framework for Inquiry-Driven Innovation includes approaches that can be inherently time-intensive, such as gathering and attending to multiple perspectives, or taking the time to observe, document, and learn about one's surrounding school context. Initially, Nargish felt some discomfort with what seemed to be the unhurried pace of this process. But by the end of the school's two years of involvement in inquiry-driven innovation, Nargish commented that she felt the framework's process and tools had ended up being an accelerant to innovation at Modern.

Underlying Structures and Supports

This chapter now zooms in on underlying structures and supports for innovation at Modern—what might be thought of as the inner and often invisible framing for the metaphorical construction project of new approaches to practice. Within the context of the study group's innovations, four such structures and supports are highlighted: an innovation-driven teaching and leadership faculty, a culture of feedback, tinkering opportunities, and friendly competition.

Innovation-Driven Faculty

The first such support for educational innovation is Modern's teaching and leadership faculty, a cadre of dedicated professionals motivated to cultivate new ideas. Members of the study group explained that they and many other colleagues have a personal drive to innovate that comes not from a sense of job responsibility or the desire to be recognized for a new idea, but instead from dedication to Modern's student body:

> *Sharada: I feel the necessity to innovate, with the implication that it's the necessity to [improve] on what you already are doing, which is already outstanding, but refining it further to sustain the standards of excellence in every pocket of the school. . . . It's not that . . . it's a game, or it's a competition that we are in, but [it's] to ensure that you are catering to the needs of the emerging learners that we have or of the ways in which society is changing, the ways in which the children are interacting outside the school, and looking at ways in which the children can learn better and be prepared for the next phase of life.*
>
> *Reshmi: . . . We're dealing with children who maybe know much more than what is there in school, so how do we keep challenging them? How do we keep up their interest level? . . . Consciously I think we are driven by that question.*

In addition to the motivation that comes from a commitment to students, Modern's faculty also seem to be pushed by the intrinsic drive to innovate and improve. Described by some as a motivation to make improvements (Demircioglu & Audretsch, 2017) and by others as the idea of "conviction" (Transcend, Inc., 2019), this internal desire is critical in launching new ideas. In the context of this case, one of the ways that school stakeholders acted on the personal drive to innovate was by stepping up to try the new practices introduced by the study group in their innovations. In line with Rogers's (1983) diffusion of innovation theory, these *early adopters* in innovation initiatives try out new approaches early on and can offer subjective evaluations of the new idea that may help later adopters to get on board. Modern's study group depended on members of the school community to self-select as early adopters of their innovation projects in order to help them get off the ground. For instance, the leadership of study group member Priyadarshini—one of the initial pilot testers of the Futurus curriculum approach—was key to encouraging adoption and broader support of the curricular approach among other teachers at the school.

Reshmi described this moment, recalling that when the study group presented the new curriculum to grade 5 teachers, "It was a big step back. They said: 'Oh my goodness, we will lose so much teaching time for this. We can't do it. Parents will be up in arms because courses won't get covered.'" Reshmi felt that the dynamic changed when Priyadarshini stepped up as an initial pilot tester. As she began to present the work she and her students had done through Futurus projects, other teachers started to see the merit of the Futurus approach and warmed up to the idea. Seeing their own colleague implementing the new practice had a more powerful effect on Priyadarshini's fellow teachers than being told about its value by those whose roles were farther away from the classroom.

A Culture of Feedback

While Priyadarshini and others' motivation to innovate was internally driven and individual, other components of the school's foundation for innovation were more social and involved ongoing communication and negotiation among different members of the school community. One example is Modern's feedback norms that helped to strengthen new ideas and practices, to engage more people in the work beyond pilot testers, and to go beyond individual pioneering to more participatory and broad-spread implementation of innovations. Feedback has been cited as one of several conditions influencing the likelihood of innovative activity in public sector organizations (Demircioglu & Audretsch, 2017) and feedback-seeking behaviors have also been noted as important for achieving creative outcomes in organizations (de Stobbeleir et al., 2011).

In the case of Modern, study group members asked teachers for candid feedback and critique about how thinking routines were being introduced and used in classrooms. This invitation not only created opportunities for teachers to push back on what they felt was not working and express frustrations, but also to support the study group's work by providing suggestions that ultimately strengthened the innovations they sought to roll out. Juliana recalled how teachers were critical of the use of thinking routines during early implementation, but were offered opportunities to voice their opinions and openly talk about the merits and drawbacks of their use. Study group members again solicited teacher feedback through interviews, surveys, and informal conversations following the initial weeks of pilot-testing thinking routines in classrooms. Sometimes this feedback was glowingly positive—but at other times, it yielded critique and concerns that members of the study group had to reflect on or address, such as concerns about classes drifting too far off-topic.

At key moments in the study group's story, principal Nargish also acted as a critical friend to the group by pushing back on core concepts they were developing, becoming part of brainstorming sessions, and pointing out logistical or practical concerns, such as constraints provided by the school schedule or concerns about overloading the curriculum.

She talked about joining the study group at key moments as they planned for next steps:

> They weren't always very comfortable conversations. . . . [The study group members] do know that when we have a meeting, I'm not the easiest person to convince or to accept things. . . . I will question 'til it hurts, just so that we all know that we're doing the right thing and don't make a decision in a hurry.

While not always easy to receive or address, the feedback garnered from colleagues and school leaders at Modern proved to be an important support for innovation at Modern.

Tinkering Opportunities

Trying new approaches in practice settings prior to implementing them in classrooms is another structural support for innovation at Modern, as it was in the Kindergarten Starters case discussed earlier in this chapter. Through their weekly meetings, study group members were asked to prototype new tools, resources, and classroom activities, and to role-play and pilot test them using the *Prototyping an Experience* tool. They also introduced role playing into workshops where other teachers could play the role of students using the thinking routines as they prepared to introduce them to their own classrooms. Teachers new to the thinking routines said that these workshops helped them to overcome inhibitions, feel a sense of pride for having tried something new, and gain confidence and clarity in using the routines. They felt this increased confidence was then passed onto their students.

> For the tool that study group members used to role-play use of their innovations, see *Prototyping an Experience* in Part Three.

These workshops were one form of practice space set up within the context of the study group's innovations. Project liaison Christine Nasserghodsi said that at Modern, pilot settings such as these provide "a place or a space to kind of tinker and do things a little bit differently, but also to train up their staff without making staff feel that their core teaching practice is under attack . . . building some confidence and competence before asking them to do this in their classroom." Principal Nargish explained the value of these safe spaces to try out new ideas: "That safety net always has to be there, whether it's for students, whether it's for teachers, or whether it's for the leadership team. And I think that has made people more comfortable in trying different things, and that's why innovation is bursting at the seam here."

Friendly Competition

As part of a cohort of schools working with the research team to develop the Framework for Inquiry-Driven Innovation, Modern interacted with other cohort schools in various ways. Periodic gatherings and online interactions among these schools provided opportunities for Modern's study group members to gather feedback from others implementing innovations, and from members of the public who attended the research cohort's exhibitions of their work (see Figure 5.20) over the course of two years. Sharada said that this type of sharing outside the school gave the study group "a sense of wanting to move deeper [and] move forward" with their work. The group's cross-cohort interactions were meant to build community and provide the structures, supports, and access to different perspectives that are part of the framework. But an unanticipated benefit was that they also created a culture of supportive and friendly competition whereby cohort schools compared notes and had to rise to the challenge of presenting work-in-progress and results of their pilot innovations to each other, and at times to public audiences.

Figure 5.20 Modern study group members presenting at an exhibition.

Beyond its involvement in the research cohort, Modern is also part of the competition and cross-comparison that are inherent in Dubai's education system.
Modern works throughout the year to maintain its Outstanding rating from
the KHDA and to consistently push the envelope on current practices. This
is important not only for its school rating, but also to demonstrate to parents
choosing between schools that theirs is a model worth paying for.

While these four supporting structures are highlighted here due to their role in the group's
engagement with inquiry-driven innovation, new approaches are also supported by countless other interpersonal, logistical, curricular, and philosophical underpinnings that are part
of the school and the communities that work within it. Together, these inner structures and
the ways of building they support can boost both the courage and confidence to innovate.

Takeaways

This section of the case study introduces some takeaways from Modern's story that may
be useful to others interested in school-based innovation.

Consider Other Ways to Build

Modern's approach to innovating by building on and around existing elements of the
school context—an approach that can be found in many schools and far beyond the field of
education—invites a consideration of additional ways that educational institutions might
innovate by building amidst existing assets and constraints. For example, are there ways in
which a school might *rebuild* by repairing or rethinking a previous initiative that did not end
up working well in its first iteration? How might a school *build through* by dismantling an
approach that is not working, and using the lessons learned to envision new pathways forward? Or could there be ways to *build by reuse* as a school upcycles materials, equipment,
resources, or ideas from programs or curricula that are no longer being used? Creating an
inventory of available resources and materials, and envisioning ways in which they might
be starting points for new or enhanced practices, could be helpful ways to start innovating
with ideas and materials already at hand in a teaching and learning context.

Think from the Perspective of a System

The prospect of working on, around, or against elements in a given environment
acknowledges that these elements are situated within an interactive system. Changing

staffing, curriculum, policies, or even the daily lunch routine will likely have knock-on effects for a multitude of other parts and pieces within the complex system of a teaching and learning environment. For these reasons, the Framework for Inquiry-Driven Innovation encourages users to examine and thoughtfully consider the teaching and learning context into which an innovation is being introduced—not just at the beginning of the process, but throughout and with the participation of an increasingly broad group of stakeholders. Systems thinking—what the Waters Center for Systems Thinking (n.d.) describes as "a transformational approach to learning, problem-solving and understanding the world" that is about "recognizing that the big picture is rarely static, but almost always a web of factors that interact to create patterns and change over time"—has been applied to fields like education and school reform by various authors (see for example Garland et al., 2018; Miller-Williams & Kritsonis, 2009–2010; Ndaruhutse et al., 2019). But it seems that a systems thinking approach could have an important benefit not only for whole-school or school system reforms, but also for the work of everyday innovation and small changes in day-to-day practice. Considering the systems that surround or are included within an innovation initiative may be critical not only in the planning and adoption of a new practice or resource, but also in its long-term stability and growth within a given context.

Go Slow to Go Fast

The trope of "going slow to go fast"—the idea that thoughtful and sometimes laborious work at the beginning of a process can ultimately lead to quicker and even better results later on—is not restricted to the field of education. This idea has been applied in fields as varied as medical and dental practice, engineering and technology, and business, just to name a few. In the midst of busy school days that often encompass hundreds of decisions, interactions, tasks, and responsibilities, the idea of slowing down and pausing to look around oneself can seem uncomfortable—if not simply impossible. Related challenges are also highlighted earlier in this chapter in the case study of GEMS Wellington International School. At Modern, as at many of the schools in the research cohort, early work in the process of inquiry-driven innovation seemed at times plodding and overly cautious in its pace, both to the study group and the principal. But the work that happened in these early days—that of blue-sky visioning and making the space to notice the school's challenges and opportunities by looking with fresh eyes—was the base on which the school's innovation work rested. Both the study group and principal at Modern over time began to see the value of slowing down. For other schools engaging in innovation initiatives, offering time, resources, moral support, and permission for slowing down may be even more important than investments in the quick roll-out or ambitious scaling of changes in practice.

Support Innovations, Innovators, and Inclusion

This case also demonstrates the importance of the broader environment within which innovations and new ideas arise—in Modern's case, many people and various kinds of support created a context that allowed the innovations to develop and spread. These structural supports for innovation are oftentimes invisible, and include factors as diverse as school culture, policies and procedures, or approaches to peer collaboration and management. The story of how Modern's innovation projects developed may prompt readers to contemplate the extent to which supportive structures for innovation are already embedded in their own contexts. Equally important may be seeking ways for these structures to support the people who innovate, and to engage a variety of stakeholders. Cataloguing supports for new practices themselves, for the people who innovate, and for the inclusion of a variety of stakeholders in innovation may be a helpful place from which to begin to take a step back and critically consider a school's preparedness to innovate in authentic and powerful ways.

Outstanding Puzzles

As for the other case studies, puzzles remain in terms of the applicability of this case to other school contexts. In particular, questions arise regarding some particularly advantageous conditions at Modern.

How Does Innovation Happen without Supportive Leaders?

One such condition involved the role of the school's principal, Nargish Khambatta, whose importance was recognized both by the school's study group and by project liaison Christine Nasserghodsi. This case outlines some of the important leadership moves that Nargish made to support innovation at her school, such as giving time to members of her Senior Leadership Team to work on innovation initiatives and acting as a critical friend to the study group's work. This begs the question: How might schools be able to innovate in the absence of such supportive leadership?

How Might Financial Implications Figure In?

Another advantage related to the school's unique context relates to the financial impact of its "Outstanding" rating, which permits the school to charge a higher tuition fee than other schools. This, in fact, makes it one of the highest–tuition Indian schools in Dubai. While availability of financial resources did not appear to be a central part of the school's innovation story, one may wonder about what role, if any, financial resources might have played in the success of the school's changes in practice.

Does Reputation Grant a License to Innovate?

A third and interconnected advantage relates to the school's "Outstanding" designation, which perhaps entitled it of creative license in innovation initiatives that other schools might not enjoy. Furthermore, its designation means it is often asked to pilot new programs, mentor other schools, and showcase best practices. The cachet of being an "Outstanding" school raises questions about whether or not such a rating grants the school a tolerance for risk-taking and experimentation that might not be so achievable for schools without such recognition, especially if they feel their schools might be judged for failed experiments or innovations that don't pan out as expected. While Modern certainly took risks, one has to wonder whether they would have had the same ability to pause, experiment, and pilot test in a context with fewer accolades for achievement and excellence.

Final Thoughts

At the start of its exploration of inquiry-driven innovation, Modern was already recognized as an excellent school with a wealth of academic and extracurricular offerings and a faculty that was challenged and supported by school leadership. But school stakeholders felt that they could—and should—push further in their ongoing pursuit of outstanding education. As the school's study group assembled, it took group members some time to find their footing in the work of developing innovation projects and to engage with the practices and tools of inquiry-driven innovation. But by immersing themselves in classroom contexts and looking at the school environment around them with fresh eyes, they began to gather inspiration, gain focus, and ultimately, shift how they were thinking about teacher performance and student learning. Working with colleagues across the school, study group members used Project Zero thinking routines to promote *visible learning* and later incorporated those thinking routines into a curricular approach focused on problem-solving skills and cross-disciplinary work. Over time, they began to scale up the new initiatives across the school and share their work with others. Along this innovation journey, engagement with the Framework for Inquiry-Driven Innovation challenged the study group to slow down, pay close attention to the existing context at the school, and gather the perspectives of multiple stakeholders in the school community. This approach led them to *build on* and *build around* existing elements of the school context as they developed their innovation projects, a process that leaned on the school's underlying structures and supports for innovation. Although Modern's story took place in a unique context, it can offer insights that may be helpful in other educational settings.

While this case looked most closely at the experiences of the adults involved, including educators, school leaders, and Modern's principal, the impact of this work on students should not be missed. The study group's innovations helped student voices to be heard, and their ideas to be more carefully considered. Both the study group and principal credited engagement with inquiry-driven innovation as having broadened the school's focus from seeing the teacher as the locus of change, to seeing both teachers and learners as possible protagonists for deepening and improving learning outcomes. As principal Nargish said, this "completely changed the culture" at Modern. Moving forward, reflecting on this case might help others to think not only of how to build new approaches to practice, but also to consider who are the builders, to reflect on the purposes of new additions, and to take a critical eye as to what might need to be torn down or repurposed in order to make room for the next new construction.

Endnotes

1. All people quoted in this case were members of one of the two study groups; however, there were additional members who are not quoted here. The research team wishes to acknowledge the following roles and job titles (as of the writing of this case) of those mentioned by name: Bhawna Sajnani (Chief Digital and Innovation Officer); Gauri Meghani (Head of Curriculum); and Mareen Mathew, Rana Sabohi, Zahra Raza Shirazi, Sharmi Rodgers, and Lourdes Oliva Mascarenhas ("Olivia") (educational supervisors/teachers). All of these individuals except Bhawna Sajnani and Gauri Meghani also taught in classes. Teachers Suby Bimal and Sreeja Unnithan are also cited in the case.

2. The research team wishes to recognize KGS Vice Principal Latha Venkateswar, who made significant contributions to the school's involvement in the research cohort but left the school faculty shortly into the project.

3. https://www.ibo.org/globalassets/publications/recognition/learnerprofile-en.pdf.

4. A seventh member, teacher Avinash Surve, had to withdraw from the group several months into its work.

5. For full text of this thinking routine, see https://pz.harvard.edu/resources/generate-sort-connect-elaborate-concept-maps.

6. For full text of this thinking routine, see https://pz.harvard.edu/resources/tug-of-war.

7. For full text of this thinking routine, see https://pz.harvard.edu/resources/compass-points.

CHAPTER 6

LIFT:

Elevating Individual Practice through Inquiry-Driven Innovation

Part Two began by taking a bird's-eye view of the innovation journeys of four schools in the research cohort (Chapter 4). Chapter 5 presented in-depth case studies of three cohort schools that drew out broadly applicable themes about inquiry-driven innovation through stories of school-level change, including some of the personal, professional, and cultural changes that accompanied them. This chapter zooms in further on some of the shifts or developments in practice reported by individual educators who participated in the project and the sense of personal and professional *lift* that appeared to be enabled by their experiences with inquiry-driven innovation. It also explores ways in which these individual-level experiences resonated with the collective journeys of the study groups, focusing attention on the ways in which the potential impacts of engaging in inquiry-driven innovation can go beyond the innovations themselves to deeply personal realizations or changes in practice. For those wishing to implement inquiry-driven innovation within their own contexts, this discussion may be helpful in thinking through what might be most valuable about the process for participating educators and what types of supports might be needed to help them succeed—such as giving them permission to take things slowly at first, enabling collaboration across departments or roles, and giving educators explicit permission to try new things out. Most importantly, this chapter highlights the ways in which teacher professional growth can be tightly bound up with promoting change in schools.

School-Based Innovation and Individual Practice: Interconnected Stories of Development and Change

From the outset of the collaborative research project on which this book is based, the research team kept track of how educators were thinking about various aspects of their work, including the specific innovations in which they were engaged. However, as noted in Chapter 1, it is fair to say that the project was initially conceived of as being about promoting innovation or change in schools rather than empowering or developing individual practitioners; the primary goal of keeping track of individual experiences was to understand the kinds of thinking that appeared to enable or hinder innovation. That framing expanded once it became clear that educators were reporting powerful developments in their individual thinking and practice due to their participation in the project.

This tight connection between individual practice and school-based change should not have been a surprise. Various studies point to the strong relationship between effective school reform and the promotion of professional development that involves educators working collaboratively to address difficult or recurring problems of teaching and learning (Hargreaves, 2019; Little, 2001; Mehta & Fine, 2019), as discussed in Chapter 2. The inseparability of empowering people and effecting change is reflected in the definition of inquiry-driven innovation developed through the research work reflected in this book. *Inquiry-driven innovation* is defined as "an ongoing process that empowers individuals and communities to pursue positive change that is relevant and responsive to their contexts." As discussed toward the end of this chapter, while features of inquiry-driven innovation echo existing best practices in teacher professional development, there appears to be something about the combination of these features that renders it particularly flexible and effective as a model for promoting both "lift" in individual practice and school-wide change or innovation.

This chapter draws primarily from interviews that were conducted with twenty-six of the approximately fifty educators involved in the research project. During these interviews, the educators elaborated and reflected on the responses they had given to a series of online surveys. The interviews show that through inquiry-driven innovation, participants experienced a lift to their practice in different ways and with different degrees of intensity depending on, for example, their roles, school contexts, existing practices and thinking, and the specifics of the innovations with which they were involved.

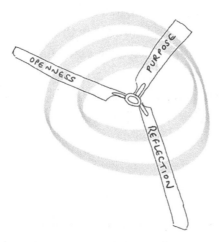

Figure 6.1 Three elements of
practice that propel lift.

As shown in Figure 6.1, three elements of practice emerged as central for propelling lift at the individual level and for promoting a sense of empowerment or increased confidence to enact change at the local level.

- **Openness**—Embracing opportunities to collaborate with new people and to learn from multiple perspectives and new ideas
- **Purpose**—Focusing on the longer-term goals of teaching and learning and feeling motivated to promote positive change
- **Reflection**—Taking the time to consider what one is doing and why, and incorporating reflection into everyday practice

Openness is promoted by the Framework for Inquiry-Driven Innovation through the opportunity to collaborate with colleagues both within and across schools, as well as by tools and strategies that foster slow looking and attentive listening. Greater openness enables educators to consider new possibilities in their practice and to account for perspectives and ideas that might be different from their own—leading in turn to more effective practice and further motivation to keep on pursuing inquiry-driven innovation. Inquiry-driven innovation also encourages educators to think about the *purpose* of specific innovations and to consider or reconsider the larger purposes of education—with an openness to new ideas and perspectives widening the possibility space for how they might conceive of these purposes. Inquiry-driven innovation can also in and of itself provide a renewed sense of professional purpose and both the means and desire to effect positive school-based change.

Finally, *reflection* is incorporated into all aspects of the process of inquiry-driven innovation; reflection is connected to openness and purpose in that individuals are encouraged to take the time to review what they are learning both with and from other people, as well as to contemplate the broader picture of what they are doing and why. Openness, purpose, and reflection variously combine to propel overall individual growth, enabling individuals to lift their practice in ways that make sense for them.

Three Elements for Propelling Lift

What did openness, purpose, and reflection look like in practice and for educators working in different contexts? This question is explored in the following section through the reported experiences of individual educators from the research cohort.

Element #1: Openness

Teaching can be a notoriously isolated profession, with teachers not necessarily aware of what their colleagues down the corridor are doing behind closed classroom doors (Hargreaves, 2019; Hargreaves & Fullan, 2012; Johnson, 2019). All the educators who were interviewed said that working as part of a team had been a highlight of engaging in inquiry-driven innovation, even in cases where it had been logistically challenging to connect and coordinate with one another. Educators spoke about how much they had learned from their study group colleagues and their new appreciation for what they could learn from different departments and schools. They also spoke of a renewed sense of the importance of paying close attention to various stakeholders, including students and parents, and a curiosity or desire to seek out new perspectives and sources of inspiration, including ones from beyond the field of education. In sum, they described a new openness to different ideas and perspectives, which they saw as beneficial both to themselves as individuals and to their schools.

Venturing beyond Their Own Departments and Schools

As the earlier chapters show, the study groups generally consisted of people playing different roles and from different departments within their schools. The importance of diverse teams with multiple perspectives is highlighted as a theme in the case study of GEMS Wellington International School (WIS) in Chapter 5, and surfaced in several participant interviews from different schools. At GEMS Wellington Academy—Silicon Oasis (WSO), for example, one educator said: "So we've learned from each other's mistakes and each other's wins. And the time, when we've had it, to sit as a group and talk has been incredible in terms of personal professional development, but also validating what you're doing." This comment points to the dual function of the teams: they enabled members to inform and teach one another, but also to offer each other psychological support, including the assurance that each of them was doing worthwhile work—benefits highlighted by other studies involving collaborative work in schools (Darling-Hammond, 2017; Hargreaves & Fullan, 2012; Opfer & Pedder, 2011). A teacher from GEMS Modern Academy (Modern) described the study group work as "very inspiring and challenging, too. So to bounce off ideas, to discuss, to review, with certain elements about the project or about best practices we have in school and making it better, that's something that I found to be the key takeaway."

Many teachers explicitly noted that inquiry-driven innovation had given them a unique and valuable opportunity to work alongside colleagues they would not ordinarily have encountered. A history teacher from WSO commented with a laugh on the way in which the experience involved "breaking down our own subject-specific prejudices" to try to consider issues within the school in a "more agnostic" and less circumscribed way. Meanwhile, a teacher from GEMS FirstPoint School—The Villa (FPS), when asked about the most important things he had learned or taken away from inquiry-driven innovation, stated: "The teamwork, the great ideas, the things I thought could never happen – thinking out of the box. And trying new things and sharing it with the team and getting information from other teachers, from other subjects, from other stages. It was amazing." This teacher went on to cite how talking to other teachers made him feel excited about what he could do in his own subject: "I was observing one of the PE [Physical Education] lessons and I was thinking, I'm teaching Islamic studies, I'm teaching stories—how could PE help with this?" Other teachers similarly talked about learning of strategies from different subject areas and applying or adapting them to their own teaching and learning contexts.

The study group structure, which was recommended by the research team but pioneered by others (e.g., Allen & Blythe, 2015), emphasized the need for a flat hierarchy even when some study group participants were in positions of authority within the school or had vastly more experience than others. One teacher from WIS referred to the equality among team members as "very refreshing." Asha from The Kindergarten Starters (KGS), the only principal who participated on a weekly basis in study group sessions, talked about learning to listen to her study group members in new ways and to take account of their perspectives. Meanwhile, a teacher from Modern talked about her appreciation not only for the sheer variety of data considered by her study group, but for the way in which group members considered different possible interpretations. Reflecting on how her group looked together at interviews they had conducted with school stakeholders, she said:

> I'm very happy with the group in the sense that there is no obvious right and wrong in the way we do things and everyone's viewpoint is totally accepted. When we sit as a group, I may look at the interview from a completely different angle and someone will look at it from a completely different angle, and that also provides very valuable insights for our discussion.

Educators similarly appreciated the opportunity to learn from peers working in different schools as they interacted on the project's online platform or during periodic cross-school exhibitions. Conversations that arose through these gatherings often brought to light new ideas or helped study groups to take a critical lens on their work to date. For example, a teacher from GEMS New Millennium School—Al Khail (NMS) commented on the inspiration she derived from other schools' innovation projects. She added that there needs to be a reason to bring schools together, in this case, provided by inquiry-driven innovation: "You need a spark of something that ignites a very focused discussion; just collaborating for the sake of it isn't enough, it needs to be focused." A teacher from FPS, a British curriculum school, talked about the frequent challenge of moving beyond existing practices at his school when teachers have received similar training and come from similar backgrounds. Referring to the cross-school exhibitions, he commented on how he learned from the Indian curriculum schools about how they manage their highly transient student populations: "I do find it interesting when we gather together and you have the mixes of the different curriculums, and I almost feel like there's more potential for change in that group . . . it could just begin to open a few more possibilities."

Attending To and Seeking Out Different Stakeholders' Perspectives

Asha, the principal of KGS, pointed to the value of being introduced to different perspectives:

> Sometimes, when I'm obsessed with an idea, I may not consider other aspects which are very, very practical. So I might need somebody to bring me down to it, to say, "Okay, this is a great idea, but you're not looking here" . . . it tempers the way you view a particular situation.

The Open Doors initiative that her school started through its innovation project invited students' parents to do observations in KGS classrooms, in part, to start dialogues that would bring to light parents' perspectives about teaching and learning at the school. This increased interest in hearing from parents was also noted by an educator at WSO.

Several teachers also noted a new commitment to hearing from students. One teacher from WIS, who like many participants was enthusiastic about introducing Project Zero thinking routines into her classroom, noted that her students "have very nice ideas, they have very smart ideas, and I think our role is to let them explore and express and develop these ideas—more than only teach them and give them information." A teacher at KGS similarly described finding more time to listen to different students' perspectives in her classroom, a theme that is highlighted in the case study of KGS in Chapter 5. Among other ways, this commitment to listening played out at KGS as educators attended to their learners' voices by documenting and reflecting on what they had to say. A teacher at NMS also described how her study group organized a more structured way to listen to student perspectives outside of the remit of their innovation project: students from each grade level were invited to become "Knights of Innovation," serving as a consulting board to the principal and providing new ideas for teaching and learning at the school.

Beyond trying to take on board a wider range of perspectives within their school contexts, several teachers talked about the value of actively searching for new ideas and perspectives and feeling motivated in the longer term to read more widely. Some talked about the value of being introduced to new readings through the process of inquiry-driven innovation and being tasked with seeking out different sources that might be relevant to their evolving innovation projects. The teachers from WIS were particularly impressed by the inspiration they drew from an article in a nursing journal. One of them noted the importance of thinking about the "crossover" with other fields and being "open to considering change or considering different ideas."

Element #2: Purpose

It would be doing a disservice to the educators who collaborated in this work to suggest that they lacked purpose in their teaching before encountering inquiry-driven innovation; in fact, given the research design that incorporated volunteer participation in the research cohort, the educators who signed up to take part already showed considerable professional commitment and a desire to develop their practice. However, a recurrent theme across many interviews was that engaging in inquiry-driven innovation had helped participants to approach their day-to-day work in a more purposeful way, with their eyes now on longer-term educational goals rather than on short-term results or time constraints. Relatedly, a number of teachers expressed a desire to pursue their innovation projects well into the future and to empower other teachers by introducing them to aspects of inquiry-driven innovation. These self-reported shifts are important given what have long been identified as three interlocking features or obstacles within the teaching profession: presentism (focusing on the short term), conservatism (concentrating on small-scale rather than whole-school changes), and individualism (performing teaching in isolation from other teachers) (Lortie, 1975 cited in Hargreaves, 2019). Others have written about the need to help teachers shift from feeling overloaded and isolated to feeling morally committed and inspired as educators, and to continually question and strive for change within schools rather than to think of their work as the completion of discrete tasks (Hargreaves & Fullan, 2012).

Zooming Out to Focus on Purpose and Process in Learning

One of the recurrent themes noted across multiple school and educator stories in the preceding chapters is the exercise of "zooming out": taking a step back from the day-to-day work of being an educator, but also making an effort to take an outside eye to practices and language that were in many cases deeply ingrained in the approach of individual educators or the schools in which they worked. Many educators indicated renewed attention to the purpose and process of what they and their students were doing in the classroom. For example, the innovation project at WIS was focused on promoting critical thinking among students. The following comment by one of the study group members reflects a particular interest in critical thinking, but also points to increased attention to the process of learning or *how* students are developing or demonstrating critical thinking capabilities:

> The questions I'm now asking are perhaps less about having a right or wrong answer, it's more about how do you get to an answer and then seeing what other people think about your answer. . . . I'm thinking less of the product, I'm thinking more of the process behind the task, which I think is more important.

One of his colleagues similarly talked about her priorities shifting from being concerned about how to deliver information in an engaging way to how to support students to explicitly reflect on how they are thinking about their answers; she said she was now more concerned with effecting lasting change on students' ways of thinking than on getting through the curriculum.

Meanwhile at WSO, one teacher emphasized the importance of introducing documentation processes into her classroom with "the idea of documenting not just your best work but how your work's developed and how you came to your final point." A colleague from her study group similarly spoke about looking beyond test results to what the students were really learning. An educator at Modern talked about a change in the way she looks at "even simple things"; she noted that although her school remains "very syllabus-oriented" as it prepares students to do well in their Indian Board exams, she is determined as a teacher to go beyond doing assigned tasks to "try to make learning visible in my class" and to enrich the collective learning experiences of her students. Similarly, at GEMS American Academy—Abu Dhabi (GAA) an educator said that she had become much more focused on the overall purpose of teaching and the kinds of people she wants her students to become rather than their immediate test scores or grades. She also noted becoming more observant of students' process of learning and using class time to observe and listen to them as they engage in learning.

Innovating for the Long Haul

Just as research cohort participants noted keeping the long-term vision of student development in mind as they innovated, a longer-term view was also discernible in the comments that some teachers made about their actual innovations. Some made comments that revealed their commitment to further developing or iterating on these innovations. For instance, a teacher from WIS noted with enthusiasm: "I can see ways in which I can tweak it and change it and make it better" as he contemplated the future trajectory of the critical thinking rubric that was the focus of his group's innovation project. Speaking in somewhat broader terms, an administrator at Modern reported that her study group had come to view the curriculum as key to enacting long-term change across the school instead of innovating more for the sake of it in different areas- here, we see a consideration of the overall purpose of introducing innovation, as well as a concern for strategically marshalling energy and resources.

Meanwhile, the study group members at WSO initially started out with four distinct projects before finding a way to synthesize their work or to find a unifying purpose. One team member described their process as follows:

> *What we found coming back was that it was more about the population and dispositions these students needed to develop in order to be successful in the online*

> *environment. Our [initial] focus was very much on introducing the innovation that would deliver the outcome. However, we've found that there was more work to be done in terms of supporting students' development and the dispositions they need to be successful in an online environment.*

Here, we arguably see a move toward considering the broader needs of students as learners and a consideration of what they will need in the long haul rather than finding quicker or more technical solutions to pedagogical challenges or opportunities. Their initial focus on blended learning in classrooms evolved over time as group members realized that their learners needed larger supports for using technology-enabled learning, be that blended learning or a multitude of other approaches involving technology. The same teacher from WSO also spoke about his study group's innovation project as something to be sustained:

> *What we need to do is figure out where we're going to go next . . . rather than viewing our innovation as a finite project that ends our involvement in [the research project] and the life cycle of this community. So how can we continue to do what we're doing? How can we start? How can we engage more people and how can we keep this innovation cycle going within our school?*

Here, a long-term motivation to sustain the specific work in which he and his colleagues had been engaged is coupled with a broader desire to introduce an ongoing cycle of innovation within the school—something that, in fact, came to pass after the official end of the research project, with many more teachers within the school engaging with an adapted version of the Framework for Inquiry-Driven Innovation. Noting the value of his study group's work for influencing teaching and learning across the school, he said, "It will definitely keep going, what we continue to do in terms of our innovations because, you know, it's an ongoing process. It doesn't end." A teacher at KGS spoke with similar passion about her desire to spread her study group's innovation in the kindergarten classes both to other grade levels within her own school and back in her home country of India: "If I passed it to more teachers and they passed it to more teachers, more teachers would spread it to more teachers; then there is innovation happening and very soon it will be widely spread." An administrator at Modern also spoke with satisfaction about innovation spreading among teachers beyond her study group: "They're taking up their own proactiveness and initiatives and doing their own research as well."

See Part Three for tools to help study groups think about the long-term trajectory of their innovations, including *Looking Ahead*, *Spheres of Influence*, and *Spreading, Scaling, and Sustaining*.

Journeys of Continuous Improvement

While the notion of educators and indeed all adults being "lifelong learners" is hardly novel, participants spoke in their interviews as if they had developed a new or renewed appreciation that they were on an ongoing journey of professional development or growth. For instance, a teacher from NMS chose to spotlight the process of pursuing an inquiry focus:

> I think, for me, the process of the evolution of inquiring questions was something that I have never engaged in before. . . . It tells of how teaching and learning practices are constantly evolving, and there is a learning in the evolution itself. Sometimes it's not as easy as taking a best practice that someone else has tried. I take something and customize it to myself.

There is a sense of agency evident here in her description of adapting practices from elsewhere to suit her particular needs and learning context; there is also a sense that pursuing an inquiry focus—in this case one connected to an innovation—helps to offer directionality to teachers' attempts to continue to improve or modify their practice. The tight connection between purpose and reflection is evident as the teacher further comments, "To me, it has been a good introspective journey"—that is, one which has enabled her both to reconsider how she is doing things, such as identifying or demonstrating learning outcomes, and to reflect on why she is doing them in that way.

Assimilating and incorporating what was learned from specific innovations into overall practice was mentioned by other teachers as well. One teacher, from WIS, commented on her new commitment to promoting critical thinking in her students: "In terms of the future, this is something that's not just done for a project, it's something that's within my practice now, and I need to keep developing it and going with it." Some participants moved back and forth between talking about their own journeys of learning and those of their students. A teacher at KGS, for example, spoke about life as a journey, which demands that we develop a range of skills to deal with many different kinds of situations; in her eyes, the idea that new questions continually arise and that education is never "done" mimics the overall project of life itself. She also commented on her new commitment to introduce deeper and more sustained learning into her classroom in contrast to her previous attitude: "We were just thinking, this is the topic, these are the questions and then this is the assessment. My job is done."

Element #3: Reflection

The growth aspect of reflection is tightly linked to the other two elements for elevating practice: openness and purpose. Meanwhile, the concept of slowing down is an important one within the Framework for Inquiry-Driven Innovation, and educators often associated reflection with *taking the time* to look, listen, and consider what was going on and why. They talked about the importance—and challenge—of periodically pausing during the rush of their life in schools to reflect on the bigger picture of what they were doing. They also spoke about the importance of trying to incorporate reflection into their day-to-day activities, including classroom teaching and learning. Variously named approaches to professional development that resonate with inquiry-driven innovation, such as collaborative inquiry, emphasize the centrality of reflection for teacher growth and the development of a sense of purpose beyond just getting a job done (Deluca et al., 2014; Nelson et al., 2015; Vangrieken et al., 2015). Here, the collaborative aspect of this work is vital, as Allen and Blythe point out: "Without the perspectives of colleagues, the capacity to reflect productively on one's own teaching and learning is sharply limited" (2015, p. 12).

Taking a Moment to Pause and Reflect

Numerous educators commented on how much they valued the opportunity to pause from the busyness of their everyday routines and the various responsibilities and initiatives they were juggling at any one time. An educator from FPS made a connection between the *Slow Looking* tool which encourages practitioners to take the time to observe their teaching contexts in new ways, with the broader importance of considering what he and his colleagues were doing day to day. An educator from WSO, meanwhile, emphasized the importance of finding the time to reflect during the process of developing an innovation project: "Having that time to stop and think about what's worked, what hasn't worked, what have the students said, and then using that to develop our innovations, that's been quite valuable."

> See *Slow Looking*, *Interviewing*, and *Documentation* for tools that study groups used to engage in slow looking and attentive listening.

Meanwhile, an administrator from WIS commented not only on the pace of the work that all teachers at the school were normally expected to embrace, but also on its fragmented nature: "This week we're going to look at this and next week we're going to look at this other thing and then we're going to look at differentiation but then the following week we're going to look at this skill. . . . " She noted that engaging in the process of inquiry-driven innovation had taught her that "you have to look at things slowly and properly." Here, there is a close link between reflection and developing or revitalizing a sense of purpose in one's practice. Other educators, for example, at Modern, commented that engaging in inquiry-driven innovation prompted them to ask new questions or reflect on their work in new ways. Indeed, study groups or professional learning communities in schools can be valuable because very few practitioners have the time or inclination to stop by themselves to reflect on their work without some kind of supportive and collaborative structure (Deluca et al., 2014; Schleicher, 2011).

Other teachers spoke more generally about the importance of reflection in the context of being on an unfolding journey both as individuals and professionals. A teacher at WIS spoke about the importance of slowing down to see where he was going on this journey rather than, as was his personal instinct, to quickly take stock and move on to the next thing. Meanwhile, other teachers spoke in terms of a bigger life mission to do something positive in the world: as in all walks of life, it is hard to disentangle what is personal and what is professional in terms of practice and growth.

Integrating Reflection into Daily Practice

Teachers also spoke about their newfound appreciation for the importance of integrating reflection into their everyday teaching practice and enabling reflection for others. A study group member from WSO noted that she was giving her students more time to reflect after class sessions:

I used to rush them through that process [of reflection] because I'd want to move on to the next part of the course, the new learning—but now I give them more time in the classroom so that they have longer to reflect on what they've done well, what they need to do to improve, even getting them to rewrite sections of work so that they are actually taking on board that feedback.

A teacher at KGS similarly spoke about giving her students more time to reflect: "We give them time to pause" instead of "this activity, that activity, this activity, I'm going to my next class." At Modern, an administrator commented that she was now asking her teachers to reflect more on what they were doing rather than to merely report if they were getting something done: "We want to look for the impact of doing that [thinking] routine, what it had on [students'] thinking, whether their responses were different from the regular." Here, we see how individual lift or professional growth can be transmitted to others.

What Lift Can Look Like for Different Individuals

The previous section unpacked what the growth elements of openness, purpose, and reflection looked like for a variety of educators working within very different schools. But what did lift look like for specific educators? Unsurprisingly, it varied considerably. This section briefly zooms in on three individuals—Helen, Vicki, and Zahra—to explore what lift looked like for them at this particular moment in their professional trajectories.

Helen

Helen, a teacher with 13 years' experience in the classroom and Head of History at GEMS Wellington Academy—Silicon Oasis (WSO), was, by her own description, a creative thinker and risk-taker well before encountering inquiry-driven innovation; in fact, her willingness to try out new ideas is what attracted her in the first place to participate in the research project that led to this book. Nevertheless, she spoke enthusiastically about the boost or lift that inquiry-driven innovation had given to her individual practice, particularly in terms of encouraging her to adopt more of an inquiry-driven stance toward her work and to incorporate reflection into her day-to-day activities.

> *Just taking two minutes to stop, to take a step back and just look at what's happening and what the students are actually doing and who is engaged, who isn't as engaged, why they are engaged, why they are less engaged. I suppose that element has changed, because I wouldn't have done that, I would have just carried on with what I was doing. . . .*

She also commented that she found herself generally questioning all aspects of her practice: "I think about stuff a lot more just generally. When I'm in the car or in the shower I just think, 'How could I do that differently, how could that work differently?'" She noted that while her teacher training program had placed an emphasis on reflective practice, it had eventually got "lost in the day-to-day of teaching, which is very busy."

By extension, she also started trying to build in more opportunities for her students to engage in reflection, both for their own benefit as learners and to "let them feed back into innovations that are taking place." Commenting on what her students had to say about her study group's innovation, which centered around a new framework to develop students' capacity to navigate new technologies, she actively reflected on what she had learned from their reflections: "I think they struggle to talk about their learning. They can talk about a website, but they aren't necessarily verbalizing how that's helping them physically learn." She went on to ponder adjustments she and her team could make regarding how they gathered data: "I think that's because we're not asking the right questions so I think we need to think more about the questions that we ask." Furthermore, she reflected on the fact that she was critiquing her own method of collecting data from students:

> The fact that I'm now saying I don't think I'm asking the right questions in the student surveys, again, it's an element of being reflective on what we're doing and improving—even improving the way that we gather documentation. Because in day-to-day classroom practice we don't stop and think and reflect because it's so fast-paced, getting students through the exams . . . doing reports, all of the day-to-day stuff often gets in the way.

Here, she is referring both to the importance of finding the time to reflect and taking an inquiry-driven approach to the process of reflection.

To be clear, Helen did not radically change all elements of her already strong practice: "I've been teaching 13 years, so what makes good practice in the classroom for me has remained the same. My understanding of what good teaching looks like and what good learning is and what good learning looks like hasn't evolved in the last 18 months." As already noted, she was already inclined to experiment and be "quite creative" with her teaching. However, the Framework for Inquiry-Driven Innovation facilitated further innovation and encouraged her to lift her practice in ways she might not otherwise have done: "It definitely has allowed me to enjoy the process of creating innovations and it's challenged me to do things that I find more difficult like the reflective element." This infusion of reflection into her practice helped her to be more discerning about how and why she was trying out new things:

> By the next week you'll be bombarded with ten more different ideas of how to do things in a classroom and it's picking out the ones that are going to be right for you ... having that time to stop and think and reflect about how you're going to implement things within your classroom is really important.

This process also gave her new ideas for the next steps in terms of her own professional development, as well as that of her colleagues. Following involvement in the research cohort, she enabled other teachers to experience the process that she herself had gone through by scaling inquiry-driven innovation throughout her school and considered pursuing more research through academic study.

Vicki

Vicki, who was featured in the case study on WIS in Chapter 5, held an administrative position within her school and was further promoted to the role of deputy head teacher during her involvement in the research cohort. She was no longer teaching in the classroom, but had until recently taught history at the school. She had also recently completed a master's degree in education, which had required her to engage in an action research project in her classroom. In fact, she was initially uncertain she wanted to get involved in the research cohort because she had found her recent experience of doing school-based action research to be somewhat draining. The underlying principles of taking an inquiry-driven approach to innovating in teaching and learning were not new ones for Vicki; however, through them she was still able to experience a considerable lift to her individual practice.

Vicki was particularly enthusiastic about her experience of working as part of a diverse team of educators, taking pride in what they accomplished together through the development of their critical thinking innovation; she also deeply valued the moral support they had offered one another along the way. This appreciation for the power of working in a team rather than pursuing solo initiatives or research projects endured over time. She wrote that the most important thing she had learned or gained was "how we can work together to bring about change using particular tools." Although in this comment she highlights the usefulness of the tools offered in Part Three, she is also signaling a new openness to working collaboratively across usual school silos, as she went on to state: "I have changed by realizing that powerful change can come about when you work with a variety of different people from different backgrounds with quite strict protocols. . . . I have learned that I should be much more open to working with people from a variety of subject areas."

Vicki also emphasized that she had come to appreciate the importance of reflection in her practice and of taking a coherent approach to pursuing positive change in schools. She noted that effective teaching and learning "happens through having small groups reflecting on their own learning and teaching and having a specific time frame to make changes and implement the differences." Here, she is valuing reflection as part of a structured process. She also commented on the importance of having a clear sense of purpose or an understanding of why she is doing her work:

> I have become more confident as a result of [inquiry-driven innovation]. I understand how to bring about change and how to engage when working with people from different backgrounds more than I did before. I understand the importance of feeling confident about my own work and thinking about the reasons behind it.

This comment also reveals an overall sense of lift to her work, as manifested by her increased sense of confidence and empowerment to enact change.

Zahra

Zahra, a teacher leader at KGS—a school featured in a case study in Chapter 5—described herself as a "very sensitive person" and someone who pays close attention to her own and other people's feelings. She was already highly committed to her students' well-being and preparing them as much as possible for an uncertain and changing future. She nevertheless spoke about inquiry-driven innovation as having had a profound effect on her practice in ways that resonate with the three elements of openness, purpose, and reflection.

Zahra was a member of the KGS study group focused on kindergarten, and stated that through her innovation work she had learned to listen to her colleagues in new ways—something she broadly described as a shift "from hearing to listening." She stated that she was now more actively trying to understand their perspectives: "I'm putting myself in another person's shoes now to find out how that person—why is she seeing what she's seeing? . . . Not superficially but in depth. . . . I felt like I was a good listener, but now I'm actually listening." Referring to the example of planning for a school event, she noted that she has become less apt to impose her ideas on the teachers she supervises. Instead, she is now more likely to ask for her colleagues' opinions and to recognize that they are offering suggestions because they think they will benefit students: "So more openness, more listening, and we can build that way." She also spoke about becoming more open to listening to the ideas of students, for example, by using thinking routines to encourage more exploratory and student-centered approaches to learning: something she described as much more difficult than simply telling them what to do. She contrasted this new openness to the more traditional teacher-centered practices that previously prevailed at KGS:

> What we were doing was—I don't know, we were not listening. It was seen as listening but we were not actually listening: we were not respecting, I felt. If a child did something, "No, that's not the way to do it." Are you respecting? No. You're just hindering his progress there. Because we have a mindset on the outcome.

When Zahra talked about trying to understand the perspectives of colleagues and students, she spoke about "reflecting a lot" as part of the process. She also commented on a desire to reflect on and make sense of changes in her own practice: "Because I don't know how far I have come—I really don't know. I need to reflect lots with my journey; what I am now." Here, we see evidence of someone who considers herself to have grown and who has a newfound appreciation for the importance of taking a moment to reflect on the path she has traversed and what she is doing now; however, it seems fair to say that compared to Helen, for example, greater openness figured more prominently in the lifting of her practice than did reflection, even if the two are closely linked.

Zahra spoke passionately about her longstanding vocation as a teacher and clearly had a strong sense of mission long before learning about inquiry-driven innovation. However, it seems that cultivating a greater openness to others' ideas and perspectives fueled a specific desire or sense of purpose to spread what she learned about the benefits of being more open to other people's ideas: "I want to bring the change that can help people identify that the key to living is to respect every opinion and create a positive change." It is worth noting that she referred to life or living writ large here; Zahra was one of a number of educators who spoke about education and growth in very expansive terms and felt that inquiry-driven innovation had helped her personally as well as professionally. She spoke of a new sense of confidence, in part, because she felt that she now had a wider range of tools or strategies at her disposal to innovate or find solutions. Commenting that she previously tended to keep what she was doing in her practice to herself, she described becoming far more eager to share her ideas and to engage with other educators. She partly attributed this change to the opportunity to share ideas across different schools through regular meetings and exhibitions: "I'm constantly in touch with other teachers: 'Look at this. Is it okay? What do you think?' Exchange of dialogue, the exchange of ideas—that's very important I think. That has developed. I was not brought up that way."

Why Inquiry-Driven Innovation Elevates Individual Practice

These brief glimpses into the experiences of Helen, Vicki, and Zahra—and the overview of how the elements of openness, purpose, and reflection played out somewhat differently in different school contexts—draw attention to the fact that there cannot be a one-size-fits-all approach to lifting individual practice. Furthermore, inquiry-driven innovation can signify different things to different people. Nevertheless, there is also a coherence to these voices and a sense that they have been involved in powerful professional learning as well as the enactment of positive change within their schools. Why?

As already noted, the Framework for Inquiry-Driven Innovation resonates with prevailing recommendations within the field of teacher professional development. Its emphasis on work that is purposeful and intentional, attentive to multiple perspectives, adapted to context, sustained and iterative, and structured and supported is a far cry from the kinds of one-off, decontextualized workshops that position educators as recipients of training rather than drivers of their own professional growth and change within their schools. Instead, it brings together the concepts of inquiry, innovation, and community in ways that allow teachers to promote changes that are meaningful and relevant within their own contexts, all the while promoting the three elements of openness, purpose, and reflection that can lift their individual practice. It arguably boosts the power of existing collaborative inquiry approaches to professional development by focusing energies on the initiation, piloting, implementation, and expansion of actionable innovations rather than more open-ended explorations into teaching and learning. And it sidesteps the perils of "contrived collegiality" by offering genuine opportunities for growth and autonomy rather than serving as a mechanism for implementing top-down policies (Hargreaves, 2019).

Furthermore, the model arguably attends to three innate psychological needs that must be met in order for professional development to be effective: competence, autonomy, and relatedness (Deci & Ryan, 1985; Noonan, 2016). In other words, educators need to be given tools that will: 1) translate into positive changes on the ground within their schools and increase their overall capacity to be agents of those changes; 2) grant them the freedom to apply their existing expertise and knowledge and to develop innovations that are meaningful within their working contexts and overall personal and professional trajectories; and 3) provide them the opportunity to learn both with and from their colleagues in ways that cultivate a sense of being part of something that is bigger than their daily list of immediate tasks.

Andy Hargreaves and Michael Fullan (2012) were not commenting specifically on the concept of innovation when they made the following assertion:

> It's not the job of bureaucrats or a few elite teacher representatives to develop curriculum while classroom teachers deliver it. Instead, within clear common guidelines, teachers and schools create, think about, and inquire into curriculum and pedagogy together. Otherwise, how can we expect children to develop 21st-century skills of innovation and creativity if their teachers don't enjoy the same opportunity?

However, their comment resonates because inquiry-driven innovation is all about offering a light, flexible structure and a set of tools to enable educators to come together to innovate in order to develop the kinds of learning experiences that make most sense for their particular students in a particular place and at a particular moment in time. And in facilitating such learning experiences, teachers may cultivate in themselves the kinds of learning or habits of mind that they aspire to foster in their students. Symmetry between adult learning and student learning is important in schools, though often overlooked (Mehta & Fine, 2019).

Situating Individual Growth within Collective Learning

While the themes of openness, purpose, and reflection emerged from an analysis of what individual educators had to say about their own personal and professional growth, these themes are also reflected in aspects of the collective learning that took place within study groups, as structured by the activities that were part of the collaborative design-based research project. This resonance is unsurprising of course; however, it underscores that inquiry-driven innovation is designed to take place in community and that it simultaneously seeks to empower individuals and groups of people to effect positive school-based change.

For instance, all study groups engaged with other stakeholders and listened to multiple perspectives as part of their work, thereby as a group cultivating the openness that individual educators reported as being so important for their personal growth. Several schools formally collected feedback about their innovations from their colleagues via surveys or interviews, and many schools also solicited feedback on their developing projects from students. The perspectives gathered often suggested changes or pivots in the design of the group's innovation project, but also helped at times to validate and strengthen new approaches that were being tried out. Modern's study group, for instance, went through a process of adjusting and iterating as it tried out a new interdisciplinary curriculum in its school and introduced thinking routines into classrooms for the first time. The group members solicited feedback from colleagues and the school principal as they pilot-tested their new ideas and made changes in response. In some cases, colleagues or students who offered perspectives and feedback went on to become an integral part of the group's work. As an outgrowth of the NMS study group's innovation project, for instance, NMS students also had their voices heard by creating a Student Thinking Routine Squad that supported scaling up of thinking routines both at NMS and in other schools.

Part of the study group work also entailed developing a strong focus or sense of purpose. Many of the schools profiled in earlier chapters used tools from the *Toolkit for Inquiry-Driven Innovation* (Chapter 8) to become more concrete and intentional about the type of change they wanted to effect in their schools, or to narrow down a specific target population that would be the focus of their innovation work. Many groups demonstrated persistence or a sense of being engaged in innovation for the long haul. This commitment to their innovations in the long term is particularly noteworthy when considering the ups and downs faced by many study groups as they brought new practices and pedagogical tools to life in their schools, often sticking with an innovation even as it changed drastically or confronted major challenges. At GAA, for example, the study group initially worked with great enthusiasm to develop assessment practices that would help students become more excited about their own learning. However, it quickly became clear that the open-endedness of the task of developing their own learning assessments was unfamiliar and even uncomfortable for GAA learners. The study group had to rethink its initial design and consider how to build more scaffolding and support for students, which ultimately helped the group to consider their long-term aspirations for learners and the overall purpose of what was trying to be achieved. The KGS study group, meanwhile, initially received strong pushback from parents and select members of the school's teaching faculty as it engaged in an ambitious and overarching school change process that fundamentally challenged assumptions about curriculum design and the role of the teacher. However, driven by a strong sense of purpose, KGS educators stuck with these changes and worked to push through transformations to school practices and philosophies. Eventually, parents and teachers became some of the most ardent and outspoken supporters of these paradigm shifts.

Finally, reflection played a vital role in the groups' learning. A theme that was part of multiple stories of school change was that of slowing down in order to see and hear the familiar with fresh eyes and ears, often supported by a practice of documentation. Importantly, this work of slow looking and attentive listening was not just about the act of noticing and recording but also about using what was learned through looking, listening, and documenting to engage in introspection and reflection. All schools involved in the research cohort engaged in these practices using tools from the *Toolkit for Inquiry-Driven Innovation* (Chapter 8). Study groups used these tools starting early on in the process of innovating in order to take an inquiry-based stance to their work and to ensure that the innovations they were developing were based on the unique teaching and learning contexts in which they were situated.

Limitations

The degree to which participating educators enthused about the process of engaging in inquiry-driven innovation and the ways in which it was impacting their overall practice initially took the research team somewhat aback; as has been noted, it helped crystallize the tight connection between teacher professional development and the promotion of innovation in schools. However, while these individual stories of personal and professional growth are compelling, some caution is warranted. For instance, educators may have been prone to exaggerating the impact of inquiry-driven innovation, unconsciously or otherwise: social connections were formed during the research project and there may have been a desire or sense of obligation on their part to sound positive, especially given the time and resources being put into the work. The research project itself, of course, created some conditions that would be hard to replicate on a regular basis—notably the educators' access to advice and resources from a university-based research team. There was also a sense of pride, and perhaps, prestige that came from being part of the project that may have helped to elevate individual practice. In addition, it has already been acknowledged that the educators were, by definition, highly motivated practitioners *before* encountering inquiry-driven innovation given their willingness to engage in a collaborative design-based research project. Indeed, they may have been particularly eager at that specific moment in their professional trajectories for such an experience. Other puzzles concern the difficulty of disentangling what educators were asked to do as part of the project and what they actually incorporated into their general practice in the long term. Further, it is hard to separate individual experiences from collective ones—although in many ways that is the point of emphasizing the importance of community within the framework.

A good deal also remains unknown. For example, were the conditions in the UAE, and within the GEMS network of schools, in particular, especially conducive to participants enjoying a sense of personal and professional growth through their participation in the project? What other conditions needed to be in place for them to benefit from the opportunity? While by design the participants had varying degrees of professional experience and played different roles within their schools, it would also be helpful to investigate if some kind of differentiation would be helpful in terms of supporting educators to get the most out of the approach of inquiry-driven innovation—particularly without the involvement of a research team. As is noted in the concluding chapter of this book, inquiry-driven innovation practices have spread to educators and schools beyond the original research cohort; however, research has not been done into the experiences of those educators. Readers of this book are encouraged to dip into, adapt, and generally make the presented framework—or select aspects of it—their own. Yet with that invitation comes uncertainty about *how much* of the framework is enough to promote individual and collective growth, let alone school-based change.

Final Thoughts

The different components of the Framework for Inquiry-Driven Innovation are tightly interconnected. Individual educators were part of school-based study groups, who were part of a broader cohort of study groups involved in a collaborative design-based research project. Educators interacted with, and indeed helped to develop, a series of tools, broader practices, and concepts that they put into practice as they developed innovations tailored to the needs of their schools. Pinpointing what exactly about this complex picture was most powerful for individuals, or the degree to which learning took place at the group rather than the individual level, would be challenging to say the least. And it would clearly be an over-statement to claim that inquiry-driven innovation is certain to encourage personal and professional growth for individuals whatever the circumstances.

Yet, through this complexity, a compelling picture does emerge of educators experiencing meaningful lift within their practice through inquiry-driven innovation. As the project liaison Christine Nassergodsi commented:

> I think the teachers who have been part of this have become pretty joyful in their work. And joy is, in my mind, so much richer than happiness. It's that sense of feeling purpose, but also feeling capable. You're purposeful in your work, but you're also capable of doing it. And you're engaged with others in the process of doing it. You're engaged with others within your school or across schools. Now, emotionally, there have been highs and lows . . . but I think that's part of the complexity, there are ups and downs.

Many educators are eager for this kind of joyfulness and satisfaction in their work, even if considerable effort is involved. Furthermore, collective efficacy among teachers is cited as the most influential factor in terms of influencing student achievement within a school (Donohoo, Hattie & Eells, 2018). All stakeholders deserve to be associated with schools where educators have experienced the kind of lift to practice that leads to a greater sense of empowerment and the motivation and desire to promote positive change. And at the heart of this lift is openness, purpose, and reflection.

PART III

CREATING *YOUR* COMMUNITIES OF INNOVATION

CHAPTER 7

ESTABLISHING AND NURTURING COMMUNITIES OF INNOVATION

As described earlier, the Framework for Inquiry-Driven Innovation emerged through a collaborative, design-based research project called Creating Communities of Innovation that partnered a team of researchers from Project Zero at the Harvard Graduate School of Education with seven schools in the GEMS Education network of schools in the United Arab Emirates (UAE). From its inception, this framework was intended to be applicable to many different educational settings without being prescriptive. This part of the book turns to the journey that *you*, the reader, could take in applying inquiry-driven innovation in your own teaching and learning context. While Chapter 8 presents a series of concrete tools to use at different moments of your innovation journey, this chapter addresses some initial decision points and stage setting. It also offers a *Roadmap for Inquiry-Driven Innovation* a bird's-eye view of the general innovation process followed by research cohort schools. You are encouraged to read on, reflect on, and get ready for the work of reimagining teaching and learning in whatever context you call home.

Part Two of this book illustrated diverse stories of inquiry-driven innovation in action at seven schools. But getting to the starting line where these stories began was not a process that happened overnight, and this is probably true of most change initiatives in schools. Generally, groundwork needs to be laid for innovations to be successful.

The Framework for Inquiry-Driven Innovation recommends a careful approach to establishing and nurturing communities of innovation—be that within a single school or across multiple sites, as in the Creating Communities of Innovation project. The preparation happens first at the level of individuals as they get ready to engage in inquiry-driven innovation with an open mind. But it also happens at the level of classrooms, departments, and schools that must prepare to help those individuals' work be successful and sustainable.

How this work unfolds in specific settings is hugely context dependent. This chapter does not provide step-by-step instructions for laying the groundwork for innovation. Instead, it presents learnings and guiding questions distilled from the experiences of the research cohort schools, external leaders who supported (and continue to support) those schools, and the research team.

Convening Your Community

One of the earliest steps of the Creating Communities of Innovation research project was to convene the community of schools that would be part of this work over an extended period of time—in this case, two years and beyond. This process involved seeking out schools that had a strong desire to participate and were also able to commit to the work, including dedicating staff time and supporting curricular and pedagogical experimentation. Bringing this community together happened by framing the *who, why,* and *how* of the work.

An important early decision point in creating your own community of innovation is deciding *who* might be part of the community. While the work illustrated throughout this book happened within one network of schools (GEMS Education), it could certainly take place across different networks of schools, or among schools unaffiliated with a network. Given the increasing prevalence of online learning, increasing opportunities exist for bringing together diverse and geographically disparate schools, and study groups could meet online rather than in person. One exciting advantage of working with schools in the UAE was the presence of curricula and pedagogies from across the globe. For this reason, members of the research team were able to convene extremely diverse study groups within the same city that shared the common bond of school inspections and governmental guidelines for schooling. For this cohort, a liaison served as a mentor and organizer for group activities, though distributed leadership across multiple organizers has worked well with subsequent groups of schools implementing the framework: following the research described in this book, a group of veteran "lead" schools emerged that collaboratively assumed the responsibility of organizing the cohort and mentoring schools new to the Framework for Inquiry-Driven Innovation.

However your community comes together, it is important to set group expectations, norms, agreements, and guiding purposes for your work together. While some groups may choose to do this in more structured ways such as writing mission statements and creating Memoranda of Understanding among involved schools, others may approach this work more organically and flexibly.

With your community established, you can begin to think about the means and frequency of ongoing collaboration and communication amongst community members. Periodic in-person or virtual community meetings might feel important as a means to share moral and intellectual support, and to give critique and feedback to each other about how innovations are developing across study groups. The concept of "exhibiting" innovation work in progress was essential for schools in the original research cohort and is explained more in the *Exhibiting Your Work* tool in the next chapter. Connecting in between structured gatherings could happen through web-based platforms, such as an email listserv or a website that enables schools to share video updates across study groups. When planning for these interactions, it may be helpful to view the *Roadmap for Inquiry-Driven Innovation* below.

In general, while a community of like minded practitioners engaging in the shared experience of inquiry-driven innovation is a critical source of feedback, it is also important to have opportunities to receive input from those outside of the study groups as the innovations progress. Study groups in the research cohort presented their work in progress to each other for the first few months of their work, then expanded out to other members of their school communities and eventually to larger public audiences as their innovations reached advanced stages of development.

Key questions to consider when convening your community of innovation:

- What do you mean by *community*? Will it be within your school, or across schools? Local, or reaching beyond your local area?

- What are the characteristics of diversity that feel important to attend to in your community, and how will you work to ensure that you honor that diversity when gathering those who might be involved?
- What commitments will you ask for both from the schools and individuals involved? How much time will you ask participants and leaders to devote to their work in this community, including meetings, work completed between meetings, and opportunities to share work with others? Does it feel important to create some kind of agreement (formal or informal) surrounding these commitments?
- How will you connect and interact as a community? With what frequency?
- How will you periodically "check in" as a community to make sure your activities and interactions are working well for all involved?
- Will there be leaders in this work? One person, or a collective?

Assembling the Study Group

In addition to the larger-scale community created across schools or within multiple schools, the "mini-community" of each study group—several individuals from a school or other learning context who meet weekly over an extended period of time to work collaboratively toward an innovation—provided the initial impetus for pushing forward innovations in a sustained and dedicated way. Within the cohort of schools involved in the original Creating Communities of Innovation project, most study groups encompassed five to eight self-selecting participants. Schools were strongly encouraged to seek out diversity within these groups by including educators working in different subject areas and those with school leadership roles. These groups met weekly for hour-long sessions during the school year over the course of two years in order to plan and reflect on their innovation projects, discuss related readings, and use the tools and resources provided in the *Toolkit for Inquiry-Driven Innovation* (Chapter 8). These sessions were nonhierarchical in nature, with rotating facilitation among group members. Study group members not only worked together, but also supported each other through the highs and lows of innovating in their schools. Their positions in different school roles and/or different departments also helped study group members to bring in diverse perspectives on how they were approaching their work. Together, these tight-knit groups embraced the work of inquiry by collaboratively envisioning possibilities, experimenting, and working through the successes and challenges that arose through the course of innovating in their schools.

Key questions to consider when establishing study groups:

- How much time will study group members be asked to devote to this work, including meetings, work completed between meetings, and opportunities to share work with others?
- How will you periodically "check in" as a study group to make sure the group's activities and interactions are working well for all involved, and that group members are honoring any agreed-upon commitments?
- How will you communicate and interact as a group, and with what frequency?
- What structural supports are needed in order for study group members to have the time and space for reflection and collaborative work (e.g., class coverage, meeting space, etc.)?
- Have study group members been given the authority and administrative support to experiment and engage in the work of innovating? If not, how can you work around this constraint or work to build support for innovation in your context?
- What diversity and equity considerations feel important for convening your study group?

Envisioning the Process

The process of innovating within a real-world context is far from something that goes from A to B in a straight line and on a predictable timeline. That said, schools that have engaged in the work of inquiry-driven innovation have found it helpful to see an overall sketch of what going through such a process might look like and how they could employ the steps and resources used by schools whose stories are told throughout this book.

The following "roadmap," shown in Figure 7.1, traces a loose route for innovating using the Framework for Inquiry-Driven Innovation. The path is meant to be fluid and winding rather than lockstep or linear. In fact, the innovation project journeys and case studies in Part Two of this book show that there is room for considerable variation from one school context to another, as well as moments of circling back or iteration. However, there is a clear overall trajectory to the process that involves creating a study group, building inquiry skills, gathering inspiration, developing an inquiry focus, making a plan, pilot testing, working with data, reflecting and sharing, and moving forward with the innovation developed by a study group. The roadmap broadly delineates these different phases of

CREATING THE STUDY GROUP

Join other interested schools to form a Learning Community cohort.

Create a study group at your school (we recommend 4-6 members with diverse backgrounds).

BUILDING INQUIRY SKILLS

In your study group, begin to learn more about your teaching and learning context. Build or refine a few core inquiry skills to use on an ongoing basis.

Related Tools:

- Slow Looking
- Interviewing
- Documentation suite of tools

FIRST DRAFT INQUIRY FOCUS

GATHERING INSPIRATION

DEVELOPING AN INQUIRY FOCUS

Take a critical lens on your draft inquiry focus and refine it further.

Considering where the energy of the study group lies and the salient opportunities and challenges in your home teaching and learning environment, frame a first draft inquiry focus.

Surface opportunities and areas of interest for innovation. Begin an on going practice of reflecting on the overall trajectory of your collective work.

Related Tools:

- Wishes, Challenges, and Opportunities

Related Tools:

- Sweet Spot of Innovation
- Population, Innovation, Outcome

REFINED INQUIRY FOCUS

FIRST DRAFT INNOVATION PROJECT

MAKING A PLAN

Articulate where you are now, where you hope to get to, and what you hope to do to explore your inquiry focus.

Related Tools:

- Theory of Action suite of tools

Envision one or more innovation projects for your teaching and learning context.

Figure 7.1 A flexible roadmap for inquiry-driven innovation.

PILOT-TESTING

Start pilot-testing one or more innovation projects, using the inquiry skills you developed to document the process.

Related Tools:

- Prototyping a Process
- Prototyping an Experience
- Prototyping a Tool or Resource

WORKING WITH DATA

Begin to collect and interpret data to understand the impacts of the innovation project so far and what more you need to learn.

Related Tools:

- Data Analysis suite of tools

REFLECTING AND SHARING

Build on this feedback, your reflections, and data analysis to continue to iterate on your innovation project(s).

Begin ongoing routines of reflection and sharing your work within your local context and giving and receiving feedback within your Learning Community cohort.

Related Tools:

- Exhibiting Your Work
- Theory of Action Tuning Protocol
- Project Journey Mapping

MOVING FORWARD

Reflect on how to further develop your innovation project(s), get more people involved in it, and/or expand its impact beyond your original target popoulation.

Related Tools:

- Looking Ahead
- Spheres of Influence
- Spreading, Scaling, and Sustaining

work, while also suggesting tools to use along the way; however, while some tools clearly fit better at one stage of the process than another, others can be frequently revisited, as indicated in specific tools in the toolkit that follows (Chapter 8). Furthermore, using one tool may prompt study group members to return to an earlier phase of the process—or to hop ahead to a later one.

Innovation communities and study groups might use this roadmap to structure their own approaches to inquiry-driven innovation, keeping in mind that it is a general process that offers a sense of the journey ahead while leaving plenty of room for customization. As you go through your own innovation journey, you may want to keep track of and reflect on how your unique roadmap is developing by using the *Project Journey Mapping* tool.

Key questions to consider about envisioning the innovation process:

- What is the timeline for your work together (keeping in mind that it is advisable to plan for at least one school year)? Where in this process do you hope to be in a month? Three months? A year or more?
- What resources do you have available to support innovation in your context?
- Are there any key challenges, constraints, or opportunities you already know about that might suggest a different process than that proposed in the roadmap above? How might you need to adapt the suggested process for your own context?
- What are some possible logistical challenges that you are likely to encounter in this process, and how might you work through them?

Knowing Your Toolkit

As noted, the preceding roadmap outlines not only a process for innovating in your school, but also pedagogical tools and resources that may help you along this journey. These tools are a component of the Framework for Inquiry-Driven Innovation, and are part of what differentiates engaging in innovation in general (doing something new or different) from engaging in *inquiry*-driven innovation: an approach that requires being reflective and intentional about the process of innovating. The tools that comprise the *Toolkit for Inquiry-Driven Innovation* (see the following chapter) are designed to support questioning, reflection, experimentation, and collaboration throughout the journey, from taking a look with fresh eyes around your context to implementing and spreading new practices in your teaching and learning context. They also support the five principles of inquiry-driven innovation that are described in Part One, helping you to consider the purpose and intention of your work and the unique contexts and perspectives that surround you. As you get ready to embark on this journey, it will be helpful to take at least a cursory look at the full toolkit in order to understand the resources available to you. The introduction to the next chapter pulls out a few particularly important tools that are referred to across the toolkit and should be part of every study group's innovation journey: a tool on the practice of slow looking, as well suites of tools on establishing a documentation practice and creating a Theory of Action diagram for your group.

Key questions to consider about using resources from the Toolkit for Inquiry-Driven Innovation:

- At first glance, which tools stand out to you as ones that you might want to explore further?
- What are some other resources (e.g., favorite protocols, reflection exercises, etc.) that you might want to add to your study group's toolkit?
- Do you have any budget or other available resources (e.g., space, materials) that might come in handy for using the tools? Note that some tools do not require any materials, and the rest depend only on basic supplies such as markers, chart paper, and sticky notes.

There is no need to have a fully worked out plan for implementing inquiry-driven innovation before you set off: the whole point of the work being inquiry-driven is that you will continually ask questions of what you are doing and why and adapt your work as you go along. However, having a sense of the journey ahead and the kinds of decision points that will arise will stand you in good stead. And establishing favorable conditions from the outset means that you are less likely to encounter serious challenges or roadblocks as you seek to effect positive change in your teaching and learning environment.

CHAPTER 8

THE TOOLKIT FOR INQUIRY-DRIVEN INNOVATION

This chapter is provided for those educators ready to try inquiry-driven innovation in their own settings. Earlier in this book, the stories of some of the schools that went through such an experience were presented as innovation journeys (see Chapter 4) and case studies (Chapter 5). Through these journeys, study groups worked together to look at their surrounding teaching and learning contexts with fresh eyes, to devise an *inquiry focus* that captured the opportunities and challenges they saw around them and eventually to craft and implement an *innovation project* in response, and to engage in ongoing reflection and learning from this process. Along their journeys, these schools made use of tools that collectively comprise the *Toolkit for Inquiry-Driven Innovation*. This toolkit, comprised of the 21 resources that follow, is meant to equip you for key points in your journey through the inquiry-driven innovation process.

The word *tool* is used here as a catch-all for pedagogical resources that will come in handy for study groups undertaking the inquiry-driven innovation approach, including protocols, activities, conversation-starters, and other materials. In line with the focus of this model on inquiry, innovation, and community, the tools are meant to support collaborative and community-based approaches to building inquiry skills and envisioning, enacting, and refining innovation projects—whether within the mini-community of a school-based study group or within the larger community created when study groups from across a school or from different schools come together to share their innovation projects and workshop ideas in progress.

Tools in the later part of the toolkit are designed to help study groups share and reflect on their innovations. Some of the tools have been inspired by existing practices and approaches, while others were created anew to suit the specific needs of the educators and administrators participating in the research cohort of schools described in this book. While some tools were designed well ahead of their use by study groups in the original cohort, others emerged more organically or were crafted from study group activities that participating educators found to be particularly helpful. Regardless of their origins, each of the following pedagogical tools has been trialed with research cohort participants and carefully refined to be useful to educators working in diverse contexts.

Key Terminology

Study groups engaging in *inquiry-driven innovation*—an ongoing process that empowers individuals and communities to pursue positive school-based change that is relevant and responsive to local contexts—will likely find it useful to have read the previous sections of this book, which describe the concept of inquiry-driven innovation in depth (Part One) and present stories of schools that have gone through their own "journeys" of innovating in this way (Part Two). However, for readers who might have skipped ahead to this section, here are a few key terms introduced earlier in the book that will help you to fully engage with the tools that follow:

- An *inquiry focus* is a question about teaching and learning in your context, similar to a research question, that is complex enough to inspire long-term investigation. It might pose a problem or challenge, put a new spin on an existing issue in your context, or propose a practice or approach that feels new and important in your teaching and learning context. An inquiry focus should feel important and compelling both to the members of your study group and to your broader teaching and learning community. A couple of example inquiry foci related to stories of school-based change in Part Two include: *How can we support secondary students at our school to develop the thinking dispositions to be successful in a digital environment?* and *How can engaging with real-world problems through interdisciplinary learning help grade 4 students think about solutions to global challenges?* Study groups work over time to develop an innovation project that grows out of their inquiry focus.

- An *innovation project* is a defined project that your study group is undertaking to develop and implement an innovation. As illustrated through the stories of school-based change in Part Two, study groups in the research cohort framed projects around developing new pedagogical tools like rubrics, curricula, and thinking routines; introducing and scaffolding the adoption of new classroom practices such as documentation of learning or student-designed assessment initiatives; and introducing technologies and learning spaces that would provide students with new kinds of learning opportunities at their schools. Note that these projects are not about general or broad concepts like "critical thinking," "interdisciplinary work," or "blended learning." They are more specific and action-oriented, and involve introducing specific strategies, tools, and resources.

How to Use the Toolkit

The tools presented in the following pages are shown in the order that they appear on the *Roadmap for Inquiry-Driven Innovation* in Chapter 7 a suggested overall trajectory for how inquiry-driven innovation might play out in a given teaching and learning context. In that sense, they are ordered in a particular sequence. However, these tools may be used very productively out of sequence, and some tools may be more useful in some contexts than others. Looking at the innovation journeys and case studies in Part Two of this book may give insight into the diversity of ways to engage with this process, and to specific tools that stood out as particularly important to individual schools in the research cohort. In this regard, you are encouraged to familiarize yourself with all of these tools and to draw on them as needed. In addition, users may also find that some tools work best as a one-time-only experience, while others might be used routinely within study groups and other contexts. Here is an inventory of the tools:

- *Slow Looking: Learning to Look beyond First Impressions*
- *Interviewing: Listening Attentively to Others*
- *Documentation, Part I: Making a Plan to Document*
- *Documentation, Part II: Interpreting Documentation as a Group*
- *Wishes, Challenges, and Opportunities: Developing an Initial Inquiry Focus*

- *Sweet Spot of Innovation: Considering Your Community's Threshold for Change*
- *Population, Innovation, Outcome: Articulating the Who, How, and Why of Your Innovation Project*
- *Theory of Action Part I: Envisioning Your Innovation Journey*
- *Theory of Action Part II: Articulating Your Rationale*
- *Prototyping a Process: Using Diagramming to Visualize Your Innovation*
- *Prototyping an Experience: Using Role Play to Get a Feel for Your Innovation*
- *Prototyping a Tool or Resource: Working on Ideas through Rough Drafting*
- *Data Analysis Part I: Identifying Indicators of Impact*
- *Data Analysis Part II: Creating a Purposeful Data Sample*
- *Data Analysis Part III: Applying Indicators of Impact to Your Data*
- *Exhibiting Your Work: Sharing Your Innovation Project with Others*
- *Theory of Action Tuning Protocol: Revisiting Your Initial Plans and Theories*
- *Project Journey Mapping: Taking the Bird's-Eye View of Your Innovation*
- *Looking Ahead: Envisioning the Path Forward*
- *Spheres of Influence: Visualizing Your Impact*
- *Spreading, Scaling, and Sustaining: Looking to the Long Term*

While you may not choose to use all of the tools in the toolkit, three tools or suites of tools are referred to across the toolkit and have been consistently called out as critical pieces of the process by those engaged in inquiry-driven innovation: *Slow Looking*, the *Documentation* suite of tools, and the suite of tools on creating a *Theory of Action* diagram. These tools are therefore considered particularly important to use throughout the process.

You should plan to spend at least an hour with each tool, though all tools could be used over longer periods of time or over multiple study group meetings. All tools are meant to be used by a study group, except in a few cases (noted within specific tools) where parts of the tool are undertaken as individual work by members of the group before coming back together to share out and reflect. As noted in the description of individual tools, many of them will be useful on a recurring basis throughout your inquiry-driven innovation journey.

While the tools are presented in a format that is printable and at times with worked examples or figures, they are not meant to be set in stone and unchangeable. You are encouraged to hack and tweak the tools to best suit your own needs and those of your students and colleagues as well as the constraints of your unique teaching and learning environment. In other words: consider this toolkit as a resource that is itself open to innovation!

Slow Looking

Learning to Look beyond First Impressions

Purpose of the Tool

Day-to-day work in teaching and learning contexts can often be rushed. The act of slow looking can help you to gain new insights about your context that might otherwise be overlooked or taken for granted. It can also be a means for better understanding the complexity of bigger systems operating in your teaching and learning context, which could, in turn, help you to identify and refine your innovation strategies.

When to Use

You might use the *Slow Looking* tool as you begin to build inquiry skills in your study group and continue to use it throughout your innovation work as you learn, document, and collect data. Its flexibility allows it to be woven into everyday practice—even for ten-minute periods—and also to be used at key points in the development of your group's innovation project.

Some of the ways in which *Slow Looking* might be particularly helpful in the inquiry-driven innovation process include:

- Using the full protocol early in your innovation project to consider how your school, classroom, or other teaching and learning context operates as a system in order to help you identify promising areas for innovation.
- Repeating the slow looking protocol once an innovation project is underway as a means for noticing any changes in your context and reflecting on the potential impact of those changes on the whole system.
- Using Steps 1 to 3 (and 6) as a general observation tool that you could incorporate into your regular practice for short periods of time—for example, to look closely at how students are behaving or to consider aspects of your teaching and learning context that you do not think about on a regular basis.

- Asking colleagues to use Steps 1 to 3 (and 6) as they observe your learning environment, even for 5–10 minutes. You could ask colleagues to look at something in particular or invite them to look closely at something that catches their attention.
- Incorporating the practice of slow looking into an ongoing practice of documentation (see the *Documentation* suite of tools).
- Using *Slow Looking* as a teaching and learning strategy with students, for example, by using *Slow Looking* to involve them more actively in the documentation process of their own learning.

Preparation and Other Considerations

Engaging in the practice of slow looking can be valuable either individually or in a group setting, and each of the following steps can be undertaken either individually or as a full study group. If using this tool as an individual exercise, you might want to reconvene with other members of your study group to share experiences as you reflect (Step 6).

Steps

1. *Select your subject for Slow Looking.*
   Choose a physical aspect or feature of your environment, a person or a group of people, or an interaction or event. This will be your observation "subject."
2. *Observe your subject.*
   Look closely at the subject for at least five minutes and note as many features as you can. Try to look at the place and/or people you're observing as if for the first time. You might want to make notes about:
   - Everything you see and hear;
   - Anything that is familiar about what you observe, and anything that seems unfamiliar or surprising to you; and
   - A close, "zoomed-in" view of a specific aspect of your observation setting.
3. *Record your "wonders."*
   Write a list of questions or "wonders" that you now have about your subject.
4. *Consider your subject within a bigger system.*
   Think of a bigger system connected to the subject (e.g., the overall system for assessment in your teaching and learning context, the systems in place for your school

to interact with parents, etc.). Try to imagine the bigger system in action and how your subject fits into it.

5. *Visualize the system.*

Sketch a diagram that shows the different parts of the system and how they might interact.

6. *Reflect.*

Reflect, either individually or as a group, on any new insights you gained from doing this activity. What are the implications for your innovation process or the innovation project(s) on which you are working?

Attributions and Additional Resources

This tool is adapted from Project Zero's Out of Eden Learn Project. The concept of "slow looking" is explored in depth in S. Tishman (2018). *Slow Looking: The Art and Practice of Learning through Observation*. New York: Routledge. It is defined more briefly in this blog post: S. Tishman (July 21, 2014). Slow Looking and Complexity. *Out of Eden Learn Educators Blog* (walktolearn.outofedenwalk.com).

Interviewing

Listening Attentively to Others

Purpose of the Tool

Interviewing is fundamentally about listening carefully and attentively to someone else, a practice that is critical for understanding a teaching and learning context, and one that can also be difficult to make time for amid the busy pace of school days. Within the Framework for Inquiry-Driven Innovation, interviewing is a core inquiry skill that can help you to better understand your surrounding context and gather data as your innovation projects develop. This tool will help you to consider how to approach interviewing and can be used at many different stages in your work.

When to Use

You can use *Interviewing* in the initial stages of developing your innovation project in order to better understand the teaching and learning context in which you are doing your work.

Later on, *Interviewing* can be an effective way to gather data on the impacts of your innovation project.

Some of the ways in which *Interviewing* might be particularly helpful in the inquiry-driven innovation process include:

- Listening to the perspectives, ideas, and needs of stakeholders early on in your work to gather insights and find out where you are starting from in your innovation project.
- Supporting students to become effective interviewers and incorporating student-to-student interviews in your overall approach to documentation (see the *Documentation* suite of tools).
- Finding out factual information that will inform your teaching and learning context or the development and refinement of your innovation project.
- Following up on survey responses or other artifacts of teaching and learning to gain a more nuanced understanding about the thinking of a stakeholder that is important to your innovation project or your surrounding teaching and learning context.
- Listening to people explain their experiences, thinking, or hopes in their own words in ways that will help you to better understand your surrounding context or your innovation project.

Preparation and Other Considerations

The practice of *Interviewing* can be done either individually or as a full study group, as could different steps in this tool (see the suggestions in each of the following steps). For example, you might want to develop a focus for your interviews and frame your questions together as a full group, but conduct the actual interviews as an individual or a pair. The first time you use the steps outlined in this tool, you might want to go through most of the steps as a group, transitioning to doing most of the work within your individual, ongoing practice as time goes on. Whichever approach you choose, making some time to interpret and reflect on your interview results together (Step 4) will likely be valuable.

Decide whether you are going to record your interview so you can listen to it later on. You could use a recording device such as a voice memo function on a phone or computer, a mobile phone app, or a digital or tape recorder. Otherwise, you can plan to take handwritten notes. Some recording or transcription apps will provide you with reasonably accurate transcripts.

Steps

1. *Consider what you want to find out and why (individual or group work).*

   Articulate what you are hoping to find out from your interviews. For example, do you want to find out more about what students find engaging and motivating as learners? Do you want to find out how teachers experience professional development at your school and how they would like to grow personally and professionally? Do you want to hear about how a student approached a class assignment in a particular way? Make sure to consider whose perspectives you most want to hear as you think about whom you will interview.

2. *Frame questions (individual or group work).*

   You may find it helpful to create the following table to help you separate what you want to find out and what you'll actually ask during your interview. It can sometimes be difficult for people being interviewed to answer direct questions; try to find ways to ask questions that will allow your interview participants to speak naturally but at the same time give you the kinds of information or insights you need.

What I want to find out	Questions I will ask

   As you develop your questions, consider the following guidelines:

   - Avoid leading questions - that is, questions that steer your interview participants to give you the answers you are hoping to hear. Try to ask your questions as open-endedly as possible.
   - Ask your interview participants to describe or tell a story about an experience ("Tell me about. . ." or "What was it like for you to. . .?"). Try asking interview participants to talk to you about a hypothetical situation or as if you or they were someone else—for example, "If I were a parent seeking advice about helping my child develop better reading habits, what would you say to me?" or "How would you explain the word 'culture' to a child in third grade?"

   You might want to do some mock interviews within your study group in order to try out your draft questions and build confidence and experience in interviewing.

3. *Conduct the interview (individual or pair work).*

   While conducting an interview, the key principle to focus on is "listen more; talk less." Actively listen to what the person is saying, what they may not be saying, and how the overall interview is going. There are a lot of similarities between good interviewing and good teaching.

Interviewing someone is a human-to-human interaction. You are an essential part of the conversation and how you do the interview will help shape what you find out. Your questions, tone, follow-up comments, and nonverbal cues will all potentially affect what the person you are interviewing chooses to share with you. Ask clarifying or follow-up questions if you are not sure what your interview participant means. Try not to rush the interview or make it sound like an interrogation.

4. *Interpret and share (individual and group work).*

Immediately after the interview, jot down your impressions, including what the interview felt like (e.g., Was the conversation relaxed? Did the interview participant seem passionate about what they were saying? Did you find yourself agreeing or disagreeing with what you were hearing?). What were the key takeaways for you? Was there anything surprising or unexpected that came up for you?

If possible, listen to an audio recording of the interview. Bear in mind what you originally wanted to find out. What did you learn? What else came up that seems important? What do you notice about yourself as an interviewer? Are there any questions you wish you had asked or which you would change?

If you've done an interview on your own, make sure to find time to share thoughts about your interview and related learnings with the rest of your study group.

Documentation, Part I

Making a Plan to Document

Purpose of the Tool

There are a wealth of reasons to document practice in teaching and learning contexts. From capturing moments of learning to reflect on later to helping inform the design of learning experiences to come, documenting learning is an essential tool for good teaching practice and is also leaned on heavily within the context of inquiry-driven innovation. The approach to documentation embraced in this framework is deeply influenced by the publication *Visible Learners* (see *Attributions and Additional Resources* at the end of this tool). From the *Visible Learners* perspective, documentation is a practice that "focuses on some aspect of learning—not just 'what we did'—and prompts questions and promotes conversation among children and adults that deepen and extend learning" (Chapter 6). It also includes the practices of "observing, recording, interpreting, and sharing through a variety of media the processes and products of learning in order to deepen and extend learning" (Chapter 5). Such media could include photographs, typed or handwritten notes, audio or video recordings, examples of student work, or other artifacts of learning. The tools of *Slow Looking* and *Interviewing* can also be used in service of gathering rich documentation.

Inspired by this approach to documentation, the tools in this suite offer several actions to help you get started in your own documentation practice. This first tool focuses on developing questions to guide documentation, while the second is about interpreting documentation together as a study group. Over time, both should become embedded in your practice as a study group and as individual group members. Many of the other tools in this toolkit incorporate *Documentation* or reflecting on documentation, and for this reason these two tools are considered especially important within the inquiry-driven innovation process.

When to Use

Engaging in the process of documentation may be useful at any stage of your innovation work. For example, you might engage in the documentation process just as you are beginning to develop an inquiry focus to gain a better understanding of a particular teaching and learning environment; as you are experimenting with a school-based innovation to gain a sense of how it is going and how it may be improved; or after you have implemented an innovation to further understand the impact of your innovation and to support student learning. To begin making a plan to document, set aside time with your study group members to discuss what you would like to learn.

Preparation and Other Considerations

Engaging in the practice of documentation can be valuable either individually or in a group setting. The following steps propose mostly group-based work and conversations, with an invitation in the last step for group members to go out and document individually. As you develop a practice of documentation over time, you might want to embed all of these steps into your individual practice.

Steps

1. *Consider what you want to learn (group work).*
   Reflect on what it is you want to learn from engaging in the practice of documentation, and then brainstorm some questions that you could explore in your classroom or school. Make sure to consider what you will look (or listen) for as you seek to learn more. For example, you could ask a general question about learning and teaching:

   - While observing students or teachers working together in a group, you might ask: What do group members do to support each other's learning? What do you see or hear? (e.g., What do they say? How do they interact? What strategies do they use to support each other?)
   - While looking at a few pieces of student work—either finished products or works in progress—you might ask: What opportunities are given to students to put their own spin on the work, and how do they use those opportunities to make their work different from the work of other students? (e.g., How does the work of one student look visually different from that of another? Are there differences in how students approached the task that was given to them?)

   You could also ask a more specific question about learning and teaching, for example:

   - What do young students do when they are learning to use scissors or glue sticks for the first time? What do you see or hear?
   - What do middle school students say when they are discussing a particular historical event or topic in social studies class? What words, questions, or phrases do they use?
   - What do students say and do to explain the steps they used to solve a math problem? What do you see or hear?

2. *Decide on your questions (group work).*
   As a group, decide if you are all going to focus on the same question to guide your documentation or if individuals are going to choose their own questions. Decide what the question(s) will be.
3. *Determine what kind of documentation each group member will collect (group work).*
   Remember that documentation can take many forms (e.g., photographs, written notes, video, examples of student work, etc.). Be specific about what you will try to capture to answer your question.

4. *Try out your documentation plan (individual work).*

    Act on your documentation plan based on your guiding question. Bring the documentation you collect to your next study group session where you can use the next tool in this suite (*Documentation, Part II*).

Attributions and Additional Resources

To learn more about documentation and access a wealth of related tools, see M. Krechevsky, B. Mardell, M. Rivard, & D. Wilson (2013). *Visible Learners: Promoting Reggio-Inspired Approaches in All Schools.* San Francisco, CA: Jossey-Bass.

Documentation, Part II

Interpreting Documentation as a Group

Purpose of the Tool

While there is learning that happens in the act of accumulating artifacts of teaching and learning through a practice of documentation, the challenging work of interpreting documentation is at least as important as collecting it. This tool invites you to step back and reflect on artifacts of learning by discussing and interpreting them as a group. As in the previous tool, this focus on interpretation is inspired by ideas described in the publication *Visible Learners* (see *Attributions and Additional Resources* at the end of this tool).

When to Use

As noted in the first tool in this suite, engaging in the process of documentation may be useful at any stage of your innovation work. Once you have collected documentation from a particular school or classroom experience, set aside time with your study group members to look closely and interpret what you collected. Collective interpretation of documentation should become a recurring part of your ongoing work together as a study group.

Preparation and Other Considerations

While the previous tool, *Documentation, Part I,* toggles between group and individual work, this tool is meant to be used as a full study group.

Steps

1. *Present the work (one presenting group member).*

   Select a piece of documentation to review from one member of your study group. The piece should enable a rich conversation about learning in a relatively short period of time; an excerpt from a larger piece of documentation may be appropriate. It is also important that all study group members be able to look carefully at the piece. The presenting group member should provide some general context and then offer the guiding question they were focused on when collecting this documentation.

2. *Ask clarifying questions (all other study group members).*

   Before engaging in discussion, the study group should ask the presenting group member any clarifying questions about the learning environment from which this documentation came, the presenting member's guiding question, or the documentation itself. A clarifying question is meant to clear up any confusion or bring to light important contextual details, as opposed to a probing question that might ask the presenting group member to interpret their work or provide extensive background.

3. *Observe and discuss (all other study group members).*

   Once all clarifying questions have been addressed, spend some time looking closely at or listening closely to the documentation, and then begin discussing the work as a group with the presenting member just listening for the time being. You might want to use a discussion protocol, such as the following:

   - *What do you see?* What do you see, hear, or otherwise notice about the documentation that you are reviewing? What stands out to you?
   - *What do you think?* Based on what you have noticed, what do you think the student and/or teacher is/are trying to figure out or understand?
   - *What do you wonder?* What questions about learning and teaching does this piece of documentation bring to the surface for you?
   - *What do you suggest?* What suggestions can you offer the presenting educators to support their work or their learners?

4. *Respond (presenting group member).*

   After discussing this piece of documentation for a sufficient amount of time, the presenting study group member should be invited to respond to what he or she heard in the discussion, and to offer some potential next steps.

5. *Switch and repeat.*

   After you have engaged in this process with a piece of documentation from one study group member, as time allows repeat the process with a piece of documentation from another group member.

Attributions and Additional Resources

To learn more about documentation, see M. Krechevsky, B. Mardell, M. Rivard, & D. Wilson (2013). *Visible Learners: Promoting Reggio-Inspired Approaches in All Schools.* San Francisco, CA: Jossey-Bass.

While different and with fewer steps, this tool has touchpoints with the Collaborative Assessment Conference (CAC) protocol developed in 1988 by Steve Seidel and colleagues at Project Zero. The CAC is another highly recommended protocol for viewing and interpreting documentation in groups, and you can learn more about it in T. Blythe, D. Allen, & B.S. Powell (1999). *Looking Together at Student Work.* New York: Teachers College Press.

The first three discussion protocols in Step 3 are inspired by the Visible Thinking project's See, Think, Wonder thinking routine. To learn more and see the full routine, visit https:// pz.harvard.edu/thinking-routines.

Wishes, Challenges, and Opportunities

Developing an Initial Inquiry Focus

Purpose of the Tool

Opportunities for innovation are all around us in the teaching and learning contexts in which we work. Narrowing down which opportunities you would like to focus on can be a challenge. This tool can help you share and reflect on the documentation you have been collecting in your own context, helping your study group to frame a long-term inquiry focus that can guide your work in the coming months.

When to Use

Use this tool after you have done some initial exploration of your home teaching and learning context (e.g., observations, conversations, collecting documentation, slow looking, etc.) and feel ready to work with your group to home in on an initial inquiry focus that will guide your work together. You might find it helpful to let this conversation unfold over multiple study group sessions or to return to this conversation multiple times throughout the process of inquiry-driven innovation.

Preparation and Other Considerations

Study group members should reflect on the in-school explorations that they have done so far (talking to students and colleagues about their experiences, collecting classroom documentation, engaging in slow looking or other types of observation, etc.), and each group member should select one piece of documentation from these explorations that feels significant. A piece of documentation might include a photograph or short video clip, a piece of student work, handwritten notes, an interview transcript, and so on. Study group members should be prepared to talk about why the documentation they selected feels significant.

Steps

1. *Share documentation and headlines as a group.*
    Gather together your study group. In no more than five minutes per person, each study group member should share 1) one piece of documentation from their explorations within the school, and 2) any "headlines" or take away thoughts that came out of their explorations. Following each group member's presentation, all group members should individually take a few minutes to note:
    *   *Wishes:* What is an aspirational or long-term goal for teaching and learning in your context that comes up as you listen?
    *   *Challenges:* Are there any explicit or implicit challenges suggested by this documentation?
    *   *Opportunities:* Are there any explicit or implicit opportunities suggested by this documentation?
2. *Share highlights.*
    After all group members have shared their documentation, go around the circle one more time and have individual group members share one or two wishes, challenges, and/or opportunities that they feels is/are most exciting or compelling. Make sure that a group member takes notes to keep track of what is discussed.

3. *Synthesize to draft your inquiry focus.*

   As a group, talk about an inquiry focus that you might want to pursue together over time. Similar to a research question, an inquiry focus is a question of practice situated in your teaching and learning context that:

   - Is personally important to the members of the study group;
   - Has relevance and importance for the broader teaching and learning community outside of the study group;
   - Poses a problem or puts a new spin on an old issue;
   - Is not too broad—contains some specifics;
   - Exhibits complexity and warrants "slow looking"—in other words, it will not be easily answered in a few sentences or a quick internet search; and
   - Encourages (or at least leaves the door open to) trying out new practices, strategies, resources, or tools.

   It will likely take multiple conversations to frame an inquiry focus that feels right for your study group. Over time, you will work to develop one or more innovation projects—a discrete project to develop new practices, strategies, curricular approaches, resources, and so on—that address a wish, challenge, and/or opportunity from your group.

Sweet Spot of Innovation

Considering Your Community's Threshold for Change

Purpose of the Tool

When envisioning your study group's innovation project, it is important to consider the threshold for change within your teaching and learning context. Innovation projects that fall below your community's minimum threshold for change may be doable, but the results of these innovations may seem underwhelming, boring, or not worth the effort. On the other hand, innovation projects that fall above your community's maximum threshold for change may seem overwhelming, difficult to grasp, or simply beyond reach. In either case, these innovations are likely to be rejected by your community because they will be perceived as being either too dull or too extreme. This tool will help your study group to consider your community's optimal threshold for change—what can be thought of as the sweet spot of innovation—and where your draft inquiry focus falls relative to that threshold.

When to Use

You can use this tool after you have developed your initial inquiry focus in order to consider where this focus lies in relation to your community's threshold for change. Your work with this tool may lead you to critique and further refine your inquiry focus prior to developing an innovation project or projects. As you develop these projects, you can return to your defined sweet spot of innovation to see if your envisioned work falls within the generative space of this "sweet spot."

Preparation and Other Considerations

Markers and chart paper are suggested materials for this group activity.

Steps

1. *Establish an innovato-meter.*

   Take a piece of large chart paper and place it on a wall. Then, with a marker, make a long vertical line. Place incremental horizontal lines on your long vertical line in order to make a scale from zero to ten. This is your innovato-meter as shown in Figure 8.1.

2. *Identify baseline practice and a minimum threshold for change.*

   On your innovato-meter, zero may be considered your baseline practice, the status quo, or business as usual in your school or learning environment. It is what you do every day, and the way you do it. This is not to say that your regular school or classroom practice is dull in any way, it is just to indicate where you are at with no change to your practice. Conversely, ten is the most radical change imaginable: a total reconceptualization of what you do—and how you do it—every day.

   Given these two points, consider what may be your community's minimum threshold for change. This is the minimum point of change your community members will get excited about. Use a different-colored marker to mark that point on your innovato-meter (see Figure 8.2).

3. *Identify a maximum threshold for change.*

   Next, using this same scale, consider what may be your community's maximum threshold for change (see Figure 8.3). Mark that point on your innovato-meter.

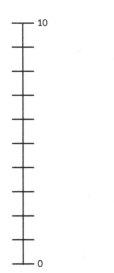

Figure 8.1 Laying out an innovato-meter.

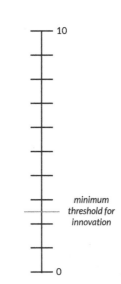

Figure 8.2 Establishing a minimum threshold for change.

4. *Identify a sweet spot of innovation.*

   Now draw a box between these two points on your innovato-meter and label it "sweet spot of innovation" as in Figure 8.4.

   Different constituent groups within your community may have different thresholds for change. If you find this to be the case in your school or classroom, consider developing multiple sweet spots of innovation that are specific to each of these different constituent groups.

5. *Situate your innovation work on the innovato-meter.*

   Depending on where you are in the process of inquiry-driven innovation, consider where either your draft inquiry focus or your innovation project(s) are currently situated on your innovato-meter and whether or not they fall within your community's sweet spot of innovation. Remember, ideas that fall below your sweet spot of innovation will likely be rejected by your community because they will be perceived as being too dull or boring, and ideas that fall above your sweet spot of innovation will likely be rejected by your community because they will be perceived as being too radical, extreme, or out of reach.

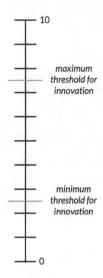

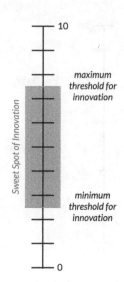

Figure 8.3 Establishing a maximum threshold for change.

Figure 8.4 Identifying the sweet spot of innovation.

6. *Use your innovato-meter often!*

    Keep your innovato-meter handy and use it often to reflect on the innovations you and your colleagues come up with in relation to your community's threshold for change. You may want to start out by developing innovations on the low end of your community's optimal threshold for change, and then gradually move up—always keeping the sweet spot of innovation in mind.

Attributions and Additional Resources

Project Zero researcher David Perkins often speaks about "wilding the tame, and taming the wild" in education. To explain this concept, he has developed a tool he refers to as a "wild-ometer." The innovato-meter presented here is a respectful adaptation of Perkins's original concept.

This tool was created by our colleague Edward P. Clapp. To cite this specific tool please do so as follows: Clapp, E.P. (2021). Sweet Spot of Innovation. In L. Dawes Duraisingh and A.R. Sachdeva, *Inquiry-Driven Innovation: A practical guide to school-based change*. Hoboken, NJ: Jossey Bass.

Population, Innovation, Outcome

Articulating the *Who, How,* and *Why* of Your Innovation Project

Purpose of the Tool

Developing innovation projects for your teaching and learning context will require the consideration of many different aspects of your practice, and it may be hard to know where to start or how to jump in. This tool pulls out three key components that should be part of the inquiry focus that will guide your study group's inquiry-driven innovation journey: 1) population: the target constituent group that will be most affected by an innovation, 2) innovation: the change in practice that will serve as the vehicle for change, and 3) outcome: the intended outcome or effect of a proposed innovation project. This tool is designed to help you refine your draft inquiry focus and begin developing an innovation project by considering these three components in a structured way.

When to Use

This tool is most useful as your study group refines its inquiry focus and prepares to begin an innovation project. You will likely return to this activity over time as you narrow the focus of your innovation project.

Preparation and Other Considerations

To begin, get a sheet of chart paper and some markers. Divide the chart paper into three columns and place the headings in the following order: "Population," "Innovation," and "Outcome(s)." Working with your study group—or the group of colleagues with whom you will be pursuing your innovation project—fill in each column using the following steps.

Steps

1. *Identify your population.*
   In the "Population" column, identify the target population for your innovation project by responding to the following question:
   - Who are the people you most hope to impact through your innovation project?
   Here, it is helpful to be as specific as possible. For instance, instead of writing down something vague and over-ambitious like "21st-century learners," it would be more helpful to focus on a specific population such as "3rd and 4th grade students at Springfield Elementary School."

2. *Identify your intended outcomes.*

   Now skip over to the "Outcome(s)" column. Considering the constituent group that you identified in the "Population" column, consider what impact you would like to have on that group by responding to the following question:

   - What specific change(s) would you like your target population to experience as a result of your innovation?

   Again, be as specific as possible and avoid writing something vague and over-ambitious. For example, instead of choosing an outcome like "become global citizens," it would be more helpful to focus on a specific outcome like "be able to consider multiple perspectives" or "be able to hold simple conversations in two or more languages featuring a range of common vocabulary words."

3. *Identify your intended innovation.*

   Now shift your attention to the "Innovation" column. The goal for this column is to develop a strategy for achieving the impact you identified in the "Outcome(s)" column for the constituent group you identified in the "Population" column. To do this, consider the following questions:

   - How can you change your practice to achieve your intended outcome(s) for your target population?
   - What other strategies can you employ to achieve your intended outcome(s) for your target population?

   As before, it helps to be as specific as possible.

4. *Move forward and revisit as needed.*

   Articulating the population you would like to focus on, the innovation(s) you would like to pursue, and the outcome(s) you hope to achieve should help you move forward with planning further details of the innovation project(s) you would like to implement in your context, perhaps using resources such as the *Theory of Action* suite of tools. As you put this plan into action, it may be helpful to return to your original Population, Innovation, Outcome chart and refine it over time.

Attributions and Additional Resources

This tool was created by our colleague Edward P. Clapp. To cite this specific tool please do so as follows: Clapp, E.P. (2021). Population, innovation, outcome. In L. Dawes

Duraisingh & A.R. Sachdeva, *Inquiry-Driven Innovation: A practical guide to school-based change.* Hoboken, NJ: Jossey Bass.

Theory of Action, Part I

Envisioning Your Innovation Journey

Purpose of the Tool

Whether or not your study group has articulated it, you likely have an implicit rationale for thinking that your group's innovation project could lead to the outcome(s) you desire. Surfacing and articulating this underlying rationale or "theory" by creating a Theory of Action diagram can help your study group clarify understandings and expectations, focus on long-term goals, and move from abstract ideas to a concrete action plan. This tool, the first in a suite of two, is designed to help you frame your *Theory of Action* ahead of using it to create a more detailed plan.

When to Use

The following tool is meant to be used when you have identified one or more innovation projects that you would like to implement as well as a target population(s) for the project. Note that this is the first of two tools that should be used in sequence to create a *Theory of Action* diagram. While not a prerequisite, creating a *Theory of Action* diagram might move more quickly if you have already used the *Population, Innovation, Outcome* tool.

Preparation and Other Considerations

Markers and chart paper are suggested materials for this group activity. While you should feel free to lay out your *Theory of Action* diagram in the way that makes most sense for your study group, the steps in this tool will lead you to a diagram formatted like the example in Figure 8.5.

INQUIRY FOCUS
How can the incorporation of experiential learning opportunities into the science curriculum help 8th grade science students to develop a greater sense of empowerment in learning?

WHERE WE ARE NOW
Students report feeling confused about scientific concepts and do not seem able to apply them. Students do not have ample opportunities to apply what they are learning in school to real-life settings.

INNOVATION PROJECT 1	INNOVATION PROJECT 2	INNOVATION PROJECT 3
Lead a workshop for educators at our school that allows them to experience first-hand how school learning can have real-world application.	Challenge students to design a learning experience for their peers that applies a concept from the 8th grade science curriculum to a real-world task or problem.	Explore ways that immersive online experiences can be used to enable students to apply their learnings in science class to real-world contexts.

LONG-TERM OUTCOME
Students become excited about scientific learning and empowered to change the world around them through science.

Figure 8.5 An example Theory of Action diagram.

Steps

1. *Articulate your inquiry focus and target population.*

    Write your current inquiry focus at the top of a piece of chart paper, in a way similar to the example laid out in Figure 8.5. Then, engage in a discussion to make sure that you have group consensus on the target population by describing the people whom you hope to impact through your innovation project. Multiple stakeholder groups might be affected by your work, but try to zoom in on one group that is your "target" population. Try to be as specific as possible.

2. *Frame your long-term outcome.*

Now, imagine the desired long-term outcome that you hope to achieve through your innovation project(s)—perhaps these are specific changes, developments, or shifts that you would like to see enacted for your target population. Think long-term and aspirationally, rather than an outcome that is constrained by systems or norms that are part of your current teaching and learning context.

Write the long-term desired outcome of your group's work at the bottom of your chart paper. Consider what might be different or what impact you would see if your group's innovation project is successful. You might have multiple desired outcomes, but try to choose one that feels like the main aim of your group's work.

3. *Identify where you are now.*

As a study group, consider the question: "Where are you now?" Just below the inquiry focus on your diagram, briefly articulate the current situation at your school. What is the problem, challenge, or opportunity that you have seen in your school that led you to your inquiry focus?

4. *Articulate your innovation project(s).*

Last, just under the "where you are now" statement, add one or more innovation projects that you want to try out in your teaching and learning context. Remember, an "innovation project" is used here to mean a defined project that your study group will undertake together to plan and implement an innovation (e.g., a new process, framework, instructional activity, tool, etc., that you want to introduce into your teaching and learning context). It is not a general concept or idea like "critical thinking," "interdisciplinary work," "blended learning," or "making learning visible." It is more specific and action-oriented, such as introducing a specific strategy in class to support students in applying critical thinking skills, starting to use thematic teaching to support interdisciplinary learning, bringing in a specific documentation tool that supports teachers in better understanding what their students are learning, etc.

In Part II of this tool, your study group will work to frame out the rationale of how you will get from your envisioned innovation project(s) to your desired long-term outcome(s).

Theory of Action, Part II

Articulating Your Rationale

Purpose of the Tool

Oftentimes, it is easy to default to accepted norms and approaches in our professional practice. These may be what we ourselves or others have done before, prevailing norms in the systems and contexts in which we work, or what seems like the most straightforward path toward the long-term outcome(s) we want to achieve. Uncovering and thinking through the rationale behind norms and practices—especially those that you plan to be part of your innovation projects—is an important step toward moving forward in the work of innovating. This section of the *Theory of Action* suite of tools asks you to frame out a rationale for why you will do the things you hope to do in your innovation project(s).

When to Use

This is the second of two *Theory of Action* tools that should be used in sequence. Before using this tool, use *Theory of Action, Part I*.

Preparation and Other Considerations

You will need the Theory of Action diagram you started using Part I of this tool as well as markers for this group activity. While you should feel free to lay out your Theory of Action diagram in the way that makes most sense for your study group, the steps in this tool will lead you to a diagram formatted like the example in Figure 8.6.

Steps

1. *Revisit.*

   To start off, look at the Theory of Action diagram you started to create using the *Theory of Action, Part I* tool. Take a few moments to remind yourselves of the target population, desired long-term outcome(s), and innovation project(s) you previously articulated as a group. If your group is planning to divide up and try out multiple innovation projects, you might want to split up into working groups for each innovation project as you engage in the steps that follow.

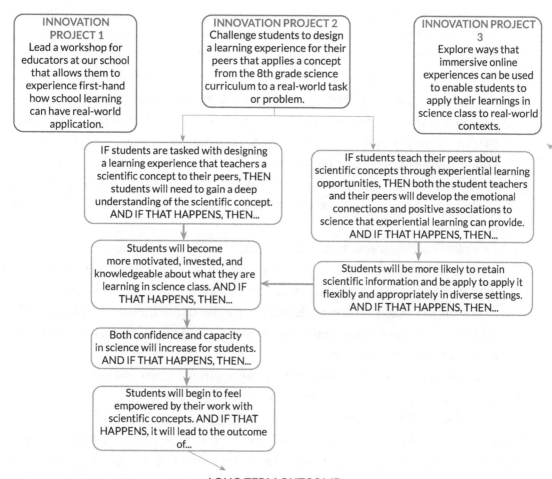

INQUIRY FOCUS
How can the incorporation of experiential learning opportunities into the science curriculum help 8th grade science students to develop a greater sense of empowerment in learning?

WHERE WE ARE NOW
Students report feeling confused about scientific concepts and do not seem able to apply them. Students do not have ample opportunities to apply what they are learning in school to real-life settings.

INNOVATION PROJECT 1
Lead a workshop for educators at our school that allows them to experience first-hand how school learning can have real-world application.

INNOVATION PROJECT 2
Challenge students to design a learning experience for their peers that applies a concept from the 8th grade science curriculum to a real-world task or problem.

INNOVATION PROJECT 3
Explore ways that immersive online experiences can be used to enable students to apply their learnings in science class to real-world contexts.

IF students are tasked with designing a learning experience that teachers a scientific concept to their peers, THEN students will need to gain a deep understanding of the scientific concept. AND IF THAT HAPPENS, THEN...

IF students teach their peers about scientific concepts through experiential learning opportunities, THEN both the student teachers and their peers will develop the emotional connections and positive associations to science that experiential learning can provide. AND IF THAT HAPPENS, THEN...

Students will become more motivated, invested, and knowledgeable about what they are learning in science class. AND IF THAT HAPPENS, THEN...

Students will be more likely to retain scientific information and be apply to apply it flexibly and appropriately in diverse settings. AND IF THAT HAPPENS, THEN...

Both confidence and capacity in science will increase for students. AND IF THAT HAPPENS, THEN...

Students will begin to feel empowered by their work with scientific concepts. AND IF THAT HAPPENS, it will lead to the outcome of...

LONG-TERM OUTCOME
Students become excited about scientific learning and empowered to change the world around them through science.

Figure 8.6 A completed Theory of Action diagram.

2. *Dissect your innovation project(s).*

   Think of whether or not there are any ways you might break down or "dissect" each of your group's innovation projects into component parts. This will help you to focus in Step 3. Here are just a few ways that you might think about breaking an innovation project into components:

   - *Separate out the stages of implementation.* Consider whether or not there are planned sequential stages in implementing your innovation project that are qualitatively different from each other. For example, staff training and in-class pilot-testing could be two elements of an innovation project around implementing a new classroom strategy for learners.

   - *Identify stakeholder groups involved in implementation.* Think about how different groups of people might be involved in fundamentally different ways in your innovation project. For example, if you are implementing a new STEAM curriculum in your school, the ways that school administrators, teachers, and language support coaches implement this curriculum might be very different. You might even have a group of students taking the lead in such a project, and their participation could look markedly different from that of adult educators who are involved.

   - *Articulate multiple core activities, if applicable.* Your innovation project might contain diverse core activities that are part of an overall strategy. For example, if your innovation project is about introducing a specific strategy in class to support students in applying critical thinking skills, core activities might include adapting teaching strategies, trying out new student assessments, and changing the language used in class routines and protocols.

   If applicable, separate component parts underneath the place where you have articulated your innovation project on your diagram.

3. *Frame a rationale ("if this, then that. . .").*

   Now, articulate the rationale behind each component of your innovation project(s) using "if this, then that . . ." statements. The idea is to start with a core activity or action that is a component of your innovation project, and then map out the rationale behind that action until you eventually reach the long-term desired outcome that you articulated on your Theory of Action diagram. Aim to show the stepwise cause-and-effect, chain reaction, or order of implementation steps that you expect to occur as you implement your innovation project. See the example Theory of Action diagram at the beginning of this tool for an idea of how this could look (Figure 8.6).

As you frame out your rationale, here are a few guidelines to keep in mind:

- *Work incrementally.* Try not to rush to arrive at your outcome at the bottom of the diagram. Think of how you expect your innovation project to play out in a step-wise manner.
- *Do not worry too much about projecting into the future.* Remember that each successive step of your "if this, then that . . ." rationale statement is an assumption or a best guess you'll need to make, even though you cannot know for sure how things will play out in your innovation project(s).
- *Make this work for you.* You might have multiple rationale statements, more than one innovation project, loops, branches, color coding, or other elements to your diagram. Frame out your rationale in whatever way makes most sense for your group and your innovation project(s).

4. *Take stock.*

   With your first-draft Theory of Action diagram assembled, take a step back and consider the following questions:

   - *Did your rationale flowchart arrive at your desired outcome?* If not, you might have a lack of alignment between your desired outcome and the innovations you hope to put into place to achieve it.
   - *Was there any disagreement within your study group about the innovations you hope to implement, the rationale, or the desired outcome of your work?* If so, now might be a good time to try to gain some consensus and engage in group brainstorming to make sure that all group members' voices are heard.
   - *Did you feel uncomfortable about trying to project forward when you do not know the future?* That is okay! This is just an exercise to help you think ahead and gain consensus and alignment across your study group.
   - *What other things do you see, notice, or wonder about that you might want to discuss as a group?*

   Keep working and tinkering over the coming weeks until you arrive at a plan that you feel will work well for your group. You might also look to your Theory of Action diagram to start conversations about the types of data and documentation you could collect at different steps of your innovation project, or what you might want to start prototyping or pilot testing as you begin to move from planning to implementation.

5. *Plan to revisit.*

   As you move forward with your innovation project, it may be helpful and orienting to periodically revisit and update your diagram using the *Theory of Action Tuning Protocol.*

Prototyping a Process

Using Diagramming to Visualize Your Innovation

Purpose of the Tool

Sometimes it is helpful to imagine the implementation of an innovation as a process. Articulating the various steps of the process can help you to get on the same page with your fellow study group members, and can also draw out points of confusion or suggest follow-up conversations that will be important to have in advance of implementing your innovation project. Visualizing your thinking by drawing and diagramming can also lead to new ideas.

When to Use

Use this tool when you have already envisioned an innovation project that has a process somehow embedded within it (e.g., a process for designing curriculum, onboarding staff, inviting parent involvement, etc.). Remember, even if your innovation project is not centered on a process (e.g., your group is innovating its process for assessing student final projects), it might still have a process embedded somewhere within it (e.g., your group is innovating by creating a new curriculum, but you know this work will require you to create a process for training teachers in the curriculum's implementation). You might find it useful to return to this activity periodically as you plan and roll out your innovation.

Steps

1. *Imagine your process.*
   Imagine a process that you want to design. List all the steps of the process.
2. *Map it out.*
   Map out your process. Consider questions such as:
   - What happens in each step of the process, and who are the people involved?
   - How are the steps arranged in relation to each other? For example: Do they connect to each other in a particular way? Are they arranged in a certain order? Is arriving at one step dependent on what happens in another?

- What does the sequence of the steps look like? Is it cyclical? Linear? Branching? Stepwise? Without structure? A combination?

3. *Think about efficiency.*

   As a study group, look at your process map and discuss how you might make the process more efficient, effective, equitable, and/or enjoyable.

4. *Try it again.*

   Revise or revamp your process map based on your conversation. Consider which parts of the process you will need to develop in order to do some initial pilot testing, keeping in mind that you might not need to develop every step before trying it out for the first time.

Prototyping an Experience

Using Role Play to Get a Feel for Your Innovation

Purpose of the Tool

Almost any innovation project involves some kind of experience—for example, the experience of using a new tool you are creating, the experience of going through a new process you are designing, or the experience of being a participant in a new practice you are planning to implement in your teaching and learning context. Using role play to try out experiences that will be part of your innovation project can provide powerful learning opportunities for the study group developing the project, and for other stakeholders outside of the study group who might be involved in the project's implementation. It can also challenge your study group to consider the innovation from another person's point of view, such as a colleague or a student. Trying out an experience in the low-stakes environment of a role play can additionally help to build confidence among those who will be involved in its eventual real-world implementation.

When to Use

This tool can be used either before you implement an innovation in your teaching and learning context, or at any time during the implementation phase of your work as you experiment with new practices.

Steps

1. *Articulate your goals.*

   Articulate the experience you want to try out, and what you hope to learn by role playing it.

2. *Determine group roles.*

   Through role playing, you will try to step into the shoes (as best you can) of those who will be the direct participants in the innovation you seek to implement in your teaching and learning context. Articulate the different people (the roles) involved in the experience (e.g., teacher and students), and determine which members of your study group will play which roles. At the same time, elect one person in the group to be an observer who will be on the lookout for aspects of the experience that connect with what you want to learn.

3. *Role play.*

   Try out your role play by acting out a scenario that incorporates the innovation you are interested in implementing in your teaching and learning context.

4. *Debrief.*

   Discuss the role play experience by first hearing from the observer, then the people engaged in the role play (the "actors").

5. *Try it again.*

   Decide as a group how you might alter the experience in a way that may yield a more optimal result, then try it again.

6. *Reflect and look ahead.*

   After you have role played your experience a few times, compare the outcomes of each iteration, document what you have learned, and consider implications for implementing your innovation in your teaching and learning context.

Prototyping a Tool or Resource

Working on Ideas through Rough Drafting

Purpose of the Tool

Many innovation projects will center around the development of a new pedagogical tool or resource—for example, a new curriculum, an online platform to connect teachers across a school, or a mindfulness podcast for school leaders, just to name a few. Innovation projects might also include the development of new resources or tools that are not the core focus of the project, but will support its development. Tools or resources in this category might include rubrics, surveys, lesson planning templates, interview protocols, slow looking guides, feedback guidelines, or even physical objects. This tool is designed to provide a structure for prototyping your own resources and pedagogical tools as you design and implement your innovation.

When to Use

This tool can be used on a recurring basis at any time throughout the development of your innovation project, but might be particularly useful during the initial phases of development. You could use this group exercise to create entirely new tools, or to refine, hack, or tweak existing pedagogical tools and resources to suit your needs.

Steps

1. *Brainstorm.*

   Working with your study group, identify an aspect of your innovation project that might require a new pedagogical tool or resource. Articulate what you would need this new tool or resource to do, then brainstorm some tools that could serve this purpose (e.g., a documentation tool, an observation protocol, a resource around starting conversations, etc.). If you have already had this conversation and you know what type of tool you want to prototype, move on to the next step.

2. *See what is out there.*

   Once you have considered what type of tool or resource you need, do a quick internet search to see if such a tool might already exist. Consider some key terms you might use to conduct your search, and then see if what you find fits your purposes. If you find a perfect match, you are in luck! More likely, you will find something close that is not a perfect fit, but has potential as a starting place. Your search may also turn up no results, which will lead you to create a new tool from scratch.

3. *Draft.*

   Have pairs, small groups, or individual members of your study group spend a short amount of time making their own rough drafts of the tool you are trying to develop—either based on an existing tool you found online or by starting from scratch.

4. *Share ideas.*

   After your study group members have come up with refinements, tweaks, or hacks of existing tools—or first rough drafts of new tools made from scratch—each person or group should articulate the different parts of their tool and the purposes of each part.

5. *Compare and select.*

   Compare the different rough drafts that were shared and discuss the strengths and weaknesses of each. Choose one tool you want to continue working on before you next meet. You could even take the most promising elements of each rough draft and combine them into a hybrid tool that you will try out or further refine.

6. *Try it out and reflect.*

   Try your tool or resource in various settings and reflect as a study group on what you learned through pilot testing.

Data Analysis, Part I

Identifying Indicators of Impact

Purpose of the Tool

As you get into the process of implementing your innovation project(s), it is important to remember to take a step back and think about the impacts of your work so far. You might have already done this in anecdotal ways, such as having conversations within your study group or using some of the reflection tools introduced throughout this toolkit. While every day and informal reflection is vitally important, it is also qualitatively different from the kind of stepping back you can do by looking formally and strategically at data you have collected through your innovation project(s).

This tool, the first in a series of three, is designed to help you to think concretely and specifically about the kinds of changes you would like to see as a result of your innovation project. It invites you to try out two broadly different approaches toward identifying indicators or signs that your innovation is making a positive impact. The first approach involves articulating the impacts you think or hope you might find before digging into your collected data (known in the research world as an "etic" approach). The second approach involves looking at your data with an open mind and identifying the indicators that emerge for you while you look at it (known in the research world as an "emic" approach). As you look ahead to further developing your innovation, you will want to build the most accurate picture you can of the impact of your innovation to date. Both etic and emic approaches are important in this work.

When to Use

This tool will be most useful at least a month into implementation of your innovation project(s) when you have collected some project-related data and documentation. It can be used at different points of your work—for example, early on to clarify what kinds of impacts you would like to see or later on to take stock of what is going on and/or what you have learned so far.

Preparation and Other Considerations

Before you meet as a study group, you will need to gather a small sample of data that you have collected through your innovation project so far. Note that throughout this suite of *Data Analysis* tools, the word *data* is used in a broad sense to mean both quantitative and qualitative information or artifacts—for example, documentation of student work, lesson plans, interviews, survey responses, test scores, and so on. Ensure that the data you gather are accessible to all group members during your study group session.

Note that this tool also presupposes that you have created a Theory of Action diagram (see the two-part suite of tools), and you should have that diagram on hand.

Steps

1. *Articulate your indicators of impact (group work).*
   Begin by trying out an *etic* approach—that is, determining the impacts you think or hope you might find before digging into your collected data. Revisit your Theory of Action diagram and consider what you hope to see in your school and/or classroom as a result of your innovation project. Write down two or three indicators that would suggest that your work is having its desired impact at this stage (see Figure 8.7). Each indicator should be something you could see, hear, or otherwise directly observe from collected data. Your indicators of impact may be overlapping but they should be distinct

If your innovation was to have 8th grade students design learning experiences for their peers that involve applying concepts from the science curriculum to real-world tasks or problems, you might identify the following indicators of impact by looking at your Theory of Action (though just two or three indicators would be fine!):

- Students demonstrate a more accurate understanding of scientific concepts in the curriculum
- Students make connections between scientific concepts and real-world applications
- Students exhibit greater engagement and attention during science classes
- Students use a variety of strategies to design interesting learning activities for their peers

Figure 8.7 An initial list of possible indicators of impact.

enough from one another so that you can usefully apply them to your data. Try to avoid categories that are too vague or abstract, or ones that are too narrow or specific.

2. *Learn from your data through line-by-line coding (individual work).*

Each member of your study group should select different pieces of data from your innovation project. For example, you could look at a few pieces of student work, some survey responses, or notes from interviews or observations. Putting aside the indicators you have just developed, try to look at the data with fresh eyes. You might want to annotate the data that you are reviewing. You may find it most convenient to make a copy of the data so that you can write directly on; otherwise, make sure you can annotate them digitally.

You will now use an *emic* approach to look at your data with an open mind to see what comes up. This strategy can help you notice unexpected or unintended consequences of your innovation and encourages you to look more carefully at what your data are telling you. For this step, it is better to look deeply and carefully at a small amount of data rather than to try to look at a lot.

If you are looking at text, have a go at a version of what is called "line-by-line coding." For this technique, force yourself to slowly read the text line by line or maybe sentence by sentence. Note down what is happening in each line or sentence, using active verbs to describe what the person is saying or doing.

If you are looking at images or objects, you can adapt these principles to look closely at different components or aspects of the images or objects.

Figure 8.8 shows what sentence-by-sentence coding looks like in action. The example involves a student's verbal reflection about his or her teacher's innovation to have eighth-grade students teach science concepts to their peers. Note that new apps now make it very easy to obtain instant transcripts of what students say. The right-hand column shows how an educator could use this coding technique to look closely at the data, using active verbs to try to stay close to what students

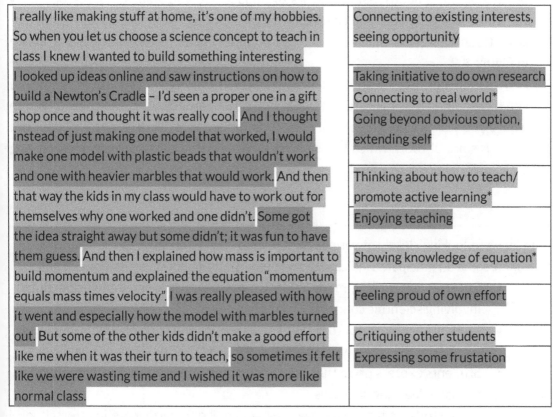

I really like making stuff at home, it's one of my hobbies. So when you let us choose a science concept to teach in class I knew I wanted to build something interesting.	Connecting to existing interests, seeing opportunity
I looked up ideas online and saw instructions on how to build a Newton's Cradle – I'd seen a proper one in a gift shop once and thought it was really cool.	Taking initiative to do own research / Connecting to real world*
And I thought instead of just making one model that worked, I would make one model with plastic beads that wouldn't work and one with heavier marbles that would work.	Going beyond obvious option, extending self
And then that way the kids in my class would have to work out for themselves why one worked and one didn't.	Thinking about how to teach/ promote active learning*
Some got the idea straight away but some didn't; it was fun to have them guess.	Enjoying teaching
And then I explained how mass is important to build momentum and explained the equation "momentum equals mass times velocity".	Showing knowledge of equation*
I was really pleased with how it went and especially how the model with marbles turned out.	Feeling proud of own effort
But some of the other kids didn't make a good effort like me when it was their turn to teach,	Critiquing other students
so sometimes it felt like we were wasting time and I wished it was more like normal class.	Expressing some frustation

Figure 8.8 An example of sentence-by-sentence coding.

are actually saying or doing. The codes marked by an asterisk are very similar to indicators of impact that were already identified in Step 1. While the emphasis in this tool is on identifying *positive* indicators of impact, educators should, of course, remain alert to unintended *negative* impacts of their innovation. In this example, the student expressed frustration at some classmates' teaching efforts and a desire for more "normal" classroom work—a concern that would need to be accounted for in thinking about the overall success of the innovation and how it might be further developed or changed.

3. *Revisit your indicators of impact (group work).*

   Compare what each of you noticed by looking closely at your different pieces of data. This exercise of looking with fresh eyes might have revealed some new or unanticipated learnings and additional indicators of impact. Can you jointly agree on two or three additional indicators of impact? Do you want to tweak or clarify the indicators of impact you came up with by looking at your Theory of Action diagram (Step 1)? An example of a list of additional, unanticipated indicators is shown in Figure 8.9.

   Articulating indicators of impact can be useful on its own to help you reflect on where you have come from, take stock of what you have learned so far, and think ahead to where you want to go. This activity also sets the stage for *Parts 2* and *3* of the *Data Analysis* suite of tools, which focus on creating a strategic data sample and applying indicators of impact to your data.

If you were looking closely at various data related to your changes to the science curriculum, some unanticipated indicators might emerge during the process. For example:

- Students are writing more extensive responses to open-ended questions involving scientific concepts
- Students are more apt to refer to news stories and current events involving science, both in their written work and during class discussions
- Students express pride that they are helping to teach the class through the design of learning activities
- More students than usual say they would like to participate in afterschool activities related to science

---

Figure 8.9 An example of unanticipated indicators of impact.

Data Analysis, Part II

Creating a Purposeful Data Sample

Purpose of the Tool

Once you have worked as a group to identify some indicators of impact (*Part I* of this suite of tools), you need to think carefully about which data you are going to examine to look for evidence of these indicators. This tool will help you to create a data sample that is broadly representative of the population and the kinds of activities involved in your innovation project. It encourages you to examine a range of different types of data in order to build as holistic a picture as possible of what is going on.

When to Use

This tool should be used after you have completed *Data Analysis, Part I*. It can be used early on in your innovation project to plan how you are going to gather data to assess the impact of your innovation or to explore initial impacts. It can also be used later when you are exploring the longer-term impact of your work.

Preparation and Other Considerations

Make sure to have on hand the list of indicators of impact that you identified using the previous tool (*Data Analysis, Part I*).

Steps

1. *Take stock.*
   As a full study group, begin by thinking about the total population that has been affected by your work so far. Which students, teachers, parents, and/or other stakeholders have experienced or been affected by your innovation so far?
   Next, make a quick inventory of all of the data you have collected (or have access to) over the course of your innovation project. Remember: here, the word *data* is used to broadly mean both quantitative and qualitative information or artifacts—for example, documentation of student work, lesson plans, interviews, class observation notes, survey responses, test scores, and so on.
2. *Determine your population sampling strategy.*
   Ideally, you want to choose a sample of data that strives for "maximum variation" of experiences, characteristics, or opinions associated with your innovation project, but

which is also a realistic quantity of information given your time constraints. When you think about who will be included or represented by your data sample, consider the following criteria:

- *Outlier cases*—for example, teachers who most strongly indicated that they liked your innovation and those who most strongly indicated that they did not, or students with the highest and lowest achievement in a particular class that experienced your innovation
- *Median cases*—for example, students or teachers who may be considered "average users," or those who fall in the middle of the outlier cases you identified above
- *Richest cases*—for example, the experiences of a few teachers or students that were particularly interesting or inspiring

You may be able to immediately identify who might fall into these categories. However, you may need to browse through your data after this activity to pinpoint the exact individuals you wish to include in your population sample. Make sure that the sample you come up with is broadly inclusive of different demographic categories within your population—for example, by gender, age, academic subject area, and/or race/ethnicity.

3. *Choose your data.*

Now that you have broadly decided who is going to be represented in the data you look at, it's time to decide what you are going to look at. Look back at the indicators of impact that you identified using the previous tool in this suite (*Data Analysis, Part I*). Consider the kinds of data that are most likely to help you learn more about each indicator. For example, if you want to look for signs of growth in student understanding, you may want to look at samples of student work from a range of students. If you are looking at overall shifts in perception or attitude, you might want to include data related to what students and/or teachers say about changes in their perceptions and attitudes or levels of motivation.

4. *Divide the work.*

Within your study group, broadly decide who is going to look at which data. Be sure to be realistic with regard to scope. You want to look at enough data to gain an accurate picture of the impact of your innovation project, but you do not want to look at so much data that you will be overwhelmed.

5. *Seek out what is missing.*

Finally, consider which data may be missing from your inventory. Are there ways to quickly obtain these data or could you plan to collect these data in the future? For example, do you need to conduct a short survey?

Now you are ready for *Part III* of this suite of tools, which will lead you through the process of applying indicators of impact to your data.

Data Analysis, Part III

Applying Indicators of Impact to Your Data

Purpose of the Tool

This tool, the last in a series of three, is designed to help you apply your indicators of impact to your data in a systematic way. At the end of this process, you should have a clearer view of the impact of your innovation project in your teaching and learning context so far, and a sense of what you can build on moving forward.

When to Use

This tool can be used early on or partway through the implementation of your innovation project(s) in conjunction with *Parts I* and *II* of the *Data Analysis* suite of tools. It can also be used toward the end of your innovation project(s) as you prepare to evaluate the overall impact of your work.

Preparation and Other Considerations

You may want to complete Steps 1–4 of this tool individually before meeting as a group to complete Step 5. You will need to have on hand the list of indicators your group developed using *Data Analysis, Part I*.

Prior to digging into this tool, group members will need to gather the data they agreed to review when going through the conversations in the previous tool (Step 4 of *Data Analysis, Part II*). Group members should make sure that their designated data are available and in a form that they can easily annotate. It might be easiest to print out or make copies of data so that you can write directly on them, or use an iPad or other tablet with a stylus. Alternatively, you can plan to do this work on the computer—for example, by using the comments function in your word processing software and/or highlighting the text in different colors that correspond to your different indicators of impact.

Steps

1. *Label your indicators (individual work).*

    Individually, revisit the indicators that your group agreed on when you used *Data Analysis, Part I.* You will probably find it useful to give each of the indicators a number, letter, or color code. To make things easier later on, everyone in your group should use the same numbers, letters, or colors.

2. *Dig in (individual work).*

    Start looking carefully through your data sample, searching for signs of your indicators of impact. Highlight or make a note of places in your data where you see evidence of a particular kind of impact using the numbers, letters, or color codes you created in Step 1. While you should keep an eye out for all of your indicators of impact as you read through your data (e.g., surveys, class notes, student work, etc.), bear in mind that some indicators of impact may be easier to find in certain kinds of data than in others.

    If you see something interesting or important in your data that does not seem to be captured by one of your existing indicators of impact, make a note of it. You should remain open to identifying unanticipated impacts. Also, you may want to suggest edits to the indicators of impact already on your list if you find that the wording does not quite capture what you are seeing in your data. Figure 8.10 is provided as a point of reference.

Let's return to the example we gave in Part 1 of this suite of tools: Identifying Indicators of Impact. The first indicator was "Students demonstrate an accurate understanding of scientific concepts in the curriculum." If you saw evidence of students showing an accurate understanding of scientific concepts—for example, in lesson observation notes or in their written work or on tests—then you would highlight that evidence and label it with a "1" (to indicate it is the first indicator on your list). The third indicator was "Students exhibit greater engagement and attention during science." If you see evidence from class observation notes, or students self-reported being more engaged in survey responses or interviews, for instance, then you would highlight that evidence and label it with a "4."

Figure 8.10 Applying the indicators of impact.

3. *Synthesize (individual work).*

   When you have finished marking up your data, flip through your annotated data to get a sense of how much evidence you have found for each of your indicators of impact—if any. Make some notes to summarize your thoughts about what you have noticed or found out.

4. *Compare notes (group work).*

   As a group, reconvene to compare what you found when trying to apply your indicators of impact to your data sample by discussing the following questions:
   - What can you learn by comparing the indicators of impact for which you found most evidence?
   - What can you learn by comparing the indicators of impact for which you found little or no evidence?
   - Do you want to change or add to your original list of indicators of impact?
   - Do you think you need to look at different kinds of data?
   - What are your thoughts at this stage about the impact of your innovation?
   - Is there anything else you learned from this process?

Exhibiting Your Work

Sharing Your Innovation Project with Others

Purpose of the Tool

Sharing your thinking, learning, and plans with others can help you to gain powerful feedback on your innovation project that may provide new perspectives on how you are going about your work. Additionally, the process of preparing to share your innovation project with others can create a goal and timeline to work toward that will challenge you to crystallize how you describe your work, to reflect on challenges or other aspects of your project that might benefit from outside input, and to curate the documentation and data you have been collecting in ways that will communicate your project and its impact to others.

Within the inquiry-driven innovation approach, these sharing moments are thought of less as presentations of work in which you, the presenter, tell the audience what they need to know about your innovation project. Rather, they are approached as *exhibitions* of work that provide ideas-in-progress that warrant slow and careful looking, invite constructive critique, and serve as starting points for thoughtful dialogue between the exhibitor (you/your study group) and the exhibition audience (your invited guests). This tool will help you to plan an exhibit that showcases your work and could be part of an exhibition with other study groups.

When to Use

You should plan to wait until you are at least a few months into implementing your innovation project to exhibit your work to an audience. Exhibitions will likely be most helpful to your study group if they are recurring over time, perhaps every three to six months.

Preparation and Other Considerations

Prior to beginning to work on your study group's exhibit, you will want to plan some basics of a project exhibition with others who are also working on implementing innovation projects—for example, other study groups in your school or across different teaching and learning contexts. Decide where and when your exhibition will take place, how long it will last, what budget you might have available, and other key logistics. Decide whom you will invite to your exhibition. Oftentimes, it is helpful to have an increasingly "outside" exhibition audience as time goes by: you might start off early in your innovation projects by exhibiting your work only among members of other study groups engaging in inquiry-driven innovation, and over the course of successive exhibitions begin to invite others from your teaching and learning contexts or public audiences that are interested in your work.

Steps

1. *Gather your materials.*
   Assemble documentation you have collected through implementing your innovation project, as well as any planning or process documents that might feel especially

important to your work so far (e.g., a Theory of Action diagram or notes from brainstorming sessions that were especially important for your group).

2. *Consider your audience.*

Based on decisions you have previously made about who will be invited to the exhibition, consider what background information your audience might need in order to engage with your work. For example, if you are exhibiting your work to colleagues within your school, then you can probably go without explaining the basics of your school context. On the other hand, if your audience is unfamiliar both with your teaching and learning context and with the inquiry-driven innovation approach, then you will need to plan to bring them up to speed on enough elements of your context and approach so that they will be able to understand and offer constructive feedback about your innovation project.

3. *Envision the kinds of conversations you want to have about your exhibit.*

Consider the conversations you might want to have with your audience, and what you will need to exhibit in order to get to that dialogue. If you would like feedback on a prototype that is part of your innovation project, you will want to make sure to have that prototype on hand. If you are working with students to create new student-driven assessment practices in your school, you might consider inviting one such student to be a co-exhibitor. If you would like feedback on a questionnaire you are designing, you might want to have draft copies available that audience members can mark up with suggestions.

However you are envisioning your exhibit, you should be sure to identify some puzzles about your innovation project that your audience might be able to help you work through, and also plan for a way to capture their suggestions or feedback (e.g., a suggestion box, having sticky notes and markers available for your audience to leave comments, etc.). Remember, an exhibition is different from a presentation in that it is not all about you telling something to your audience; it should be an exchange where both the visitor and the exhibitor get something out of it.

4. *Create an exhibit.*

Now it is time to create your exhibit. Think creatively about the form of your exhibit and what will work best in terms of engaging your audience in conversation. For example, your exhibit might take the form of a digital product that can be projected, or it might be in a physical format such as a poster board display. Whatever format you choose, you might want to include the following information:

- *Basic information about you:* for example, the names, school name, and professional roles of your study group members;
- *Innovation project description:* a concise framing of your innovation project;
- *Population:* a description of the people or students you are hoping to impact through your innovation project;
- *Project rationale:* a brief outline of the rationale or plan behind your innovation project, possibly including a Theory of Action diagram;
- *Documentation:* samples of images, audio, video, text, observation notes, student work, or other artifacts that show what you have done in your innovation project and where you are now; remember, this could include digital assets such as short video clips or physical products such as prototypes;
- *Insights:* key insights or "*aha* moments" you have had as a result of exploring your innovation project; and
- *Puzzles:* questions, challenges, or puzzles that have emerged through the process of planning and implementing your innovation project; you might want to choose one or two big questions or puzzles on which you would like feedback from your invited audience.

5. *Work together to plan the exhibition.*

   As you work as a study group to create your own exhibit, continue working with your exhibition co-exhibitors to plan and publicize the exhibition. For example, you might want to include exhibition elements such as a brief overview presentation for your audience about the process of inquiry-driven innovation, a shared protocol or format for audience members to give feedback and input to all exhibitors, or a process debrief after the exhibition is over so that all study groups can share how the exhibition went and what they learned from audience feedback.

Attributions and Additional Resources

Past study groups have found it helpful to use the Dialogue Toolkit from Project Zero's Out of Eden Learn research initiative to encourage meaningful feedback and dialogue during project exhibitions. To learn more about the Dialogue Toolkit, see https://learn.outofedenwalk.com/dialogue-toolkit/.

Theory of Action Tuning Protocol

Revisiting Your Initial Plans and Theories

Purpose of the Tool

Diagramming a Theory of Action can be a powerful exercise to get you started on planning to implement your innovation project and articulating the rationale behind it. However, the best-laid plans can change and the process of implementation will likely lead to learnings that might impact the underlying rationale that you originally framed. This tool should be used to revisit a Theory of Action diagram that was previously created by your group in order to consider the ways in which your innovation is playing out as planned—or not!

When to Use

You will probably find it most helpful if you use this tool when you are at least one month into trying out the rationale framed in your Theory of Action. You will likely want to return to the questions in this tool as often as once a month throughout the implementation of your innovation project.

Preparation and Other Considerations

Make sure to have on hand the Theory of Action diagram you created previously using the *Theory of Action Part I* and *Part II* tools. Make sure your diagram is available in a format that will allow all group members to easily see it at the same time.

Steps

1. *Tune up the basics.*
   Start by checking in on some of the elements that articulate the basic premise of your Theory of Action. Discuss these questions:
   - Has your group's inquiry focus changed at all?
   - Has your desired outcome changed at all? Are you still going toward the long-term outcome that you outlined initially?
   - Have you tried out one or more of the innovation projects outlined in your diagram?

If you have gone in a new direction and have not pursued one of the innovation projects on your Theory of Action diagram, map out the rationale ("if this, then that . . .") behind the other innovation project(s) you have been pursuing. If your inquiry focus or desired outcome has changed, make adjustments to your diagram to reflect those changes.

2. *Check in.*

   If you have tried out one or more of the innovation projects articulated in your diagram, do a check-in on the rationale ("if this, then that . . .") statements you outlined for your project(s):

   - Has your rationale played out as expected? What information have you collected (including at least some documentation or student work) to help you decide how it is working?
   - Pinpoint the places where your rationale has not played out as expected. Engage in a conversation about why things might not have gone as anticipated, and revise your diagram as needed.

3. *Determine where you go from here.*

   Think about implications and next steps:

   - What have you learned through implementing your innovation project(s) so far? Maybe you have learned things about the project that you are trying out, about your teaching and learning context, about innovation in general, and so on.
   - What are your next steps for moving your innovation project(s) forward? How will you amend your Theory of Action diagram either to keep you on track toward your school innovation goals, or to chart a new path?

Project Journey Mapping

Taking the Bird's-Eye View of Your Innovation

Purpose of the Tool

While you are likely doing frequent check-ins about what has happened and what you have learned through the process of innovation, at times it may be helpful to zoom even further out and take a bird's-eye view of your study group's story from its beginning to present day. Reflecting on where you began and the key points of your story can help you to both appreciate the changes and developments that you have experienced thus far and capture some of the learnings from these experiences that might otherwise be missed.

This tool will help you create a project journey map, similar to the Innovation Journeys in Chapter 4, that tells the story of your group's innovation project. It is designed to help you reflect on your study group's journey of innovating together and to capture what you have learned along the way. It might also be useful in helping you to communicate your innovation and its impacts to others outside of your study group, including in exhibitions of your work for other study groups or public audiences.

When to Use

The following conversation and activity protocol is meant to be used at least a few months into implementing your innovation project, and revisited periodically throughout the process of innovating.

Preparation and Other Considerations

Prior to engaging with this protocol, study group members should refresh their memory about the group's work so far—for example, by reviewing any documentation collected from your innovation project or from past study group meetings, your Theory of Action diagram, or any products or prototypes created as part of your innovation project.

You should also have writing utensils, a stack of blank paper or sticky notes, and chart paper on hand.

Steps

1. *Articulate significant moments in your group's story (individual work).*
   Individually, take a few moments to draw on your memory and reflect on the documentation and artifacts you looked at in preparation for this session. Identify any significant moments of change or development in your study group's story of developing and implementing your innovation project(s). For example, you might want to consider:
   - any big realizations that had an effect on your group's work;
   - moments when your study group encountered challenges;
   - questions or big decisions you faced;

- times when your study group's work took a notable turn toward a new or unexpected direction; and
- other moments or events that feel significant.

Write each significant moment you identified on a separate sheet of paper or sticky note.

2. *Reflect as a group (group work).*

    Take a look at what all group members have written and engage in a conversation about the following:

    - Were there any moments that stood out as significant to multiple study group members? Why did these moments feel so significant, and what were the circumstances that led up to them?
    - Were there any moments that stood out as significant to some group members, but not to others? Why might these moments not have felt equally significant to all group members?

3. *Define the actors (group work).*

    Now, think of the *actors* in your group's story. Actors in this instance are catalysts to change or development within a study group's innovation process. While actors may be people, they could also be inanimate objects such as policies, test schedules, school inspections, technological platforms, tools and materials, or physical spaces. As a group, discuss the following:

    - Who or what were the actors involved in some of the moments of change or development that you just identified?
    - How did they serve as drivers or obstacles to the development of your innovation project(s), or to the way your study group developed?

4. *Reflect on your journey through the inquiry-driven innovation process (group work).*

    Look at the *Roadmap for Inquiry-Driven Innovation* in Chapter 7. As a group, discuss where in this process you are right now. Does this roadmap resonate with your journey so far? Why, or why not? Does your group's process follow the same order and flow as the roadmap? If not, in what ways is it different? What tools from the *Toolkit for Inquiry-Driven Innovation*, or elsewhere, have stood out to you as especially helpful in envisioning and developing your innovation project(s)?

5. *Map out your innovation journey (group work).*

    Now, put together the full narrative of your group's story: where you started from, key points along the way, elements of the inquiry-driven innovation process, and tools or resources that were important to your journey. Feel free to be creative with how your story comes together! Perhaps you can best tell your story in a digital format, by drawing it out on chart paper, or by combining text and documentation you have collected to create something in the spirit of the Innovation Journeys shown in Chapter 4.

6. *Share and repeat periodically.*

   While there is great value in creating your group's own project journey map, that value can be enhanced by sharing your map with another study group—perhaps another group at your own school or at another school that is also engaging in inquiry-driven innovation. Periodically revisit this tool to update your project journey map and reflect on the road you have traveled together.

Looking Ahead

Envisioning the Path Forward

Purpose of the Tool

Whether your innovation project is moving ahead full-steam or has hit a roadblock that is raising questions about how to move forward, it is a good idea to regularly make time as a study group to reflect on what you are learning and where you might want to take your work next. This tool offers some suggestions that can help you envision how you will advance your innovation project over the next few months.

When to Use

You will likely find it most helpful to use this tool for the first time when you are at least a month into piloting your innovation project(s), and to revisit it periodically throughout project implementation.

Steps

1. *Consider what you have learned so far (individual work).*

   Within your study group, take some time to individually write your responses to the following questions:

   • What have I learned so far in terms of my group's inquiry focus?

   • What more do I want to learn and figure out about the inquiry focus?

   Note that considering what more you want to learn might include continuing what you have been doing in a deeper way, or trying something new.

2. *Envision where you might go next (group work).*

   As a study group, share your responses to the previous questions with each other. Then, work as a group to envision what the upcoming three to four months might hold for your innovation project by discussing one or more of the following questions.

   How might your study group...

   - *Go deeper?* If your group is feeling as though it has already "finished" implementing an innovation project, take another look. Are you pushing your ideas far enough into the innovation space and getting at something that is a significant departure from what has happened before in your teaching and learning context? You might find it helpful to revisit the *Sweet Spot of Innovation* tool as you consider this question.

   - *Take a different tack?* If your group is feeling that you might be missing something important, consider how you might take your work in another direction. Can you think of ways to gain a deeper understanding of the needs or design challenges related to your project, the impacts of the innovations you have tried out already, or ways to apply what you have learned so far to other aspects of your practice?

   - *Play with size?* Look inside your teaching and learning context. Is there a compelling reason to try to expand the scope of your innovation project, or to scale it back? You might think about expanding the model you are implementing, including more people, and so on—or about reducing its size and scope if the project is feeling unwieldy.

   - *Expand your thinking?* Think outside your teaching and learning context. What networks, communities, and/or ideas might you want to work with beyond your teaching and learning context? Perhaps you would like to expand the network associated with your innovation project by reaching out to other education practitioners or connecting with a relevant expert. You might also want to expand on the ideas that are influencing your work by making connections to existing literature, both within and beyond the field of education.

3. *Share out and discuss next steps (group work).*

   Decide on a few actionable steps that your group will take in the near term to move your innovation project forward.

Spheres of Influence

Visualizing Your Impact

Purpose of the Tool

As you become increasingly immersed in the work of implementing your innovation project, it can be helpful to take a step back, look beyond your immediate environment, and
consider the broader impact your innovation project may have on different stakeholder
groups. This tool can help you to engage in that work and reflection.

When to Use

Use this tool when your study group is at an advanced stage of implementing its innovation project. You might choose to return to this activity periodically over time.

Preparation and Other Considerations

You will need chart paper, markers, sticky notes, and pens or pencils to map out the
spheres of influence related to your innovation work.

Steps

1. *Name your spheres of influence (group work).*
   As a group, come up with a list of "spheres of influence": contexts in which your innovation project is having (or could have) an impact. For example, you might imagine
   your project having a local impact in individual classrooms, across multiple classrooms
   within a department, or throughout your larger school community. You might also
   imagine your project one day having broader or more far-reaching impacts—such as
   those that affect other teaching and learning contexts within your local geographic
   area, the broader community surrounding your teaching and learning context, or even
   the field of education writ large. Think in aspirational terms and try to envision a
   range of types of impact from local to far-reaching.
   Try to narrow your list to no more than five or six spheres: those where it feels most
   important to have an impact through your innovation project. On a large piece of

chart paper, draw concentric circles and label each one with the name of one of your spheres of influence. Start in the center with the spheres that are closest to school or classroom practice, moving to spheres that are increasingly farther from your specific teaching and learning context (such as the broader field of education) as you move outward. An example of how this might look is shown in Figure 8.11.

2. *Reflect on impact (individual work).*

   Take personal reflection time for each group member to think about how your innovation project has had an effect on each of these spheres. Keep in mind:

   - Reaching more or larger circles does not necessarily mean greater impact—there is no one "best" circle in which to have impact.
   - Impacting others might not only happen through direct, in-person interactions; consider the reach of any dissemination of your project's work or ideas that might have happened through participation in professional learning communities, presentations, online or printed materials, and so on.

   Each group member should take some sticky notes and write the ways in which the innovation project has had an impact within the identified spheres, then place the sticky notes at the appropriate points on your spheres of influence diagram. Use a separate sticky note for each impact. Place sticky notes in between the spheres or in multiple spheres if needed. Note that you might not have anything in one or more of the spheres you identified.

3. *Take a look (group work).*

   Once all group members have contributed their sticky notes, take a few minutes of quiet looking time to read each other's contributions.

4. *Debrief as a group.*

   Reflect through a group conversation on the following questions:

   - Are we having impact (and if so, the right kind and amount or degree of impact) in the spheres of influence that are most important to us?
   - Are there any spheres where we are not having an impact right now, but might like to in the future?
   - Are there any spheres we are influencing that we might want to step back from, in order to focus that energy on other aspects of our work?

5. *Looking forward.*

   Take a moment to think about any implications for moving your work forward.

Spheres of Influence

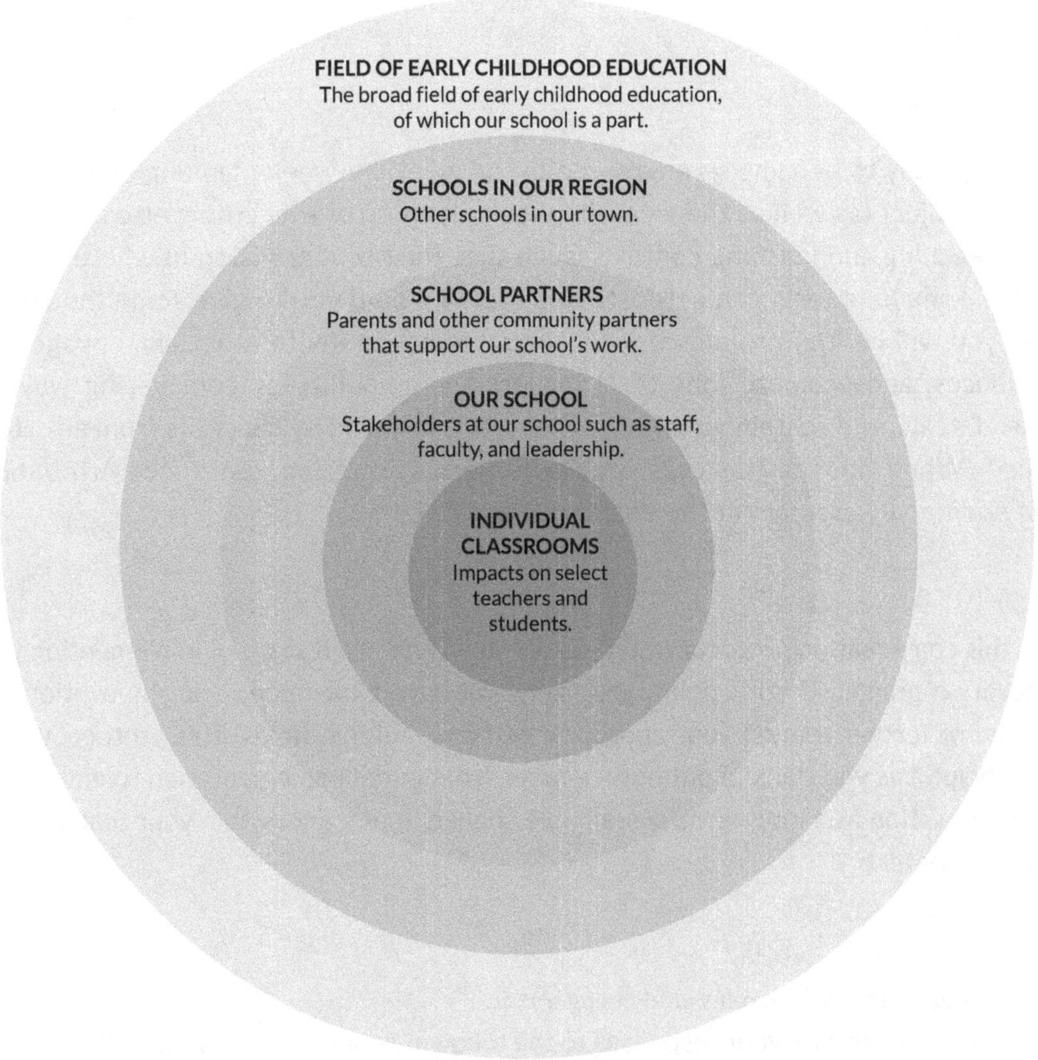

FIELD OF EARLY CHILDHOOD EDUCATION
The broad field of early childhood education,
of which our school is a part.

SCHOOLS IN OUR REGION
Other schools in our town.

SCHOOL PARTNERS
Parents and other community partners
that support our school's work.

OUR SCHOOL
Stakeholders at our school such as staff,
faculty, and leadership.

**INDIVIDUAL
CLASSROOMS**
Impacts on select
teachers and
students.

Figure 8.11 An example of a spheres of influence diagram.

Attributions and Additional Resources

The concept of spheres of influence and the accompanying activity and diagram are loosely based on Bronfenbrenner's well-known ecological systems theory first presented in U. Bronfenbrenner (1979). *The Ecology of Human Development: Experiments by Nature and Design*. Cambridge, MA: Harvard University Press.

Spreading, Scaling, and Sustaining

Looking to the Long Term

Purpose of the Tool

It can be easy to become so engrossed in the week-by-week planning of your innovation project (as well as the week-by-week planning of everything else going on in your teaching and learning context), such that the broader vision of where you are going in the long term can get lost. This tool will help you to give some thought to how you will lay the groundwork for your project to invite others in, engage new audiences, and promote long-term project sustainability by considering ways to spread, scale, and sustain your innovations. It is inspired by concepts from an article called "When Change Has Legs" by David Perkins and Jim Reese (see *Attributions and Additional Resources* at the end of this tool).

When to Use

Use this conversation protocol when you are in an advanced stage of implementing your innovation project. By this point, you likely will have pilot-tested your innovation and revised or further refined your approach, perhaps multiple times. This protocol will be most helpful as you think about how to move from initial implementation to embedding your innovation as a long-term, sustainable change in practice within your teaching and learning context.

Steps

1. *Consider adaptability, roles, and engagement.*
   As a group, discuss your responses to the following questions inspired by Perkins and Reese's article:
   - *Is your innovation adaptable?* How have you adapted your study group's innovation project to suit individual needs, opportunities, contexts, or styles of practice in your teaching and learning context? How will you make your innovation project adaptable so that a variety of teachers or administrators from outside of your study group can engage with it?
   - *What is the role of "visionaries" in your innovation?* Who in your teaching and learning context has helped you with your innovation project so far? Looking ahead,

who might be what Perkins and Reese call the *political visionaries* (e.g., school principal/headteacher, a member of the school leadership team, the director of an afterschool program, a community organizer, etc.) and *practical visionaries* (e.g., teachers, school counselors, youth workers, those working on day-to-day implementation, etc.) who could help make sure your innovation project both grows and thrives?

- *What is the communication and engagement strategy behind your innovation?* How have you let others in your community know about your innovation and what opportunities, if any, have you created for them to get involved? How will you ensure that there is awareness of your innovation both within your teaching and learning context, and beyond? How will you keep various stakeholders updated on your progress? How might you offer people from outside of your study group different "degrees of participation," as Perkins and Reese put it, in your work—for example, those who want to try out some small changes in practice versus those who want to commit to becoming study group members?

2. *Draw up an action plan.*

   From your discussion around these questions, draw up an action plan for how you might spread, scale, and sustain your innovation project(s). As you consider scaling up or spreading your work, be specific in terms of what growth looks like (e.g., number of students served, depth of inquiry, new levels reached, etc.).

3. *Generate questions and puzzles.*

   Generate a list of questions or puzzles you currently have about how you might put your ideas for spreading, scaling, and sustaining your innovation into action. If possible, make plans to share these questions with people from outside your study group in order to gather feedback. Be specific and try to word the questions so that someone who does not know your context could reasonably help you to generate ideas.

Attributions and Additional Resources

This tool is inspired by the following article: D. N. Perkins, & J. D. Reese (2014). When Change Has Legs. *Educational Leadership, 71*(8), 42–47.

CHAPTER 9

CONCLUSION:

A Call to Action

Writing about the ongoing work of envisioning and designing what education can and should look like, Hargreaves and Fullan (2012) put forth a challenge to schools:

> [T]here needs to be a mix of committing to best practice (existing practices that already have a good degree of widely agreed effectiveness) and having the freedom, space, and resources to create next practice (innovative approaches that often begin with teachers themselves . . .). (p. 51)

This book presents and illustrates the concept of *inquiry-driven innovation*: an ongoing process that empowers individuals and communities to pursue positive school-based change that is relevant and responsive to local contexts. The Framework for Inquiry-Driven Innovation sits in this space of "next practice" in that it offers grounding concepts (Part One of this book), real-life examples of innovation in practice (Part Two), and tools and guidelines that will help other schools to engage in this process within their own unique and diverse contexts (Part Three). But given that school-based innovation frameworks already exist, what is the value of this particular approach?

Contributions to the Field of Education

The Framework for Inquiry-Driven Innovation was developed through collaborative, design-based research that partnered a team of researchers—which included the authors of this book—with seven schools in the UAE's GEMS Education network through a research initiative called Creating Communities of Innovation. The results of that work, illustrated in the three previous parts of the book, point to the benefits of conducting collaborative design-based research that leads to usable knowledge. There is, of course, a time and a place within the ecosystem of educational research for randomized con-trolled trials involving new or existing programs, or for observation-based investigations into effective and less effective practices in schools. However, if we are to envision what schools and classrooms *could* look like, then collaborative design-based research offers a way to develop new approaches—and, crucially, to have those approaches be piloted, iterated on, and further developed by practitioners in conjunction with a research team. The fact that the research was conducted in the UAE also provided a special opportunity to work across international boundaries and to collaborate with practitioners working in schools serving different communities and following different curricula and pedagogic traditions. The result is a product that could only have come from this type of research: a framework that is flexible and general enough to work in a variety of teaching and learning contexts, yet specific enough to offer concrete, actionable guidance to busy edu-cators, including supports to understand what their schools might be ready for in terms of innovation.

This approach to innovation also shines a spotlight on the mutual dependence and intertwining of individual educator growth and community-based change, and asserts that change at the individual and school levels can and should be attended to simulta-neously. This point is important because teachers and administrators cannot be expected to enact the kinds of teaching and learning practices that they themselves have not had access to; there should be consistency between professional development experiences and the kinds of learning and development desired in schools. The research behind this book further brought out the idea that individual professional growth is greatly enhanced when individuals are part of a community that is doing meaningful work together and over which they have some ownership. This community ideally extends beyond the four walls of a single school, and indeed, the Creating Communities of Innovation project included in its design a cross-school research cohort that included eight different study groups across seven schools considering different questions, different student populations, and different curricula.

Another contribution of this work is that it illustrates the power of what might be called "everyday innovation." In most cases, the innovations initiated by the study groups were not high-profile or radical changes such as ones involving cutting-edge technology, expensive infrastructure, or a reorganization of teaching and learning at the school (although they could be). While inquiry-driven innovation led to important new resources and practices, the study groups generally built on existing practices within their schools or adapted ones that existed elsewhere but which were new to their schools. Everyday innovation can also be interpreted in a different way: while each school study group started with the charge to develop an innovation, the work of each group eventually moved beyond the bounds of a particular project and helped inquiry-driven innovation to become integrated into the daily practice of teaching and learning at its school.

The Framework for Inquiry-Driven Innovation also presents five principles of inquiry-driven innovation, detailed in Chapter 1. According to these principles, inquiry-driven innovation is: purposeful and intentional, attentive to multiple perspectives, adapted to context, sustained and iterative, and structured and supported. Articulating the principles of inquiry-driven innovation is helpful because the principles lend language and specificity to aims that should guide educational change at the intersection of innovation, inquiry, and community. These principles help give a sense of the breadth and depth of the work entailed for those who wish to take up the charge of inquiry-driven innovation for themselves.

Real-World Impacts

Beyond contributing ideas and invitations for further consideration within the field of education, inquiry-driven innovation has also had concrete and immediate impacts on the ground. On a practical level, the schools engaged in inquiry-driven innovation through their participation in the research cohort—each of whose stories are shown in Part Two—were impacted by the specific innovations they developed. For example, at GEMS Wellington International School (WIS), the study group was gratified when its annual school inspection report praised its school's promotion of critical thinking through its WISical Thinking innovation, citing it as an element that contributed to the school's renewed

Outstanding designation. At GEMS Modern Academy, its Futurus curriculum innovation has been incorporated in various ways across all aspects of the school curriculum, helping both teachers and students to approach and solve problems in new ways. Meanwhile, The Kindergarten Starters' (KGS) Open Doors initiative and integration of student-centered, inquiry-driven practices into its pedagogy continue to attract attention: at the time of writing, KGS had been selected as one of the best one hundred schools in the world and as such was set to present at a global showcase event for World Education Week.

> For more background on the stories of school-based and individual change mentioned here, see Part Two of this book.

Individual teachers involved in this work were also promoted to positions of leadership either within their existing school or in new ones, with several of them noting that inquiry-driven innovation had given them the confidence, motivation, and set of skills to pursue leadership positions—although, of course, their very participation in the project reflected their commitment to promoting change in education and continuing to improve their own practice.

Although staff turnover and other administrative challenges within GEMS—not to mention the onset of a global pandemic and an ongoing economic downturn in the Middle East—have impeded attempts to roll out inquiry-driven innovation more expansively, the impact of this work has extended beyond the seven schools that participated in the original research cohort. With very light support from Project Zero, five GEMS schools beyond the original cohort have been actively engaging in inquiry-driven innovation by joining the informal "Creating Communities of Innovation network" that was spearheaded by educators involved in the original research project as a way to keep up the momentum of their work and help spread inquiry-driven practices to more schools. The three co-leaders of this network—Nicholas Bruce, Vicki Hallatt, and Helen Loxston-Baker—have written the Afterword that follows this chapter. Educators from four of the original cohort schools play a mentoring role to those who are new to inquiry-driven innovation, and several exhibitions and conferences have been organized so that schools can continue to exchange ideas and support one another in their efforts to promote positive school-based change. TELLAL (Teaching and Learning for All), the professional development provider for GEMS Education and beyond, has played a supportive role in these endeavors since the completion of the two-year research project on which this book is based.[1] In addition, TELLAL has incorporated a number of the tools featured in Part Three into its regular teacher professional development and also tapped study group members to help deliver professional development for other schools.

The impact of inquiry-driven innovation also lives on in the work of Project Zero, the authors' home research institution. A significant collaborative design-based research project called Creando Comunidades de Indagación (Creating Communities of Inquiry) builds off the framework laid out in this book. A collaboration with the Innova Schools of Peru, the project uses a similar study group model and many of the inquiry-driven tools and practices featured in Part Three to support this network of schools in developing a system-wide culture of inquiry-driven teaching and learning.

The Imperative of Inquiry-Driven Innovation: A Responsibility to Reflect, Critique, and Act

Beyond making an intellectual contribution and having an impact on those schools using inquiry-driven innovation in their practice, the ideas and stories shared in this book also imply another offering: that of a call to action to reflect and critically consider the practices and possibilities of school-based innovation—and to act on them.

To be sure, there is no one single way to effect changes in practice across schools. Indeed, many different approaches to "next practice" could be seen within a single school—from a new strategy that a teacher makes up on the fly to address what is happening on a particular day in class to a department-wide initiative to try out a new pedagogy to the schoolwide introduction of a more student-centered or inquiry-driven curriculum. No matter what school-based innovation looks like in a particular context, those involved in teaching and learning owe it to the individuals and communities with whom they work to consider how they can make positive changes in practice happen, and how those changes might happen in better, deeper, more meaningful, and increasingly equitable and respectful ways. Chapter 6 shows how changes in practice within schools impact not only teaching and learning, but also the individual development of educators. And the stories of school-level and personal change detailed throughout Part Two show how this impact, in turn, can also extend to the experiences of students and their parents. With all of these stakeholders affected, everyone has an imperative to think about the role of inquiry and innovation in schools—and to put that thinking into action. Why? In the following, we offer some reflections.

Innovation Should Be Part of the Experience of *All* Learners, Schools, and Communities

For those working within school systems or who have a vested interest in them from a different point of view, it is part of our call to action to ensure that "next practice" is not restricted to schools that have the money and social connections to gain access to expensive equipment, paid consultants, or myriad other assets that come with a price tag or other barriers to access that might put them out of reach of other schools.

Ongoing innovation is important for all schools. However, to only think of the impacts of innovation at the school level would in many ways be missing the deeper purposes behind those innovations. Even though the research described in previous chapters focused on the adults who were leading the innovations and the schools in which the work was enacted, the innovations were essentially driven by a desire to focus on students in new and deeper ways—be that through promoting their critical thinking skills; using thinking routines to give them greater opportunity to express their ideas; or creating interdisciplinary, problem-based curricula.

While promoting greater justice and equity in schools was not articulated as an explicit innovation focus for the research cohort schools featured in this book, inquiry-driven innovation projects certainly could and *should* be developed with this crucial goal in mind. But the stated focus of study group-led projects is not the only way that educational equity could be embraced by those who take up the charge of inquiry-driven innovation. Fostering school-based innovation can in and of itself be viewed as a move toward advancing more just practices in education. It should be a charge that all schools take on—one that involves listening to and respecting different perspectives and experiences and one that is grounded in paying close attention to unique and diverse contexts. All learners, schools, and communities deserve innovation. Ensuring that school-based innovation is both a priority and a possibility for all schools is essential in providing an excellent education for every learner, and the approach to developing locally adapted innovations described in this book may be a resource to help bring this vision closer to reality.

What Seems Impossible May Not Be So

Amid the many demands placed on schools on a daily basis—curricular requirements, budgetary constraints, or benchmarks and standards to name just a few—it can be tempting to postpone the introduction of school-based change to next week, next month, next year, or even the next five-year plan. Reflecting on the impact of inquiry-driven innovation on educators in the research cohort, project liaison Christine Nasserghodsi said:

> I think we've seen them go from, "This'll be great but I'm not sure what I'm doing" to periods of frustration—"I'd like to do this, but I just don't have time"—and competing priorities. . . . And really having to be in that pit of "we're learning as we're doing this" and tinkering and the messiness of it and developing some comfort with ambiguity. But then also seeing themselves as capable of leading and driving change in the process.

The world has learned that when there is immediacy and urgency behind the push to innovate, changes in practice can and will happen—no matter the messiness or competing priorities. At the time of writing, educational practices have been hugely disrupted by the global COVID-19 pandemic—presenting an important opportunity to shake up the status quo in education and offer young people the kinds of learning experiences that will help equip them for the realities of a complex and challenging world. Among countless lessons, this worldwide crisis has taught us that at least some of what might have been pushed off to "next year" or "when we have the budget" is, in fact, achievable or at least possible to try out in much more immediate timeframes. With so many aspects of education requiring new thinking and new energy given the realities of our contemporary world, there should be a constant and ongoing urgency to strive to effect positive changes to practice—and not just in response to a global crisis that has arguably affected in one way or another every country, school system, and individual.

Our Schools Are Already Filled with Innovators, Inquirers, and Researchers

Another call to action of this book is that it is high time to recognize educators—a term used throughout this book to include teachers, administrators, educational support staff, and school leaders—as innovators who are experts about their own contexts and who can operate more creatively in the absence of siloed work that restricts them to thinking solely about their own departments or roles. At the very core of many educators' work lie driving purposes, questions, and values that may have led them to the field in the first place. And at the heart of every strong educator's practice are skills such as listening, collaboration, and inventiveness. Educators are already inquirers and researchers, but they need to be granted both the trust and support to develop and use those capacities.

The stories of innovation profiled throughout this book show that helping educators to take on the mantle of innovation requires commitment at the individual, group, and school levels. This work is not always easy, nor does it travel in straight lines. But as shown in the stories of school-based and personal change in this book, the returns on investing in educators as inquiry-driven innovators in their own right can be powerful.

Everyone Benefits from Working in Community

A final critical reason for paying attention to the practices and possibilities of school-based innovation is that both learners and educators deserve to be part of a community of innovation: innovation should not be left solely to lone teachers trying to push forward changes from within their classrooms, or technology developers toiling away at new educational apps that may be disconnected from real teaching and learning contexts. While both of these examples have their place within the overall ecosystem of school-based innovation, the idea of *inquiry-driven innovation* taps into the type of change that can take place only when innovation happens in communities, driven by inquiry-based approaches that help educators to attend to and be responsive to their local contexts.

Study groups in the Creating Communities of Innovation research cohort actively supported one another intellectually, practically, and personally. Even though their projects were not particularly alike, as project liaison Christine Nasserghodsi noted, "They were invested enough in one another's work that they were able to find common ground and actually spur each other on at different points." GEMS Education, the network to which the research cohort schools belong, had previously encouraged its educators to engage in action research. But Christine said there was a sharp contrast between teachers trying something out by themselves for several months and, as she put it:

> a community coming together and looking closely at their school environment, identifying areas that were ripe for innovation, identifying stakeholders that would need to be engaged in developing and carrying out an innovation and thinking really critically about themselves as people who can effect change within their schools.

This combination of innovation, inquiry, and community within the Framework for Inquiry-Driven Innovation amplifies each of these important elements for school-based change such that the total is greater than the sum of its parts. The benefits of study group-led inquiry-driven innovation can accrue to students, educators, parents, and even surrounding communities—as the various stories embedded in this book clearly and sometimes dramatically show. We live in vexing times. There has arguably never been a more pressing moment to commit to pursuing and promoting meaningful educational change than now.

Endnote

1. More information about TELLAL can be found at www.tellalinstitute.com.

AFTERWORD

By Nicholas Bruce, Vicki Hallatt, and Helen Loxston-Baker

At the time of writing, Nicholas Bruce and Vicki Hallatt both worked at GEMS Wellington International School (WIS), and Helen Loxston-Baker worked at GEMS Wellington Academy— Silicon Oasis (WSO). They all joined the Creating Communities of Innovation (CCI) project in January 2016. Collectively, they have gone on to co-lead a network of GEMS Education schools committed to the development of inquiry-driven innovation in a variety of school settings.

Beginning in January 2016, a small research team from Project Zero joined us in the United Arab Emirates to support us and our colleagues on a journey toward inquiry-driven innovation. *Slow Looking* was just one of the many tools introduced to us through the Creating Communities of Innovation (CCI) project. It was also one that every participating school struggled with at the start of the process. In Dubai, we are all used to working at a fast pace and schools are expected to achieve a lot every month. Therefore, slowing down and thinking carefully about an issue we wanted to develop was difficult for us. Each one of us individually remembers a meeting that we were in where we laughed and groaned about "slow looking" and couldn't fathom how it could work. Fast-forward six months: we each remember being in an exhibition at one of the schools and realizing how much progress we had made with our mindsets, tools to innovate, routines of thinking, and constant evolution of ideas.

We did, however, have slightly different experiences. From the outset, engaging in the process of inquiry-driven innovation challenged Helen as she wanted to see instant change and results. Over time she learned that there is great value in slowing down and spending time really analyzing the effect of innovations on learning. Now she leads multiple study groups—or what at WSO they call CCI projects—across her entire school. Vicki, meanwhile, already had an interest in research having just completed her master's in education and she was keen to continue her work in this area. However, she did not realize when she began just what an impact inquiry-driven innovation would have on her professional outlook and work. Meanwhile, Nick signed up wanting to make changes in learning and teaching at WIS and instead learned a whole new way of approaching change in schools. Vicki and Nick have since helped facilitate multiple new CCI study groups across WIS, as well as co-leading with Helen a broader network of GEMS schools committed to trying out CCI ideas and practices.

All three of us have found that the process for inquiry-driven innovation presented in this book has been invaluable for supporting teachers to carry out innovations in teaching and learning within a clear framework. The CCI process has taught us that all innovations need points of iteration. Quite often the first idea is not the one that will create the magic in a classroom; rather, innovation is a process and a journey. We found tools such as *Sweet Spot of Innovation*, *Theory of Action*, and *Population, Innovation, Outcome* to be a huge support in allowing us to frame our research and to slow down and think carefully about the process of inquiry.

The value of sharing ideas and discussing pedagogy with colleagues has likewise been of great value. Having opportunities to meet colleagues from different content areas, experiences, and cultural backgrounds is invaluable in developing teaching practice in all classrooms. The perspectives that others brought allowed us to challenge, adapt, and develop our ideas beyond what we could do individually and within our own schools. In addition, the feedback we received from other schools was different to the feedback from our own colleagues: teachers from other schools do not have the same biases, and therefore their feedback was essential to help us adapt and change our ideas.

Moreover, the process of inquiry-driven innovation is one that continues past the end of one academic year and one cycle of school inspections. It was important to us that our innovations endured beyond that initial development process and continued despite changes of staff and leadership, and the demands of continuous inspection and government initiatives. We believe that this is the case in many of our cohort member schools—as it may also be for other schools around the world.

We hope that the network we have created within the UAE to help spread inquiry-driven innovation practices will help support more schools in the UAE and more broadly in the world to engage with the ideas in this book. There is real importance in sharing ideas and best practices in education. In a highly connected world where ideas are plentiful, having opportunities to discuss, debate, download, and digest new ideas with colleagues is so valuable and often overlooked in the congested school calendar. The Framework for Inquiry-Driven Innovation supports the whole community in developing and improving the quality of education for students.

As we write these words, the world is gripped by the COVID-19 pandemic. While the pandemic clearly poses additional challenges to educators, it has made us reflect further on the importance of this work. We no longer work in the silos of our own school buildings and our own teams. Our work has entered homes across the world in the last few months and will possibly continue to do so in the near future and beyond. Therefore, it is important that we continue to work in groups to reflect, change, and innovate our teaching methods by working collaboratively far and wide.

Nicholas Bruce, Deputy Headteacher—Teaching & Learning, The International School of The Hague, The Netherlands

Vicki Hallatt, Head of the Centre for Excellence, GEMS Wellington International School, Dubai

Helen Loxston-Baker, Director of Teaching, Learning & Innovation, GEMS Wellington Academy—Silicon Oasis, Dubai

APPENDIX
Index of Participant Schools

School	Abbreviated name	School curriculum	Grade levels offered
GEMS American Academy—Abu Dhabi	GAA	American	K–12
GEMS FirstPoint School—The Villa	FPS	British	K–9
The Kindergarten Starters	KGS	Indian (CBSE)	K–5
GEMS Modern Academy	Modern	Indian (ICSE)/International Baccalaureate	K–12
GEMS New Millennium School—Al Khail	NMS	Indian (CBSE/IGCSE), Cambridge Assessment International Education	K–12
GEMS Wellington International School	WIS	British, International Baccalaureate	K–12
GEMS Wellington Academy—Silicon Oasis	WSO	British, International Baccalaureate	K–12

GLOSSARY

Some of the terms in this glossary can have varied meanings. They are defined in the context of the Framework for Inquiry-Driven Innovation as follows:

- **artifacts:** closely tied to the concept of documentation (see below), artifacts are sources of evidence that can help make teaching and learning visible; they may include photographs, typed or handwritten notes, audio or video recordings, or examples of student work
- **Creating Communities of Innovation (CCI):** the collaborative design-based research project led by researchers at Project Zero, Harvard Graduate School of Education in conjunction with and funded by the GEMS Education network of schools; this work led to the development of the Framework for Inquiry-Driven Innovation
- **documentation:** the practice of closely observing, recording, reflecting on, and sharing learning in order to deepen learning and make it visible to others; documentation can involve gathering a variety of media such as photographs, typed or handwritten notes, audio or video recordings, examples of learners' work, or other artifacts of learning
- **Framework for Inquiry-Driven Innovation:** key concepts and principles, a suggested process, and a range of practicable tools for enacting inquiry-driven innovation
- **inquiry-driven innovation:** an ongoing process that empowers individuals and communities to pursue positive school-based change that is relevant and responsive to local contexts
- **inquiry focus:** the question of practice that motivates and focuses the work of innovation

- **innovation:** the act or result of trying out anything that is new within a given school context, even if it involves practices that are commonplace elsewhere
- **innovation project:** a defined project that a study group is undertaking to develop and implement an innovation
- **learning community:** a broader cohort of study groups that periodically gathers to learn from one another and to support one another's work; the study groups that comprise a learning community can be from within the same school or from across different schools
- **study group:** several individuals from a school or other learning context who meet regularly over an extended period of time to work collaboratively toward an innovation
- **thinking routine:** a short, simple structure or protocol that invites learners to practice and routinize ways of thinking to help engage them in deeper inquiry

REFERENCES

Acar, O.A., Tarakci, M., & van Knippenberg, D. (2019). Creativity and innovation under constraints. A cross-disciplinary integrative review. *Journal of Management, 45*(1), 96–121.

Adarves-Yorno, I., Postmes, T., & Haslam, S.A. (2007). Creative innovation or crazy irrelevance? The contribution of group norms and social identity to creative behavior. *Journal of Experimental Social Psychology, 43*(3), 410–416.

Admiraal, W., Kruiter, J., Lockhorst, D., Schenke, W., Sligte, H., Smit, B., & de Wit, W. (2016). Affordances of teacher professional learning in secondary schools. *Studies in Continuing Education,* 38, 281–298.

Allen, A.S., & Topolka-Jorissen, K. (2014). Using teacher learning walks to build capacity in a rural elementary school: Repurposing a supervisory tool. *Professional Development in Education,* (40)5, 822–837.

Allen, D., & Blythe, T. (2015). *Facilitating for learning: Tools for teacher groups of all kinds.* New York: Teachers College Press.

Baumfield, V., Hall, E., & Wall, K. (2013). *Action research in education: Learning through practitioner enquiry* (Second ed.). Los Angeles, CA; London: SAGE.

Bronfenbrenner, U. (1979). *The ecology of human development: Experiments by nature and design.* Cambridge, MA: Harvard University Press.

Bunderson, J.S., & Sutcliffe, K.M. (2002). Comparing alternative conceptualizations of functional diversity in management teams: Process and performance effects. *The Academy of Management Journal, 45*(5), 875–893.

Cheung, S.Y., Gong, Y., Wang, M., Zhou, L., & Shi, J. (2016). When and how does functional diversity influence team innovation? The mediating role of knowledge sharing and the moderation role of affect-based trust in a team. *Human Relations, 69*(7), 1507–1531.

Christensen, C., & Raynor, M. (2013). *The innovator's solution: Creating and sustaining successful growth*. Boston, MA: Harvard Business Review Press.

Clapp, E.P., Ross, J., Ryan, J.O., & Tishman, S. (2016). *Maker-centered learning*. Somerset: John Wiley & Sons, Incorporated.

Cochran-Smith, M., & Lytle, S.L. (2009). *Inquiry as stance: Practitioner research for the next generation*. New York: Teachers College Press.

Cochran-Smith, M., & Lytle, S.L. (1999). Relationships of knowledge and practice: Teacher learning in communities. *Review of Research in Education, 24*, 249–305.

Collinson, V., & Cook, T.F. (2001). "I don't have enough time": Teachers' interpretations of time as a key to learning and school change. *Journal of Educational Administration, 39*(3), 266–281.

Couros, G. (2015). *The innovator's mindset: Empower learning, unleash talent, and lead a culture of creativity*. Dave Burgess Consulting, Inc.

Csikszentmihalyi, M. (1997). *Creativity: The psychology of discovery and invention*. New York: Harper.

Darling-Hammond, L. (2017). *Empowered educators: How high-performing systems shape teaching quality around the world*. San Francisco, CA: Jossey-Bass.

Datnow, A., & Park, V. (2018). *Professional collaboration with purpose*. Milton: Routledge.

Deci, E., & Ryan, R.M. (1985). *Intrinsic motivation and self-determination in human behavior*. Springer Science & Business Media.

Dede, C. (2020). Introduction. In C. Dede & J. Richards (Eds.), *The 60-year curriculum: New models for lifelong learning in the digital economy* (pp. 1–24). Milton: Routledge.

Deluca, C., Shulha, J., Luhanga, U., Shulha, L.M., Christou, T.M., & Klinger, D.A. (2014). Collaborative inquiry as a professional learning structure for educators: A scoping review. *Professional Development in Education, 41*(4), 1–31.

Demircioglu, M.A., & Audretsch, D.B. (2017). Conditions for innovation in public sector organizations. *Research Policy, 46*(9), 1681–1691.

de Stobbeleir, K.E.M., Ashford, S.J., & Buyens, D. (2011). Self-regulation of creativity at work: The role of feedback-seeking behavior in creative performance. *Academy of Management Journal, 54*(4), 811–831.

Dewey, J. (1916). *Democracy and education*. New York: Macmillan.

Dewey, J. (1963). *Experience and education*. New York: Collier.

Donohoo, J., Hattie, J., & Eells, R. (2018). The power of collective efficacy. *Educational Leadership, 75*(6), 40–44.

Garland, J., Layland, A., & Corbett, J. (2018). Systems thinking leadership for district and school improvement. Available at: www.corbetteducation.com/ILCSI_ImprovementSystems_June18.pdf

Giudici, C., Krechevsky, M., & Rinaldi, C. (Eds.) (2001). *Making learning visible: Children as individual and group learners* (1st ed.). Cambridge, MA: Reggio Emilia, Italy: Project Zero, Harvard Graduate School of Education; Reggio Children, International Center for the Defense and Promotion of the Rights and Potential of all Children.

Gonzalez-DeHass, A.R., Willems, P.P., & Holbein, M.F.D. (2005). Examining the relationship between parental involvement and student motivation. *Educational Psychology Review, (17)*2, 99–123.

Hardy, Q. (2011, July 16). Google's innovation—And everyone's? *Forbes.* www.forbes.com/sites/quentinhardy/2011/07/16/googles-innovation-and-everyones/?sh=34e1d9143066

Hargreaves, A. (2019). Teacher collaboration: 30 years of research on its nature, forms, limitations and effects. *Teachers and Teaching, 25*(5), 603–621.

Hargreaves, A., & Fullan, M. (2012). *Professional capital: Transforming teaching in every school.* New York: Teachers College Press.

Henderson, A.T., & Mapp, K.L. (2002). *A new wave of evidence: The impact of school, family, and community connections on student achievement.* Austin, TX: National Center for Family & Community Connections with Schools.

Hill, H.C. (2009). Fixing teacher professional development. *Phi Delta Kappan, 90*(7), 470–476.

Hofhuis, J., Mensen, M., Ten Den, L.M., Van den Berg, A.M., Koopman-Draijer, M., van Tilburg, M.C., Smits, C.H.M., & De Vries, S. (2018). Does functional diversity increase effectiveness of community care teams? The moderating role of shared vision, interaction frequency, and team reflexivity. *Journal of Applied Social Psychology, 48*(10), 535–548.

Hong, L., & Page, S.E. (2004). Groups of diverse problem solvers can outperform groups of high-ability problem solvers. *Proceedings of the National Academy of Sciences—PNAS, 101*(46), 16385–16389.

IDEO. (n.d.). Design thinking defined. Available from: https://designthinking.ideo.com/

Johnson, S.M. (2019). *Where teachers thrive: Organizing schools for success.* Cambridge, MA: Harvard Education Press.

Jones, E., & Nimmo, J. (1994). *Emergent curriculum.* Washington, D.C.: National Association for the Education of Young Children.

Juliani, A.J. (2018). *Intentional innovation: How to guide risk-taking, build creative capacity, and kead change.* Taylor & Francis.

Ketelaar, E., Beijaard, D., Boshuizen, H.P.A., & Den Brok, P.J. (2012). Teachers' positioning towards an educational innovation in the light of ownership, sense-making and agency. *Teaching and Teacher Education, 28*(2), 273–282.

Knowledge and Human Development Authority. (2012). Inspection report: The Kindergarten Starters. Available at: https://www.khda.gov.ae/DISB/AttachmentDownload.aspx?DOC_ID=mGSz7qa6zyQ%3d

Krechevsky, M., Mardell, B., Rivard, M., & Wilson, D. (2013). *Visible learners: Promoting Reggio-inspired approaches in all schools.* San Francisco, CA: Jossey-Bass.

Kreikemeier, A., & James, C. (2018). Commenting across difference: Youth dialogue in an inter-cultural virtual exchange program. *Digital Culture & Education, 10,* 49–66. https://static1.squarespace.com/static/5cf15af7a259990001706378/t/5cf417c6b3ed2e00010ee713/1559500749222/Kreikemeier_and_James+%28sep+2018%29.pdf

Litchfield, R.C, Karakitapoğlu-Aygün, Z., Gumusluoglu, L., Carter, M., & Hirst, G. (2018). When team identity helps innovation and when it hurts: Team identity and its relationship to team and cross-team innovative behavior. *The Journal of Product Innovation Management, 35*(3), 350–366.

Little, J.W. (1982). Norms of collegiality and experimentation: Workplace conditions of school success. *American Educational Research Journal, 19*(3), 325–340.

Little, J.W. (2001). Professional development in pursuit of school reform. In A. Lieberman & L. Miller (Eds.). *(2001). Teachers caught in the action. Professional development that matters* (pp. 23–44). New York: Teachers College Press.

Lortie, D. (1975). *Schoolteacher: A sociological study*. Chicago: University of Chicago Press.

Mayer, M.A. (2006). *Creativity loves constraints*. Bloomberg Businessweek. www.bloomberg.com/news/articles/2006-02-12/creativity-loves-constraints

McWilliam, E. (2008). Unlearning how to teach. *Innovations in Education and Teaching International, 45*(3), 263–269.

Mehta, J., & Fine, S. (2019). *In search of deeper learning: The quest to remake the American high school*. Cambridge, MA: Harvard University Press.

Meirink, J.A., Imants, J., Meijer, P.C., & Verloop, N. (2010). Teacher learning and collaboration in innovative teams. *Cambridge Journal of Education, 40*(2), 161–181.

Mertler, C.A. (2017). *Action research: Improving schools and empowering educators* (5th edition). Thousand Oaks, CA: SAGE Publications, Inc.

Miller-Williams, S.L., & Kritsonis, W.A. (2009–2010). A systems approach to comprehensive school reform: Using the realms of meaning and the Baldridge Approach as a systems framework. *National Forum of Applied Educational Research Journal, (23)*1–2, pp. 1–8.

Mills, G. (2017). *Action research: A guide for the teacher researcher* (6th edition). New York: Pearson Education.

Nagji, B., & Tuff, G. (2012). Managing your innovation portfolio. *Harvard Business Review, (90)*5, pp. 66–74.

Ndaruhutse, S., Jones, C., & Riggall, A. (2019). Why systems thinking is important for the education sector. Available at: https://www.educationdevelopmenttrust.com/EducationDevelopment-Trust/files/17/17fec588-e413-461b-a107-78b6569304cc.pdf

Nelson, T.H., Slavit, D., Perkins, M., & Hathorn, T. (2008). A culture of collaborative inquiry: Learning to develop and support professional learning communities. *Teachers College Record, 110*(6), 1269–1303.

Noonan, J. (2016). *Teachers learning: Engagement, identity, and agency in powerful professional development*. Dissertation: Harvard Graduate School of Education.

OECD. (2006). *Demand-sensitive schooling? Evidence and issues*. Paris: OECD Publishing.

Opfer, V.D., & Pedder, D. (2011). Conceptualizing teacher professional learning. *Review of Educational Research, 81*(3), 376–407.

P21 (Partnership for 21st Century Learning: A Network of Battelle for Kids) (2019). Framework for 21st century learning. Available from: https://www.battelleforkids.org/networks/p21

Perkins, D.N., & Reese, J.D. (2014). When change has legs. *Educational Leadership, 71*(8), 42–47.

Pierce, J.L., Kostova, T., & Dirks, K.T. (2001). Toward a theory of psychological ownership in organizations. *Academy of Management Review, 26*(2), 298–310.

Project Zero. (n.d.). Visible thinking. Retrieved from http://www.pz.harvard.edu/projects/visible-thinking

Project Zero & Reggio Children. (2001). *Making learning visible: Children as individual and group learners.* Reggio Emilia, Italy: Reggio Children.

Robertson, D. (2017). *The power of little ideas: A low-risk, high-reward approach to innovation.* Boston, MA: Harvard Business Review Press.

Rock, D., & Grant, H. (2016, November 4). Why diverse teams are smarter. *Harvard Business Review.* https://hbr.org/2016/11/why-diverse-teams-are-smarter

Rogers, E.M., (1983). *Diffusion of innovations.* (3rd edition). New York: The Free Press.

Sawyer, R.K. (2006). Educating for innovation. *Thinking Skills and Creativity, 1*(1), 41–48.

Schleicher, A., OECD. Secretary-General, & OECD iLibrary. (2011). *Building a high-quality teaching profession: Lessons from around the world.* Paris: OECD.

Spann, A. (2018). *Teacher's description of multiple initiatives implementation: A phenomenological study.* ProQuest Dissertations Publishing.

Stringer, E.T. (2013). *Action research* (4th edition). Los Angeles, CA: Sage Publications.

Tishman, S. (2018). *Slow looking: The art and practice of learning through observation.* New York: Routledge.

Tishman, S. (2014, July 21). Slow looking and complexity. *Out of Eden Learn Educators Blog* (walktolearn.outofedenwalk.com). The Design-Based Research Collective. (2003). Design-based research: An emerging paradigm for educational inquiry. *Educational Researcher 32*(1): 5–8.

Transcend, Inc. (2019). *Transcend's conditions for innovation framework.* https://static1.square-space.com/static/55ca46dee4b0fc536f717de8/t/5d6bf722be3d8f0001886e3e/1567356707060/Transcend%27s+Conditions+for+Innovation.pdf

Vangrieken, K., Dochy, F., Raes, E., & Kyndt, E. (2015). Teacher collaboration: A systematic review. *Educational Research Review, 15,* 17–40.

Wagner, T. (2012). *Creating innovators.* New York: Scribner.

Wagner, T., & Dintersmith, T. (2015). *Most likely to succeed.* New York: Scribner.

Waters Center for Systems Thinking. *What is systems thinking?* https://waterscenterst.org/systems-thinking-tools-and-strategies/what-is-systems-thinking/

Watkins, C. (2017). Developing student-driven learning: The patterns, the context, and the process. In N.A. Alias & J.E. Luaran, *Student-driven learning strategies for the 21st century classroom* (pp. 1–9). Hershey, PA: IGI Global.

Weinbaum, A., Allen, D., Blythe, T., Simon, K., Seidel, S., & Rubin, C. (2004). *Teaching as inquiry: Asking hard questions to improve practice and student achievement.* New York: Teachers College Press.

Wien, C.A. (2008). *Emergent curriculum in the primary classroom: Interpreting the Reggio Emilia approach in schools.* New York: Teachers College Press.

INDEX